Early Childhood Curricula: Reconceptualist Perspectives

stories created and lived

that is singular

in the single

Discovery begins

the bright particulars. Disco

the blind street

they lose themselves, the

to draw up water like the roots of a tree

substantially transformed

to the child dancing to herself in a swirl of sunlight

In the green and silver chorus of the grass

the possiblity of another way

Luigi Iannacci & Pam Whitty
Editors

DETSELIG

Early Childhood Curricula: Reconceptualist Perspectives
© Luigi Iannacci & Pam Whitty 2009

Library and Archives Canada Cataloguing in Publication

Early childhood curricula : reconceptualist perspectives / Luigi Iannacci & Pam Whitty, editors.

Includes bibliographical references.
ISBN 978-1-55059-370-9

1. Early childhood education--Curricula--Canada. 2. Postmodernism and education--Canada. I. Whitty, Pam II. Iannacci, Luigi, 1970-

LB1139.4.E15 2009   372.19   C2009-904224-X

Detselig Enterprises Ltd.
⊛
210, 1220 Kensington Road NW
Calgary, Alberta, T2N 3P5
www.temerondetselig.com
Phone: (403) 283-0900   Fax: (403) 283-6947

We acknowledge the support of the Government of Canada through the Book Publishing Industry Development Program (BPIDP) for our publishing program.

We also acknowledge the support of the Alberta Foundation for the Arts for our publishing program.

SAN 113-0234
ISBN 978-1-55059-370-9
Cover Design by David Casey

Contents

Reconceptualizing Children's Image and Agency

Reconceptualizing Literacies in ECE

Acknowledgements

Luigi Iannacci and Pam Whitty would like to acknowledge the UNB Faculty of Education Graduate Studies office for initiating this publishing project through their visiting scholar programme. They would also like to thank all of the researchers who contributed chapters to this book. Their commitment and dedication to the volume was greatly appreciated.

Luigi would like to acknowledge family, friends, and mentors who have supported him, and all of the children and teachers he has learned from and with.

Pam expresses appreciation to all members of the UNB Early Learning Curriculum Project, the Early Childhood Unit in the New Brunswick Department of Social Development and, especially, to the educators and children who contributed to the immense NB curriculum-making project.

Luigi and Pam are grateful to Ted Giles and Shane Riczu from Detselig Enterprises for their support and dedication to this volume.

The cover image was provided by Nicholas Muia. We thank him for the use of his painting.

1

Introduction to Reconceptualist Perspectives

Luigi Iannacci & Pam Whitty

> Our responsibility, as educators and as social scientists, is to understand to the extent that it is possible, the complex conditions of our mutual formation. And we must seek to understand our own contribution to creating and withholding the conditions of possibility of particular lives. In order to achieve that understanding we must ask what it is that makes for a viable life and how we are each implicated in constituting the viability and non-viability of the lives of others.
>
> Davies & Gannon, 2006, p. 183

Wide-ranging discussions and actions related to the viability and nonviability of children's lives, now and into their futures, has earned Early Childhood Education (ECE) a place of prominence on the political agendas of many countries throughout the world. Given such prominence, it is not surprising that ECE is fraught with tensions and fuelled by political agendas, competing stakeholders and taken-for-granted notions about children, childhood, and learning. As Peter Moss (2007) notes, "the situation that is emerging in early childhood is troubling" (p. 233) because of an increasing paradigmatic divide in ECE between modernist and postfoundational thinking. One need look no further for an example than the dominant discourses shaping the on-going debate over whether to finally develop a national system of early learning and child care that would address the chronically "underfunded patchwork of programs" (OCBCC, 2007) currently in place across Canada. Long standing economic arguments have continuously validated the need for increased funding and the development of a coherent ECE system. These arguments have positioned parents primarily as consumers, their children as economic collateral, and ECE as having the prime purpose of creating future viable workers: all of which reinforces the construction of childhood as a time to invest in to ensure later dividends. This notion of ECE perpetuates early learning and care as a vehicle for monitoring developmental norms in order to create future producers/consumers able to meet labor market demands. Economic discourse continues to be dominant in a time where more and more attention has been placed on the rights of the child (Hallett & Prout, 2003; O'Neill & Zinga, 2008), a growing awareness of shifting and commodified childhoods (Hughes, 2005; Kapur, 2005; Steinburg & Kincheloe, 1997), and an increasing recognition that the future of childhood studies must be interdisciplinary (Kehily, 2004; Prout, 2005).

Tensions, troubles, and divides, however, offer within themselves significant possibilities. They can open up spaces for policymakers, educators, and researchers alike to think, feel, and converse about how children, childhood, and learning might be reconceptualized. It is our desire to live and speak within such spaces that prompted this volume into reconceptualist perspectives in the Canadian ECE context. A growing global emphasis on early childhood policies and curricula has produced an extensive body of literature on policy and curriculum concerning our youngest citizens. International ECE initiatives and curricular practices in place for several years such as Reggio Emilia, Italy (Boyd-Cadwell, 1997; Fraser, 2006; Rinaldi, 2006), and the Te Whariki, (Carr, 2004; New Zealand Ministry of Education, 1996) have started to influence the Canadian ECE context. The promising effects of these influences create a need for current pan-Canadian research grounded in reconceptualist early childhood curriculum theorizing that draws on socio-cultural, feminist, critical, postmodern and decolonizing understandings about early childhood and education to examine the limits, problematics and possibilities of Canadian ECE.

These curricula and curriculum frameworks invite educators to act in ways that are responsive to children's and educators' socio-cultural contexts and their "funds of knowledge" (Moll, 1992). They are representative of a shift from the economics to the pedagogies and ethics of ECE, and from developmental to socio-cultural and critical understandings of children and learning. These shifts have resulted in significant changes in the way pedagogy, assessment, the learning environment, and relationships are configured and understood within ECE. Some of the work that provinces have done or are in the process of doing to establish new curricula, curriculum frameworks and policies in ECE are reflective of these shifts. Dr. Pam Whitty, for example, is currently co-leading a curriculum project discussed within the book, one focused on the co-construction of a socio-culturally inspired early childhood curriculum framework in the province of New Brunswick. Other provinces such as British Columbia and Saskatchewan have begun to similarly rethink and renew their early year's curriculum frameworks and policies. Quebec is already operating with an ecological model.

With this in mind, we have invited contributions from established and emerging Canadian scholars who are working with reconceptualist thought and practice. We recognize that the volume – any volume for that matter – is by no means comprehensive or representative of the diversity of research presently being conducted. We offer this text as a way of contributing to a growing field with the hope that it will foster further conversations and contributions by and among other ECE researchers and educators. This collective contribution is intended for a) teacher educators working with teacher candidates at the primary level, b) professors teaching graduate courses about early childhood education and learning, c) college instructors working with future early childhood educators, and d) ECE policy makers and curriculum developers.

Reconceptualist perspectives act as counter narratives to dominant ECE discourses such as developmentalism, economic investment, and the universal child. As reconceptualist perspectives inform the collection, we thought it helpful to provide a sense of reconceptualist thought and practice as it questions, troubles, and provides alternatives to the dominant discourses that have shaped ECE. We illustrate how and why reconceptualist perspectives are vital to its future.

(De)constructing Norms as the Ideal

Reconceptualist theorizing as applied to ECE, resists and is a response to the overwhelming influence developmental/maturationist notions of child development and learning have had on ECE. These notions are inextricably connected to and rooted in the history of normative theory. Historically, the development of the norm coincides directly with the idea of grades organized around age, marks, a set curricula and the development of special education (Woodill 1992, p. 7). Norm-referenced understandings of the "ideal" have created divisions and hierarchies that construct those who do not mirror norms as deficient and Other than normal. These hierarchies "enable the articulation of standards so that people can be compared and differentiated on the basis of their relation to standards" (Toohey, 2000, p. 8). The development and mass application of the norm has consequently furthered a "hegemony of normalcy" (Davis, 1997, p. 26). Davis argues that the entire "social process of disabling arrived with industrialization and with a set of practices and discourses that are linked to late eighteenth and nineteenth century notions of nationality, race, gender, criminality, sexual orientation, and so on" (pp. 9-10). These divisions can be understood as a coalescing of particular discourses and practices such as the development of statistical science, the creation of numerical representations of normalcy, and the eugenics movement to form an overarching dominant discourse (Moss, 2007).

The pursuit of statistical measurements of human normalcy has deceptively communicated that such measurement gathering "helps to improve humans so that deviations from the norm diminish" (Davis, 1997, p. 14). Dominant theoretical discourses and practices that shape ECE have traditionally been informed by these understandings of and investments in statistical constructions of normalcy. Such notions are reflected within research conducted by early-twentieth-century child development researchers such as Stanley Hall (1826-1924) and further developed by his student, Arnold Gesell (1880-1961). Hall and Gesell's botanical model constructed child development as similar to that of plants in that both occurred according to a predetermined plan and with reasonable nourishment, unfolded automatically. Nurturing a child's biologically preprogrammed development held greater priority to Hall and Gesell than considering the role of environment and its contribution to the quality of life in the present and the future (Krogh & Slentz, 2001).

Decades of utilizing this botanical model helped Hall and Gesell produce normative data that defined what children are like and what they should be able to do for each 6-month period of their lives (Krogh & Slentz, 2001; Mayfield, 2001). These maturationist theories base "ages and stages on norms derived from data on predominantly white, middle-class children, which raises questions about the validity of applying the ideas to the development of other children" (Mayfield, 2001, p. 217). Gould (1995) argues that such models place too much emphasis on heredity and subsequently "rehashes the tenets of social Darwinism as it was originally constituted" (p. 4).

This has been significant to ECE since the constructed norm has created the comparative base line in which children's failure and abnormality can be discerned and diagnosed. Despite its contentious development and mass-application by societies that have fully invested in its certainty, Canadian ECE has been largely committed to the idea that there is a quantifiable norm which allows for measurements and comparisons of development and ability (Thompson, 2002). These commitments and the taken-for-granted practices they have fostered have been reinforced by other prominent child development researchers as well.

Although researchers such as Hall and Gesell are inextricably linked to the development of staged understandings of child development via normative data (Almy, 1979), the overwhelming influence of translations and interpretations of Piaget and his research affixed the focus on individual development rather then social interactions, thus maintaining and validating age and stage models of child development. In keeping with the biological model, these translations and interpretations of Piaget asserted that each of his stages (sensory-motor-birth to two, preoperational-2 to 7, concrete operations-7-12, formal operations-adolescence, etc.) evolved from the previous in a fixed sequence and were universal across cultures (Piaget, 1993/1970), thus reinforcing Gesell and Hall's work.

An adherence to norms, and the unilinear understandings of child development they help organize, has encumbered ECE's ability to provide specific programming that is responsive to children's socio-cultural contexts and their "cultural, intellectual, historical and political legacy" (Delpit, 2003, p. 14). Since developmental progression is viewed as inevitable, children are understood and constructed as an analogous group rather than individuals. Differences are ignored and what is deemed normal for an age group becomes the primary pedagogical focus of programming and instruction for that age group, with little room for variation.

Developmentally Appropriate Practice: Reinscribing the Norm

Developmentally Appropriate Practice (DAP) as outlined by the National Association for the Education of Young Children (NAEYC) has further complicated these issues. In 1984, a commission on appropriate education for four and five year olds was established by the NAEYC to develop standards and curriculum for early years educators. From its inception, the reports and position statements published by the committee in 1986 and 1987 have been controversial. One of the earliest criticisms of the NAEYC's statement on DAP concerned the overrepresentation of child developmentalists on the committee who wrote it. The "heavy reliance on child development, specifically Piagetian theory . . . and the relative exclusion of other theoretical bases" (Mayfield, 2001, p. 492) was especially contentious for many prominent ECE researchers. These theoretical leanings were said to have contributed to the narrowness of the initial definition of DAP and its subsequent failure to recognize the importance of cultural and social contexts with regards to development and learning (Mayfield, 2001). One of the initial purposes of DAP was to help end "inappropriate" practices and as such, emerged from binary thinking (i.e. in opposition to inappropriate practices). It is therefore a modernist artifact that picks up on the construction of binaries and, by doing so, reinscribes them and rejects other possibilities.

The overall appropriate/inappropriate structure of the document "oversimplified educator decision-making into an either-or situation" (Mayfield, 2001, p. 492). O'Brien, (1996/1997) questioned the dominant ways of knowing and culturally bound conceptions of appropriateness the report took for granted as well as its depiction of structured, teacher-directed learning as inappropriate. Cannella (1997) challenged the "pedagogical determinism" and universal construction of the child the report reified and argued that DAP objectifies and creates the child as Other as it "perpetuates the modernist discourse of oppositional thought; adult/child, right/wrong, white/black, male/female, appropriate/inappropriate" (p. 131). A revised edition of the report published in 1997 addressed some of the criticisms with regards to direct instruction (DI) and cultural factors. The new guidelines attempted to "recognize the complexity and variability in human development and learning . . . [and] at the same time . . . retain many of the normative and "universal" features that characterized the initial version" (Lubeck, 1998, p. 286). The document took a "both/and" approach that ECE researchers found unsatisfying and problematic.

The main contention continued to be that DAP was negligible in rectifying and combating the legacy of developmentalism. As such, developmental norms and the idea of a universal childhood were not destabilized. Essentially, those in favor of DAP argued that it was for "everyone" and that there are developmental commonalities "that cut across socio-economic, cultural and language groups such as maturation, sequential developmental stages, and a learning mode based on, concrete-based experiences" (Escobedo as cited in Charlesworth, 1998, p. 277). Researchers and theorists operating from reconceptualist perspectives that draw on critical, postmodern, poststructuralist, and feminist perspectives challenge the idea that DAP is for "everyone" and believe that alternative perspectives of childhood acknowledging the importance of power have been largely unrecognized and poorly considered in the field of ECE (Grieshaber & Cannella, 2001;

Lubeck, 1998). Although another iteration of the report published in 2008 addressed some of these concerns, it continues to reinscribe others. As a result, child development continues to be understood as an inevitable static series of steps, rather than a fluid web of mediating factors that include gender, time, social and economic status, as well as cultural and linguistic diversity.[1] These notions and practices have maintained and reinforced a deficit orientation.

The Deficit Model and the "At-Risk" Phenomenon

The impact of normative theory including the taking up of Piaget's "genetic epistemology" (Sigel, 1979, p. 219) has led to ECE reinforcing a "cultural deficit theory" (Sleeter & Grant, 2003). This theory constructs children as "'at risk' and suggests that their only chance for academic and professional success is by adopting the norms of the majority culture" (Falconer & Byrnes, 2003, p. 197). This consequently transmits a dominant culture and language to children and families and reinforces singular ways of constructing the goals and purposes of ECE. As a result, the deficit-oriented thinking embedded in the professionalization of well-meaning and, often well-educated ECE educators is left unchallenged. Consequently, diversity continues to be framed as disadvantageous, problematic, and a factor that places children "at-risk" (Siraj-Blatchford & Clarke, 2000).

Swadener (2000) questions whether the at-risk label is simply a retooling of the deficit model. She argues, "The problem of locating pathology in young victims of oppression is . . . the most objectionable tenet of the at risk rhetoric" (p. 118) and concedes that inequity, educational funding, race, and class-based stratification are at the helm of being at risk.

The at-risk phenomenon reinforces society's ability to blame the victim and locate pathology within them rather than looking at social and economic factors that create the need for the label. Once again, the child is understood to be somehow socio-culturally detached. Swadener (2000) demonstrates the importance of contextualization by examining how children's experiences are connected to social and organizational constructs. Moreover, she questions conceptions of normalcy that secure deficit models that work to Other the marginalized as they continue to dominate approaches to ECE. Rather than take for granted the Swadener insists that we explore the work society *pathologies* foster "at-promise" children and urges us to focu. determining our collective deficits in doing so rather tna. pathologies we create to mask our failures. In ECE this would mean an abandonment of normative understandings of child development that blame those constructed as deficient for their inability to demonstrate and perform developmental norms. This would also necessitate ecologically theorizing children's care and learning to guide our professional and institutional responses to them. In short, it would necessitate embracing reconceptualist perspectives within the field of ECE. Without this shift, deficit models will continue to prevail in ECE ensuring domination rather than transformation (Ghosh, 1996), thus furthering the negation of Otherness and sustaining colonial relations of power within ECE.

The Universal Child and Colonialism in ECE

Dominant discourses of development and at-risk children have led to constructions of children and childhood that have fortified specific relations of power within early childhood education. ECE is "related to both colonization of much of the world by European powers and the spread of industrialization throughout the world" (Woodill, 1992, p. 3). What has furthered the presence and replication of colonial relations of power in ECE is the notion of the *universal child*. It is founded in the scientific construction of childhood as a predetermined universal truth in which one group creates beliefs about and values for the other (Viruru & Cannella 2001, p. 160). These perspectives have ensured that younger human beings have been "unrestrictedly colonized" (p. 160) by adults. When we question how children have been understood and constructed throughout history,[2] we begin to see the roots of the universal child construction and the colonial relations they sustain.

Friquegnon (1997), argues that the "historical development of the idea of childhood shows increasing tension between emphasis on the potential superiority and reverse emphasis on the actual inferiority of child to adult" (p. 12). Throughout history, children's contradictory roles have demonstrated these tensions. In the ancient world children were assigned a similar status to slaves.

Christianity later glorified and sentimentalized them. During the middle ages, children were treated as indistinguishable from adults and subject to sexual abuse. Subsequently, the seventeenth and eighteenth centuries saw a growing division between adults and children that culminated in grouping them in schools according to their age (Friquegnon, 1997). During this time, "people vacillated between the Christian-Rousseauian view of the child as angelic and the older view . . . of the child as barbarian" (p. 13). Education reflected these particular paradoxes.

By the mid-nineteenth century, schools outside of France (still heavily influenced by Rousseauian romanticism) mirrored the idea that childhood was a necessary evil that required a punitive approach. Schools were renowned for abusing children in an effort to civilize them (Friquegnon, 1997). Late-nineteenth-century thinkers such as Froebel and Pestalozzi and early-twentieth-century educators such as Montessori and Dewey, altered the focus of schooling toward a more liberal paradigm which tapped into the possibilities of childhood and the importance of personal (and in the case of both Pestalozzi and Montessori, spiritual) development. Although Friquegnon (1997) calls for a balance between permissiveness and authority in education, she concedes that the present wave of conservatism has made our inadequacy in understanding childhood and approaches to education for children even more conspicuous.

Dominant economically focused arguments, for example, fortify the role of ECE as responsible for producing future viable workers and operates from the perspective that children are "weak" and "ignorant" and "because of their inferiority should be forced to unquestionably obey" (Friquegnon, 1997, p. 14). The teacher's role in this conception of education is to "shape children like Japanese Bonzai trees, to satisfy . . . social needs and achieve predetermined goals" (p. 14). Such an approach reinscribes biological models of child development that construct children as unfinished passive objects and economic discourses that similarly stress the importance of ECE in addressing children's incompleteness, their intellectual inferiority and their subsequent economic vulnerability. Importantly, this conception of children and learning has often ensured that when a child fails to demonstrate developmental norms, the colonial gaze as manifest within ECE becomes fixed on their specific dysfunctional elements and "processes of pathologization" (Heydon & Iannacci, 2008) occur through isolating and fixating on the body parts of the child that "don't work" (e.g., the brain, the mouth). The child is no longer whole, but rather parts that need fixing. The threat the deficient child poses on the system ensures that these punitive and pathologizing processes are employed in an effort to transform the child from the anxiety-provoking object he/she is, to that which the system recognizes – the normal child. Otherness can therefore be understood to connote *to-be-altered-ness*.

Research, Children, and Colonization

ECE has not in and of itself been responsible for reinforcing problematic constructions of children, childhood and learning and the colonial relations of power these constructions reinforce. Research has also ensured that these constructions and relations were furthered and maintained:

> The empirical study of children in the West has, for the last 150 years, been regarded as the domain of psychology. Within this discipline children have been treated as the (passive) objects of study; scrutinized, tested and measured (Burman, 1994; Rose, 1985). The focus has been on what happens to them (and the processes they undergo) rather than what they do or say. The psychological construction of the individual which underpins this is hegemonic and has provided the foundation for sociological thinking too. However, for children, it is confounded with developmentalism: the construction of a linear, sequential and normalized process by which children become adults. (Alldred, 1998, p. 150)

The influential Canadian research report in the field of early years education and care, *Reversing the Real Brain Drain: Early Years Study: Final Report* (McCain & Mustard, 1999), has reinforced "taken-for-granted representations of childhood as an economic resource in which adults must invest to reap future profits and of child development as a combination of exclusively biological processes" (Stooke, 2003, p. 91). The report's findings are heavily based on particular forms of neuroscience and present a story of Ontario's children as "not doing well because they are not receiving enough of the right kind of brain stimulation in the first five years of life" (p. 93). Although the creators of the report see the value of early years and take an advocacy role, it is important to note that the particular neuroscience story they tell "tends to conflate child development with brain development ... [and] privileges a view of childhood as a set of biological processes and parenting as a set of clinical practices" (Stooke, 2003, p. 97). The report calls for communities to respond to the neglected needs of children in order to remain competitive in the global economy and as such, constructs communities as marketplaces responsible for investing in children in order to ensure capital return. The actual quality of the children's lives and their relationships seem to take a back seat to current investments for a future productive citizen. In addition, there is a sense that if a child is not fixed by three, it may be too late; as such, fear is incited in parents if their child cannot meet norms.

This "neuroscience story" has also been taken up in news media. In a series of articles in *The Globe and Mail* (McIlroy, 2004, April 10), entitled, "Starting From Zero: The Children of the Future," several articles such as, "We Can Build A Better Brain" and "Coming Soon Your Baby's Brain: The Manual," discuss controversial magnetic resonance imaging (MRI) research currently being conducted by Max Cyndar of the Brian Research Centre at the University of British Columbia. Cyndar argues that within the next ten years he and his team can determine a "timeline of optimal brain development, to help parents and caregivers ensure that kids get the kind of stimulation they need when they need it," Cyndar declares, "It is exciting to think we can train better people ... That we can build better brains" (McIlroy, 2004). Dr. Alan Evans, a researcher at McGill University's Montreal Neurological Institute is also working with MRI technology to create an "'atlas' of brain development in children [that] could provide an even more precise road map for doctors and children." Evans states, "The whole idea is to capture what is normal" (McIlroy, 2004). At best, this new research continues to fuel biological understandings of children that position them as hegemonous groups that are the Other in relation to the adult world responsible for monitoring and fostering their brain development to ensure future economic viability. At worst, the work further reinforces science over other forms of data and can be seen as rehashing notions commensurate with eugenics.

It is important to note that there are counterviews within the neuroscience field that take up different positions than those espoused by the dominant developmentalist discourse that Evans' research underwrites. Marianne Wolf (2007), for example, cautions about singular "one size fits all" applications of neuroscience, noting that contributions from neuroscience are in their early phases, and recognizes the inappropriate push down of print cognition to younger and younger children, while at the same time detailing the complexities of reading.

Ethnography, which avoids some of the problems inherent in MRI-based research, is often held up as an ideal method for conducting educational research with children in homes, communities, and schools. It has been considered useful in exploring "the everyday lives and real-world practices of human beings" (Viruru & Cannella 2001, p. 165). However, ethnography is not without its problems. It too has reinforced the universal child construction and colonized children since "the researcher is considered to hold all the power, deciding who and what to study, and how the voices of others will be recorded and represented" (p. 165).

Alldred (1998) has critically examined several ethnographic studies of children. Her work suggests that ethnographers have not always fully considered the ethical dilemmas inherent in studying children and have had a tendency to reproduce adult-centric understandings of childhood culture. Viruru & Cannella (2001) contend that ethnographic studies have cast children as things to be raised rather than people to live among and a sub-species to be studied rather than heard and understood. Alternatively, they urge that "decolonization become a major focus of our struggle as educators" (2001, p. 210) and call for research involving children to be reconceptualized using post-colonial alternatives (2001). These alternatives have the potential to effectively challenge and destabilize the universal child construction and colonizer/colonized relationships in ECE. In order for this to come to fruition, they suggest that inquirers view research "as a process of continual self-conscious critique" (p. 168) and that constantly examining "the social and political forces influencing participants, researcher[s] and methods of inquiry illustrates this self-conscious functioning" (p. 168). Viruru and Cannella (2001) confirm the need for researchers to integrate themselves into their research and fully examine and critique the interpretations of data they proffer. The placement of these interpretations in compounded contexts, as seen through multiple lenses (Brown & Barrera, 1999) helps to ensure that the subjectivity of a researcher's analysis is fully described, thus challenging the notion of a universal truth that constructs knowledge production as value free. This process is reconceptualist in focus and orientation and may combat discourses and research paradigms that have objectified and marginalized children.

Counter Narratives: Reconceptualist Perspectives

Reconceptualist perspectives that have countered these notions of children, childhood, research, and learning initially focused on the social dimensions of learning and development. Lev Vygotsky was a forerunner in forwarding socio-cultural perspectives for examining children's development and learning. His ideas contrasted starkly to those of Hall, Gesell, Piaget, and many of their contemporaries. In *Mind and Society* (1978), Vygotsky argued that child psychology's appropriation of botanical and zoological models was problematic and led to a biological basis of study of human behavior. His work countered dominant discourses by not subscribing to norms and stages, but rather by describing the importance of developing a child's "zone of proximal development" (ZPD), defined as "the distance between the actual development as determined by independent problem solving and the level of potential development as determined through problem solving under adult guidance or in collaboration with more capable peers" (p. 86). One of the premises of ZPD is that social and cognitive skills that have been scaffolded today will be independently performed tomorrow. To that end, the adult's role in children's learning "is understood to be one of supporting the child's agenda in a more contingently responsive manner of co-construction of meaning" (Ritchie, 2001, p. 137). Underpinning these understandings of how children learn is the importance of the environment.

Vygotsky emphasized the role of linguistic, cultural, and social factors in understanding learning. His theories and approaches to examining development were much more concerned with the context in and through which children learn (Mayfield, 2001). In his estimation, maturation is

> a secondary factor in the development of the most complex, unique forms of human behaviour. The development of these behaviours is characterized by complicated, qualitative transformations of one form of behaviour into another ... The conception of maturation as a passive process cannot adequately describe these complex phenomena. (Vygotsky, 1978, p. 19)

The environment that Vygotsky conceptualized was always in flux and subject to change. He believed that "every age presents the child with an environment which has been organized in a special way, so that the environment, in the purely external sense of the word, keeps changing as the child passes on from one age to another" (Vygotsky, 1994, p. 339). The factors that constituted the environment were multiple and dynamic, and these factors needed to be fully considered when assessing a child's social, cognitive and physical growth. Vygotsky argued that "the influence of the environment on child development will, along with other types of influences, also have to be assessed by taking the degree of understanding, awareness and insights of what is going on in the environment into account" (1994, p. 343). The de-emphasis of biology on child development allows for a more ecological perspective of cognitive growth, and consequently challenges the construction of the child as a "decontextualized organism" (Bronfenbrenner, 1979, p. 9).

It is important to note that socio-cultural perspectives were not developed from a single body of work. Gee (1990) points out for example that that a "sociocultural approach to literacy has emerged out of several different disciplines. This body of literature, combining work in linguistics, social psychology, anthropology and education, constitutes an emerging interdisciplinary field" (p. 49). He adds that various movements, stemming from different disciplines that have also reflected the "social turn away from a focus on individual behavior ... and individual minds toward a focus on social and cultural interaction" have been influential and converge in current work on socio-cultural approaches to literacy (Gee, 2000, p. 180). Similarly, some of the perspectives that have been important to further developing a reconceptualist orientation include feminist, postmodern and decolonizing understandings about early childhood, children, learning and education. The use of a theoretical pastiche is a common characteristic of reconceptualist theorizing.

The pastiche has ultimately allowed critical perspectives to begin to destabilize some of the dominant discourses and conceptualizations plaguing ECE and children that have been discussed throughout this introduction. Giroux (1988), among others, describes the need for educators to become politically-minded in order to foster transformative and critical pedagogies through their refusal to act as tour guides and keepers of the dominant tenets of education. In short, the ultimate goal of the critical project requires a reconceptualization of what is and what can be.

Reconceptualization invokes a tradition of curricular theorizing that sees as its crucial goal the social transformation and reconstruction of educational institutions such as ECE. This transformation is brought about through an understanding of what was, an analysis of what is, and an envisioning of what can be and realized through a process of text construction, deconstruction, and reconstruction. By challenging the grand narratives or dominant discourses that have shaped ECE, new stories can be shared that inform a refashioned vision for the future. The hope is that this process will yield more equitable approaches to ECE, and also a constant reflexive monitoring of what is done in the name of educating and caring for children.

Pinar (1994) asserts that reconceptualization is neither arrested nor ever complete and "to imagine it a finished product, a doctrine, is to miss the point. What is essential about the reconceptualization . . . is its constant redefinition" (p. 73). Reconceptualist orientation holds that educators be in a constant state of (re)learning what they know so that curriculum is constantly being reconceived. ECE as a field can only be reconceptualized through a critical revelation of the power relations sustained within it, which ultimately may forward hope and possibility. It is from these perspectives that the remaining chapters work. They offer hope and possibility as they interrupt limited and limiting understandings about children, childhood, learning, and education that have sustained colonial relations of power within ECE.

The Volume

We have organized the book into three sections, with each section examining particular aspects of reconceptualizing within Early Childhood Education. In the first section, each chapter centres upon an aspect of reconceptualizing curriculum-making, professional development, and documentation. In the second chapter, Pam Whitty takes the reader into a large scale curriculum development project created and implemented within licensed Anglophone child care centres in New Brunswick. In the context of this project, she examines how the co-construction of curriculum documents contributes to conversational crossings across modernist-postfoundational thinking. Using conversations as traces of the pedagogical, she provides insights into local and global curricular connections, discursive connecting within the New Brunswick Curriculum Framework for Early Learning and Child Care (English), and how the interruption of time and literacies of places contribute to reconceptualizing ECE. In the next chapter, Emily Ashton, a member of the University of New Brunswick Curriculum Team and one of the editors of the curriculum support document series, focuses upon ethical issues that surface in the process of co-constructing curriculum documents. Through a process of folding ethical-textual tensions, Emily examines her role in the ethical editing process of this large curriculum-writing project, taking care to distinguish between editing and editorializing in the creation of multimodal, polyphonic curriculum documents.

The next two chapters shift our geographic location to British Columbia and scholars there working with/in reconceptualist thought and practice. Chapter Four is co-authored by Veronica Pacini-Ketchabaw, Laurie Kocher, Alejandra Sanchez, and Christine Chan. The reconceptualizing of professional development in this case occurs within another large-scale curriculum project. In this instance, the authors draw upon posthumanist thinking from philosophy and physics and deconstruct notions of developmental stages of professional development. They demonstrate how the professional development process can be theorized as a process of becoming rather than a series of discrete stages. In particular, they draw upon pedagogical documentation written by educators that demonstrate how they are in a constant state of becoming and learning as they engage in this large-scale project. In the last chapter in this section, Laurie Kocher discusses how pedagogical documentation connects with the practice of phenomenology. She weaves together observations from her research study, that of the classroom educator Ann, and researcher Max van Manen. Phenomenology serves as a lens through which to write and read pedagogical documentation as a narrative rendering of the learning of children and educators.

In the next section, "Reconceptualizing Children's Image and Agency," the focus shifts from curriculum and documentation to examples of children's and adult's agency and participation within various learning sites including school, home and an intergenerational art program. In chapter six, Tara-Lynn Scheffel, asks the question "how can we be confident that our understandings represent children's thoughts, behaviors and experiences?" Referring to the United Nations Conventions of the Rights of Children and in particular children's rights to participate or not in ethnographic research, she examines her role in the construction of children as research partners. Her reflections on an ethics committee's review of children's role calls for a serious reconceptualizing of both researcher's and children's agency within ethnographic studies. In the next chapter, Sherry Rose critically reflects upon her life as a principal and classroom teacher through an examination of the ways in which schooled practices can crystallize socially constructed identities. In retelling the stories of Lion and Landscaper, she exposes how transgressing "normalized boundaries of teacher" can open up a series of possibilities for students positioned in these instances as *bad boy* and *class brain*. Retelling stories in a self-critical way makes visible the messiness, contradictions, and emancipatory possibilities of teaching and learning.

Chapter eight takes us out of schooled sites and into Maureen Kendrick's interpretation of a multilayered home play narrative in which she plays the dual role of researcher/playmate with a five-year-old Chinese-Canadian girl. Consciously relinquishing the direction of play to Leticia, and drawing upon Bahktinian notions of carnavelization, Kendrick presents a "detailed portrayal of the literacy related rules and routines of a kindergarten classroom." Leticia's play also reveals ways that children's ideas can inform reading-writing practices in the classroom, ideas such as sibling pairing and a pay centre. Closing this section Rachel Heydon's study takes us into intergenerational sites; artspaces shared by children and elders in three different care settings. Weaving childhood memory with curricular questions on the place of death and dying within an IG artspace, Heydon brings forward the poignancy and transience of life and death. Ironically, (given the context), death and dying were not part of the intended curriculum.

The remaining four chapters in the last section of the book offer insights into "Reconceptualizing Literacies in ECE." In chapter ten, Roz Stooke focuses upon a case study where she reclaims the multimodal affordances of interactive storytelling with seventeen kindergarten children in a culturally and linguistically diverse classroom. She argues that an interactive flannel board approach to storytelling is a "fertile context for literacy" and she seeks to "reposition storytelling as a pedagogical resource for twenty-first century early primary classrooms." This interactive approach emphasizes co-creation of texts with children, appropriation of texts by children, and contributes to children's narrative, expository, and metacognitive language. In the next chapter, Kim Bezaire and Linda Cameron claim play as one of many multiliteracies and make the case for toys as texts. They then take us into their *toytexts* action research project and uncover gendered and raced readings of mass marketed toys. Through this study they make explicit the transforming of childhood from one generation to another and a perceived shift from innocence to consumerism.

In chapter twelve, Kelly Young provides a critical reading of the Ontario environmental education curriculum and maps out a historical trajectory of the ways in which environmental education has been and continues to be dominated by a science model, one that perpetuates division between science and Indigenous notions of environmental education. In turn, she offers an eco-justice framework as a reconceptualist approach to early childhood literacy curriculum, one that could help foster critical cultural and ecological curricula in early childhood education.

With chapter thirteen, Luigi Iannacci takes up a critical narrative research approach to ethnographic work in primary classrooms. In his work with culturally and linguistically diverse children, Iannacci brings to fore the issues of power inherent in culture, language, and participation. The privileging of transmission-based pedagogies emphasizing phonics and physical colonization of students' bodies particularly for cultural and linguistically diverse children, run contrary to notions of a democratic and participative education.

Returning to the words of Bronwyn Davies and Susanne Gannon (2006) that open this chapter that we "seek to understand our own contribution to creating and withholding the conditions of possibility of particular lives" (p. 183), we invite you to enter into the pedagogical possibilities offered by the scholarly work that follows.

Notes

1 Although the new iteration continues to use developmental language, we recognize that it contains significant differences and that some notions have been seriously rethought. We also recognize that the field will require time for significant change to occur and understand the importance of creating conceptual and organizational bridges and alliances that address what has been described here (i.e., what has been and what is), and facilitate a shift toward what can be.

2 We recognize that the information provided here provides a very brief and perhaps essentialist history of childhood. The intent of this section was to succinctly demonstrate the social construction of childhood over time, and how these constructions have been limited and limiting. For a fuller examination of childhood see Aries, 1963 (often credited with being the first in this area of study and greatly critiqued.) Also see Higonnet, 1998; Shahar, 1990; Stearns, 2006; Suransky, 1982.

References

Alldred, P. (1998). Ethnography and discourse analysis: Dilemmas in representing the voices of children. In J. Ribbens & R. Edwards (Eds.), *Feminist dilemmas in qualitative research: Public knowledge and private lives* (pp. 148-170). London, Sage.

Almy, M. (1979). The impact of Piaget on early childhood education. In F.B. Murray (Ed.), *The impact of Piagetian theory on education, philosophy, psychiatry, and psychology* (pp. 159-190). Baltimore, MD: University Park Press.

Aries, P. (1963). *Centuries of childhood.* New York: Vintage Books.

Bronfenbrenner, U. (1979). *The ecology of human development.* Cambridge, MA: Harvard University Press.

Brown, W., & Barrera, I. (1999). Enduring problems in assessment: The persistent challenges of cultural dynamics and family issues. *Journal of Infants and Young Children, 12*(1), 34-42.

Cadwell, L. B. (1997). *Bringing Reggio Emilia home: An innovative approach to early childhood education.* New York: Teachers College Press.

Cannella, G. S. (1997). *Deconstructing early childhood education: Social justice & revolution.* New York: Peter Lang.

Carr, M. (2004, September). *Actual and possible selves: Kei tua o te pae.* Keynote address to EECERA 14th Annual Conference, Malta. Retrieved May 10, 2005, from http://www.educ.um.edu.mt/Computing/Eph/Presentations/Margaret%20Carr.pdf

Charlesworth, R. (1998). Developmentally appropriate practice is for everyone. *Childhood Education, 74*(5), 274-282.

Davies, B., & Gannon, S. (2006). *Doing collective biography.* Berkshire, UK: Open University Press.

Davis, L. (1997). Constructing normalcy. In L. Davis (Ed.), *The disability studies reader* (pp. 9-28). New York: Routledge.

Delpit, L. (2003). Educators as "Seed People": Growing a new future. *Educational Researcher, 32*(7), 14-21.

Falconer, R. C., & Byrnes. D. A. (2003). When good intentions are not enough: A response to increasing diversity in an early childhood setting. *Journal of Research in Childhood Education, 17*(2), 188-200.

Fraser, S. (2006). *Authentic childhood: Experiencing Reggio Emilia in the classroom* (2nd ed.). Toronto: Thomson/Nelson.

Friquegnon, M. L. (1997). What is a child? *Thinking: The Journal of Philosophy for Children, 13*(1), 12-16.

Gee, J. P. (1990). *Social linguistics and literacies: Ideology in discourses.* London: The Falmer Press.

Gee, J. P. (2000). The new literacy studies: From 'socially situated' to the work of the social. In D. Barton, M. Hamilton, & R. Ivaniè (Eds.), *Situated literacies: Reading and writing in context* (pp. 180-196). London: Routledge.

Ghosh, R. (1996). Multicultural teacher education in Canada. In M. Craft (Ed.), *Teacher education in plural societies* (pp. 45-56). London: Falmer Press.

Giroux, H. (1988). Teachers as transformative intellectuals. In H. Giroux & P. McLaren (Eds.), *Teachers as intellectuals: Towards a critical pedagogy of learning* (pp. 121-128). Granby, MA: Bergin & Garvey.

Gould, S. J. (1995). Mismeasure by any measure. In R. Jacoby & N. Glauberman (Eds.), The Bell Curve Debate (pp. 3-13). New York: Times Books.

Grieshaber, S., & Cannella, G. S. (2001). From identity to identities: Increasing Possibilities in early childhood education. In G. Grieshaber & G. S. Cannella (Eds.), *Embracing identities in early childhood education: Diversity and possibilities* (pp. 3-22). New York: Teachers College Press.

Hallett, C, & Prout, A. (2003). *Hearing the voices of children: Social policy for a new century.* New York: Routledge.

Heydon, R., & Iannacci, L. (2008). *Early childhood curricula and the de-pathologizing of childhood.* Toronto: University of Toronto Press.

Higonnet, A. (1998). *Pictures of innocence: The history and crisis of the ideal childhood.* New York: Thames & Hudson.

Hughes, P. (2005). Baby, it's you: International capital discovers the under threes. *Contemporary Issues in Early Childhood. 6*(1), 30-40.

Kapur, J. (2005). *Coining for capital. Movies, marketing, and the transformation of childhood.* Piscataway, NJ: Rutgers University Press.

Kehily, M. (2004). *An introduction to childhood studies.* Berkshire, UK: Open University Press.

Krogh, S. L., & Slentz, K. L. (2001). *Early childhood education; Yesterday, today and tomorrow.* New York: Routledge.

Lubeck, S. (1998). Is developmentally appropriate practice for everyone? *Childhood Education, 74*(5), 283-292.

Mayfield, M. I. (2001). *Early childhood education and care in Canada.* Toronto: Prentice Hall.

McCain, M., & Mustard, F. (1999). *Reversing the real brain drain: Early years study, final report.* Toronto: Canadian Institute for Advanced Research.

McIlroy, A. (2004, April 10). Starting from zero, the children of the future: 'We can build better brains'. *The Globe and Mail*, pp. F1, F6.

Moll, L. (1992). Funds of knowledge for teaching: Using a qualitative approach to connect homes and classrooms. *Theory into Practice, 31*(2), 132-41.

Moss, P. (2007). Meetings across the paradigmatic divide. *Educational Philosophy and Theory, 39*(3), 229-245.

New Zealand Ministry of Education. (1996). Te Whariki: Early childhood curriculum. Wellington, NZ: Learning Media Ltd.

O'Brien, L. M. (1996/1997). Turning my world upside down: How I learned to question developmentally appropriate practice. *Childhood Education, 73*(2), 100-102.

OCBCC. (2007). *Child care still a patchwork of underfunded programs.* Media release from Ontario Coalition for Better Child Care. Retrieved July 22, 2009, from http://action.web.ca/home/ocbcc/alerts.shtml?x=105734

O'Neill, T., & Zinga, D. (2008). *Children's rights; Multidisciplinary approaches to participation and protection.* Toronto: University of Toronto Press.

Piaget, Jean (1993/1970). The intellectual development of the child. In W. Coney, C. Cross, & B. Trunk (Eds.), *From Plato to Piaget: The greatest educational theorists from across the centuries and around the world* (pp. 251-267). Lanham, MD: University Press of America, Inc.

Pinar, W. (1994). *Autobiography, politics and sexuality: Essays in curriculum theory 1972-1992.* New York: Peter Lang.

Prout, A. (2005). *The future of childhood: Toward the interdisciplinary study of children.* London: Routledge.

Ritchie, J. (2001). Reflections on collectivism in early childhood teaching in Aotearoa/New Zealand. In G. Grieshaber & G. S. Canella (Eds.), *Embracing identities in early childhood education: Diversity and possibilities* (pp. 133-147). New York: Teachers College Press.

Rinaldi, C. (2006). In dialogue with Reggio Emilia: Listening, researching, and learning. London & New York: Routledge.

Shahar, S. (1990). *Childhood in the middle ages.* London: Routledge.

Sigel, I. E. (1979). *Piaget and education: A dialectic.* In F. B. Murray (Ed.), *The impact of Piagetian theory on education, philosophy, psychiatry, and psychology* (pp. 209-224). Baltimore, MD: University Park Press.

Siraj-Blatchford, I., & Clarke, P. (2000). Supporting identity, diversity and language in the early years. Berkshire, UK: Open University Press.

Sleeter, C. E. & Grant, C. A. (2003). *Making choices for multicultural education: Five approaches to race, class, and gender* (4th ed.). Toronto: John Wiley & Sons, Inc.

Steinberg, S. R., & Kincheloe. J. L. (Eds.). (1997). *Kinder-Culture. The corporate construction of childhood.* Boulder, CO: HarperCollins Publishers.

Stearns, P. (2006). *Childhood in world history.* New York: Routledge

Stooke, R. (2003). (Re)Visioning the Ontario early years study: Almost a fairy tale – but not quite. *Journal of Curriculum Theorizing, 19*(2), 91-101.

Suransky, V. (1982). *The erosion of childhood.* Chicago: University of Chicago Press.

Swadener, B. B. (2000). "At risk" or "at promise"? From deficit constructions of the "other childhood" to possibilities for authentic alliances with children and families. In L. Diaz Soto (Ed.), *The politics of early childhood education* (pp. 117-142). New York: Peter Lang.

Thompson, G. (2002). "Not an attempt to coddle children": Dr. Charles Hegler Gundry and the mental hygiene division of the Vancouver school board, 1939-1969. *Historical Studies in Education, 14*(2), 247-278.

Toohey, K. (2000). Learning English at school: Identity, social relations and classroom practice. Clevedon, UK: Multilingual Matters Ltd.

Viruru, R., & Cannella, G. S., (2001). Postcolonial ethnography, young children, and voice. In S. Grieshaber & G. S. Cannella, (Ed.), *Embracing identities in early childhood education; Diversity and possibilities* (pp. 158-172). New York: Teachers College Press.

Vygotsky, L. (1978). *Mind and society: The development of higher psychological processes.* Cambridge, MA: Harvard University Press.

Vygotsky, L. (1994). The problem of the environment. In R. Van Der Veer & J. Valsiner (Eds.), *The Vygotsky reader* (pp. 338-354). Oxford, UK: Blackwell.

Wolf, M. (2007). *Proust and the squid. The story and science of the reading brain.* New York: HarperCollins Publishers.

Woodill, G. A. (1992). International early childhood care and education: Historical perspectives. In G. Woodill, J. Bernhard, & L. Prochner (Eds.), *International handbook of early childhood education* (pp. 147-154). New York: Garland Publishing.

Reconceptualizing Curriculum and Professional Development in ECE

Discovery begins in the single that is singular

stories created and lived

the possibility of another way

to draw up water like the roots of a tree

2

Towards Designing a
Postfoundational Curriculum Document[1]

Pam Whitty

> The meaning we give and make of things, actions,
> people and feelings, is collectively constituted and
> formulated within specific cultural and societal con-
> texts; ie: negotiated and re-negotiated as a co-con-
> structive process of meaning-making in time and
> place.
>
> Hillevi Lenz Taguchi, 2007, p. 277

My involvement in the conceptualization and creation of Early Learning and Care curriculum documents for the province of New Brunswick has allowed me, and many others,[2] to closely and critically experience and examine, in a first-hand manner, the dominance of developmentalism (Moss, 2007) in early childhood curriculum-making provincially, nationally, and inter-nationally. My hope in this chapter is to share with you a look into a more post foundational approach to early years curriculum, in part, through the co-constructing of multimodal, polyphonic representations of educators', and children's knowledge and know-how (Dyson, 2003) as they have been negotiated in published and forthcoming curriculum documents. The published documents, to date, include *The New Brunswick Curriculum Framework for Early Learning and Child Care – English* (*NBCF*) (University of New Brunswick [UNB], 2008) and the *Well-Being Curriculum Support Document* (Ashton, Hunt, & White, 2008). These documents have been and continue to be co-constructed by members of the University of New Brunswick (UNB) Early Learning and Child Care Curriculum (ECC) Project Team with childcare educators in licensed centres in New Brunswick.[3] My telling and interpretations can only be partial, while inviting alternative understandings and providing me a place to begin to examine this immense curriculum project.[4]

In these co-constructed documents, we have drawn upon curriculum theorizing that emphasizes a social-cultural approach to children's learning and care, one that recognizes children's and educators' interests, passions and strengths.[5] As a means to interrupt the grand narrative of developmentism (Dahlberg & Moss, 2005, p. 166), we have taken up Valerie Walkerdine's (2004) proposal that rather than viewing humans as developmental subjects on a developmental path from birth to death, we see ourselves, and children, as subjects produced by and producing various subject selves – or identities – within various contexts, the intent being to value the "many and varied childhoods in their local variants and global forms." (p. 107). This type of postfoundational thinking and practice within this project emphasizes the local; it makes central New Brunswick children, educators and families, New Brunswick practices, provisions and places within co-constructed, New Brunswick documents. It is a local project with global resonance.

Throughout the course of this project, close to 1300 child care educators[6] and approximately twenty-five curriculum team members at the UNB-ECC have taken part in the research, development, and implementation of a provincial curriculum[7] for early child care educators working with infants, toddlers, and young children in licensed centres.[8] Members of the UNB curriculum team have worked side by side with each other and with child care educators both on and off sites via telephone and email. My work within this project work resonates with Taguchi's (2007) sensibility that negotiating and renegotiating a meaning-making process is collectively constituted within specific cultural and societal contexts, within a particular time and place.

Conversations As Traces of the Pedagogical

For some time, I have been drawn to the philosophical notion of reclaimed and reconstituted conversations as a way to articulate educational thought by and about women and children (Ashton & Whitty, 2007; Nason & Whitty, 2007; Rose & Whitty, 1995; Whitty 1993; Whitty, 1995; Whitty, Rose, Baisley, Comeau, & Little, 2008). I trace my initial influence to the work of feminist philosophers Jane Roland Martin (1985, 1992) and Elisabeth Young Bruehl (1987): Martin for her philosophical thought and practice of reclaiming epistemological thinking by and about women in the form of philosophical conversations; and Young-Bruehl's notion of conversational moments, an ontology of being in the moment with a cast of encouragers, courage and encourage deliberately intertwined. The notion of reclaimed conversations and conversational moments coincides with reconceptualist early childhood literature. In particular, a pedagogy of listening (Rinaldi, 2006) enacts a deeply conversational approach to pedagogy. It emphasizing responsive and reciprocal relationships and co-constructed curriculum that emerges out of educators' conversations and careful observations of their own knowledge and interests and those of the children they teach (Fraser, 2006; Rinaldi, 2006).

Janet Miller (2005) writes that the paradox of the pedagogical is that "it leaves no visible trace of its happening" (p. 115). Within the context of this curriculum materialization, much was made visible through reclaiming, reconstituting, and textualizing conversations and conversational moments of pedagogical learning and care from child care educators. In this chapter, I am interested in making the pedagogical visible by examining how forms of *discursive conversing* within/across modernist and postfoundational ideas and spaces have been animated in our co-constructed curriculum documents (Gorodetsky & Barack, 2008; Moss, 2007; Taguchi, 2007). At the same time, I wish to make visible a sense of our indebtedness and contribution to *international policy and cur-*

riculum conversations in early childhood education. In particular, in terms of the co-construction of curriculum materials by educators within their centres, I am intrigued by how interrupting the taken-for-granted nature of time and place is integral to reconceptualizing early childhood curriculum (Kearney, 2008; Bachelard, 1988; Pink, 2008; Somerville, 2007; Whitty, Rose, Baisley, Comeau & Thompson, 2008; Wien & Smith, 1998).

Global-Local Connections: Co-constructing the NBCF

> The *NBCF* is about living a good life with children. It is strongly rooted in early childhood internationally and it links New Brunswick with Scandinavia, New Zealand and Reggio Emilia. It is both local and global and inclusive (in text) of aboriginal communities. It demonstrates sensitivity about children and acknowledges that these proposed curriculum changes present a challenge. That is unusual. It is not prescriptive – it doesn't tell you what to do. It asks questions and invites your responses. . . . I could read about the various childcare centres across the provinces and as an outsider to New Brunswick, it gave me an image of life with children in New Brunswick. It is promising and positive. (Carol Anne Wien, 2008)

During the creating of the *New Brunswick Curriculum Framework* (*NBCF*), we had many opportunities to carefully examine and converse over official early childhood curricula from other places. Of the many official curricula that shaped our thinking about the who, what, where, and how of curriculum-making in the province of New Brunswick, two were particularly foundational: Te Whariki (New Zealand Ministry of Education, 1996) and Essential Learnings (Department of Education, Tasmania, 2004). Similarities that these two early learning and care curricula hold in common with the *NBCF* include: a) curriculum frameworks that outline values and broad areas of learning; b) a social-pedagogical/social-cultural approach to children's knowledge and know-how that make explicit a positive, competent image of children

and childhood including the critical role in learning of relationships, cultures, languages and environments;[9] and c) an effort to
topple traditional developmental psychology as the singular
grand narrative of early childhood education (See Whitty, Rose,
White, & Langille, 2006). In part, due to the proliferation of the
English language, access to the Internet and extensive minority
world publications (Pence, 1998), we at UNB-ECC have been able to
benefit from the work of numerous educators and researchers
who have taken a generally social-cultural/social-pedagogical,
postfoundational approach (Cannella & Viruru, 2004; Dahlberg &
Moss, 2005; Edmiston, 2008; McNaughton, 2006; Rinaldi, 2006) to
the (re)visioning of curriculum for infants, toddlers, and young
children – prior to their entry into the school system.

In proposing forums for engaging people from different paradigms in discussions about early childhood policy and practice,
Peter Moss (2007) suggests these forums might be "in seminars,
conferences, journals, and other media, which might provide
space for political argumentation" (p. 236). In this revisiting of the
NBCF, it strikes me that through the process and publication of the
NBCF, the curriculum framework is a forum that reaches across
modernist-postfoundational paradigms through various forms of
discursive conversing. These forms of discursive conversing
include: visual form and format, use of language, and narrative-
reflective possibilities. I explore these notions of discursive conversing in the following section.

Discursive Conversing: Form and Format

The form and format of the *NBCF* consists of numerous double
page spreads. In this way, the *NBCF* looks similar in form to both
Te Whariki and Essential Learnings. This was intentional on the
part of the authors and designers. The two pages and the
non–paragraph format give a breathing space, if you will, while
explicating various aspects of each of the four goals: well-being,
play and playfulness, communication and literacies, diversity and
social responsibility. Belonging, an aspect of the well-being goal, is
presented on the next page. This form and format is not unlike
school curriculum documents, and thus it allows educators,
administrators, and policy makers to recognize the *NBCF* as a curriculum documents and engage with it as such.

Children build respectful and responsive relationships.

Educators provide time and spaces for children to develop and maintain relationships

WHAT'S INVOLVED IN LEARNING	SAMPLE NARRATIVES
Developing cherished as well as casual friendships	"I like everyone in our class," states Julie (4 years). "But Isaac is my best friend," she adds, while talking to her educator.
Forming close relationships with a range of adults	After Tommy's fourth birthday he moves from Mildred's room to a new group in the centre. Every time something especially exciting happens, Tommy returns to share the stories with Mildred.
Growing in their awareness that their actions contribute to the well-being of others	Children in the four-year-old room take pleasure in pushing the infants on the swings. The infants respond to the interactions with spontaneous, contagious laughter. *100 Aker Woods Daycare*
Participating in group initiatives	Claire (3 years) exclaims, "Let's have a parade," and begins to march. Her friends see her and join in. A line of children makes its way through the classroom. The educator, noticing their excitement, pulls out the rhythm instruments and hands them out as the children march by.

For Reflection

What opportunities does your centre provide for children to develop friend-ships across ages? How do the centre's polices and procedures support and/or limit such multi-age interactions?

How do you provide space, time, freedom, and support for children to develop friendships? Think about indoor and outdoor activities, on-site and beyond-site relationships. Think about scheduling, physical space, staffing ratios, indoor and outdoor activities.

How do you encourage the participation of every child? Think about children's friendships, patterns of exclusion, activity choices, gender, race, and class.

SUGGESTED PROVISIONS AND PRACTICES

Allow children private social spaces to make and sustain friendships within their own and other age groups.

Let families know about their children's friendships so that they can choose to extend them beyond the centre.

Acknowledge and maintain the special bonds that form between children and adults within the centre.

Provide for multi-age groupings in which caregivers get to know all the children.

Consider following a group of children through their daycare experience.

Provide spaces for children to work together and learn from one another.

Model appreciation of others with positive talk; encourage children to listen, support, celebrate, question, and care for other children; talk through and point out how their actions affect others.

Be open to unplanned changes in scheduling.

Build upon children's spontaneous and recurring activities; be playful in following their lead.

Be aware of how each child participates within the centre community.

How are children's contributions to your centre invited and accepted? Think about toys, stories, cultural artifacts, ideas, questions, and children's theory building.

How do educators and families learn from and about each other at your centre? Think about how you ensure time and space for authentic and personal communications, and consider relationships between families, between educators, and between educators and families.

As in Te Whariki, we used shading to designate one section from another and like Essential Learnings; we included photographs of children and educators – all taken in New Brunswick pilot sites. Unlike either document, we have woven explicit values in a banner form at the bottom of the pages; collected sample narratives from eight pilot sites and included children's art work – in this case the hearts icon, which represents well-being. In a visual sense the curriculum is quite approachable, in part because of its similarity to other curriculum documents and through the invitational feel offered by photographs and children's icons. Thus it may have the flexibility to be read by those who locate themselves within modernist and postfoundational discourses, thereby providing a starting point for conversation to begin. As Kate Pahl (2009) noted when she was speaking of the *NBCF*, her first read through was instrumental, in that she read the *NBCF* as a standard curriculum document. During her second and third read, she gained a better sense of the depth of the document and made the explicit shift from modernist to postfoundational thinking and practice.

Discursive Connecting: What Language to Use?

> The discourse (developmentalism) has a distinct (and English) vocabulary: words like "development," "quality," "readiness for school," "best practice," "benchmark," and "outcomes" figure prominently. It draws on a few disciplinary perspective, notably child development and economics. It privileges instrumental rationality and technical practice; its prime questions being "what are the outcomes?" and "what works?" In doing so, it sets up a binary opposition between process and outcomes. (Moss, 2007, p. 229)

In the case of creating curriculum documents for this project, process and outcomes are deconstructed as binaries and the published documents serve as a way to illuminate both. As one of the many writers of the *NBCF*, I am aware of the careful and deliberate way in which we chose language – from one paradigm or another or both – that in retrospect may serve as a kind of conversational crossing between modernist and postfoundational spaces. For the most part we avoided the identifiable language of developmentalism that Moss discusses above; however other linguistic turns were made visible to us by Susan Fraser, our first outside reviewer.[10] She helped me (and I believe others on our project) see how much I still was sitting inside the progressive developmentalism language. As I recall it, this was particularly the case with the use of the phrase *the child*; an emphasis on the child's autonomy; and an apparent lack of linguistic emphasis on children, collective learning, and pedagogical documentation. As a consequence of her review, we reconceptualized parts of the framework prior to taking it to the field for further consultation and review.[11] It is likely that other modernist tendencies will be uncovered in time.

Discursive Connecting and Redefining "What's Involved in Learning"

Because the New Zealand writers textualized *outcomes,* the designers of the *NBCF* could think about the language of outcomes and ask questions such as how does this work here in NB, or is there a different choice? What linguistic term (linguistic turn) can we take textually and politically as we engage in this conscious effort to shift more fully into postfoundational theories and practices? How will this shift work for educators, children, families, and policy-makers? Instead of using the language of outcomes, we decided to go with broad-based learning goals. We moved away from foregrounding developmental outcomes and deficit-based assessment to much broader based learning goals and narrative assessment (Carr, 2001) encompassing rather than foregrounding developmental domains; once again, these integrated broad-based learning goals are well-being, play and playfulness, communication and literacies, and diversity and social responsibility.

My interpretation of our aim was that we intended to accentuate "what's involved in learning" and to disrupt outcomes; outcomes call attention to the normative-performative, sometimes to the exclusion of learning occurring in the present moment. Attention to a checklist and what is or is not going on falls in line with a deficit view of children, childhood, and curriculum. It is this deficit, modernist view that we were aiming to disrupt.

On the other hand, *goal* is a familiar term, but it can be mis-construed to be synonymous with an outcome. There exists an inherent danger that in making the complex simple, goals, when put into practice, could become checklists. Did we disrupt? As we meet, converse, and workshop with educators around the province, I think it is fair to say that there are mixed reviews. A formal evaluation is in the works; however, anecdotally, many educators find broad-based goals more open and relaxing and more related to the what and how of children's learning. Moreover, these educators report that these goals inform and expand their own pedagogical practice.

Into the Postfoundational: Narrative-Reflective Possibilities

Sample Narratives

The Essential Learnings curriculum document created in Tasmania outlines *little narratives* as a way to story short examples of children's learning within their curriculum framework. It was my sense that the authors of Essential Learnings chose little narratives as a way to deconstruct the grand narrative of development-mentalism that so permeates early childhood education. Picking up from the Tasmanian example, and to be inclusive of the pilot project educators, we decided to go with sample narratives. We created the sample narratives initially from our own collective experience and research. For the most part, sample narratives from the eight pilot sites replaced these initial narratives. These sample narratives highlight a positive image of children and educators. The reviewers and pilot participants have indicated that these textualized conversational moments resonate with their experiences and make the document readable and tangible.

Learning Stories

We did embrace the idea of learning stories, though not uncritically. Learning stories are accessible forms of narrative assessment intended to document children's strengths acting as a credit rather than deficit form of assessment (Carr & Lee, 2004; Rose, 2007). It was while visiting New Zealand (Whitty, Rose, White, & Langille, 2006) that I experienced first-hand how observing and documenting moments of children's learning including their own words, acted as a kind of *narrative connecting* between home and centre, between child and child, between adult and child, and within the child – bringing the textual and conversational together with the visual in a "positive and promising way" (Wien, 2008). There was clearly a "can-do" notion in New Zealand in relation to children, a phrase I heard repeated the entire length of the country.

Reflective Questions

The questions we created were largely co-constructed by members of the UNB team. They were surprisingly time consuming and intended to act as a series of possibilities. Although right answers can be read into the questions, I think it is fair to say that it was our collective sense, that reflective questions remain a less prescriptive approach to communicating with educators than directives. Examples of questions include:

> How do people and policies at your centre honour children's initiatives – through careful planning, documentation, and/or responses. Think about how your centre builds upon children's interests.

> How does your conception of childhood and what it means to be a child influence your responses to the different identities children take on? Describe how your responses to a child's gestures, verbal expressions, and work help to increase a child's belief in herself or himself? (*Well-Being*, p. 23)

Changing our Image of Children, Curriculum, and Ourselves

> We acknowledge children as curious and communicative individuals in their own right; young children actively constructing, co-constructing and re-constructing their understanding(s) of their world(s). (*NBCF*, 2008, p. 8)

This image of children and childhood is not what we typically encountered as we began the project in 2005. At that time, when consulting across the province and visiting child care centres, health and safety regulations and planning documents posted by educators or administrators were in evidence in all centres. Typically, the curricular postings outlined the daily schedule and weekly themes; in very few cases, themes were posted for the entire year. This public posting of themes appeared to be a fairly common interpretation of New Brunswick government regulations, that required curriculum planning be visible to parents and Early Childhood Services Coordinators. Such an interpretation resulted in curriculum and accompanying activities that were fairly prescriptive, and often the same from year to year. Children and educators were thus regulated to plan well in advance and to provide evidence of this planning typically in advance. Co-constructing curriculum is difficult to do when much is preplanned.

Emergent curriculum (how the field has named the curriculum)is defined as working from children's and educators' interests within a meaning-making paradigm (Dahlberg, Moss, & Pence, 2007; Wien, 2008), was largely an unfamiliar concept within the field; typically children and educators were guided through the day by the clock and through the year by the weekly themes. In some cases, when the numbers of children decreased during the day, and ratio requirements shifted accordingly, it was not uncommon for educators to be sent home by their directors. This is in part because day care in New Brunswick is a mostly a private enterprise, though not a corporate enterprise.[12] In either case, early education suffers from limited funds, and such a practice limits planning and reflection time.

Pedagogical Poetics: Interrupting Clock Time

> Bachelard claims that every "real " poem signals a stopping of ordinary clock time introducing instead a dimension of "verticality" in depth and in height a stopping of ordinary clock time. Where prosaic time is horizontal and continuous, poetic time is discontinuous and disruptive. (Kearney, 2008, p. 38)

Linda Gould, childcare educator, director, and currently onsite curriculum support staff, created what Bachelard might recognize as "an event of temporal rupture" (Kearney, 2008, p. 41) when she asked educators at her centre to remove the clocks from their walls for two weeks (Wien, 2008). As a centre director, working with the curriculum framework during the piloting phase, she had noticed that engagement with the curriculum seemed to be hampered by an overriding engagement with clock time. Attention to clock time seemed to supersede attention to a child's/children's interests and knowledge – a key component of the curriculum framework.

When Linda articulated her insight to her staff and made the clock request, she suggested that they see what happens. When she retold this event at a large workshop (Wien, 2008) and later in conversation with me, she freely admitted that the initial response was: "Are you crazy?"[13] In effect, Linda ruptured horizontal time with her request that educators remove clocks. Without the clock, the educators felt the children were more relaxed; they themselves were more relaxed and within this more relaxed ambience better able to attend to children's conversations, engage with their interests, and co-create curriculum. Without the clock, the educators seemed able to practice what Bachelard (1988) calls "an ethic of attention," in this case to children and creating curriculum and noting learning rather than chronological time. To date, one room remains clock-free, other rooms have restored the clock, but reportedly not clock time.

Linda's observation and experience resonates with Wien's (1995) findings that close adherence to time can act as a systemic constraint to the implementation of co-constructed curriculum. In "Untiming the curriculum: A case study of removing clocks from the program," Wien and Kirby-Smith (1998) write,

> Once the clock was removed from Tanya's and Elizabeth's work patterns, a new curriculum began to emerge. It did not focus on an arbitrary program that teachers believed was good for the children. Rather now the children begin to co-own the curriculum with the teachers. Observations were more astute and precise and more cohesively tied to programming. (p. 12)

Over this ten-month period, the complexities of removing the clock and shifting to co-creating curriculum with children are made visible. The untiming of the curriculum has the potential to shift educators from horizontal time to a more fluid style of pedagogical poetics, one infused with an ethic of attention to children and pedagogical possibilities rather than an over strict adherence to clock-time.

Playing With and For Time:
Conversations about Interrupting Horizontal Time

Two examples of other ways that educators have played with/for time are materialized within the *Well-Being* support document. When engaged in the pilot project workshops, we noticed that a more fluid structure of the day, as a way to attend to children and create blocks of uninterrupted time for and with them, was argued against by some educators for a number of legitimate reasons including: the need for routine and predictability; cooks' schedules; staff breaks; lunches and snacks; and ratio requirements.

The examples we chose to textualize were worked out with educators through conversations that took place within Curriculum Project workshops, onsite visits, and numerous emails and telephone conversations; these educators were playing *with* time in an effort to open up the day for children and themselves. We hoped that these examples might inspire educators in the field to try their own time shifting. One example features a visual routine of the day with photographs of children engaged in various activities marking major shifts in the day such as arrival and departure times, lunch and tidy-up. The visual routine example from Maria Gillis of Unicorn Children's Centre in Moncton was placed in an educator reflection section within the personal care aspect of physical health, one of the well-being facets. In her words:

> The photographs story the children's day from arrival to departure. The photographic timeline of the day is a much more realistic and practical way to help children understand the passage of time as opposed to counting abstract numbers on a calendar or chart. The children are actually experiencing these events

each day in the centre...We talked about these events and the photos seem to inspire the children to take control of their own tasks and responsibilities. (Ashton, Hunt, & White, 2008, pp. 34-35)

Another textualized example that illustrates a way to play *for* time is open snack. Snack time, as a ritualized practice, often was cited as a reason for ending periods of play, interrupting some children and educators' capacity to engage in sustained activities or projects. Angela Thompson, then at King's County in Sussex, New Brunswick, had heard about open snack at one of the curriculum workshops we had organized – a deliberately created participative edge community of learning where sharing between educators formed a significant portion of the day. Encouraged by her peers, she tried it out. Initially, open snack was unsuccessful so she and her colleagues "stepped back afterward and re-thought the approach" (Ashton, Hunt, & White, 2008, p. 38). The next time, instead of calling everyone at once, snack was made available to the children by quietly informing them while they were working-playing in the groups that snack was there if and when they wanted it. After some thoughtful adjustments, Angela comments, "We have a true buffet style snack that is very relaxed and the children love it!" (p. 39).

Open snack discussions were often highly controversial and initially took on a mythological status as something that must be done rather than an option of the new curriculum. As a counterpoint, we ensured that other possibilities including the reasons for sharing food together were included in the *Well-Being* support document (Ashton, Hunt, & White, 2008, p. 39); however, it seems that discussion around the new controversial practice took on a either-or binary life of its own. Over time, we noticed that the opposition became less vocal, and we hope that in the same way that Angela was inspired by her peers, so too will her detailing of open snack inspire others to open up time for children and educators.

Co-creating Curriculum – A Complex Instant

We are concerned here with a "complex " instant which gathers and concentrates many simultaneities at once. So doing, it cuts across the continuity of sequential time." Time no longer flows, as he puts it, it shoots up. (Kearney, 2008, p. 38)

Making curricular change is a complicated process and can be frustrating. Identifying and co-constructing curriculum with children takes time and expertise. Although we encouraged people "to take their time" (Whitty, 2007) in making a shift from prescribed, preprogrammed curriculum to co-constructed curriculum, that engages children's minds and hearts (Katz & Chard, 2000), we recognize that planning with and for children's interests takes knowledge, know how, and a bit of a leap. This is where curriculum making can become dangerous (Ashton & Whitty, 2007). In fairness to childcare educators, children, and families, something must replace something. The *complex instant* as theorized by Bachelard has the capacity to dislodge horizontal time, a poetic instant that entails listening to children and engaging in self-reflection. Being with/in time seems to be one way to engage.

Beep-Beep – A Complex Instant of Recognition

Shawnda Farquhar, Kelly Trenholm, and Leanne Donavan work at the Unicorn Day Care in Moncton and have done so for a number of years. For many of these years, a garbage truck has done a weekly pick-up from the centre. Recently, this weekly occurrence produced an unexpected opportunity for co-constructing curriculum. Both Kelly and Shawnda were taking part in the curriculum pilot and had voiced questions about how to make a shift from more prescribed programming to engaging children's interests. Up until their involvement in the pilot project, the beep-beep sound of the garbage truck reversing was merely a novel bit of weekly background noise. However, it was in this one moment, when the children's attention was arrested by the sound, that Shawnda, Kelly, and Leanne saw the garbage truck an authentic point of engagement for the children and their educators. The educators realized this was an interest that could provide curricular content. Acting on the beep-beep moment, these two educators co-constructed an extensive recycling and landfill project.

Kelly and Shawnda were part of a group of educators creating learning experiences for children and themselves; experiences that when reflected upon provided the basis for co-constructing curriculum. They graciously shared their excitement at a pilot site meeting and at orientation sessions – noting that they had not been keen on the curricular change initially. They enacted what Carol Anne Wien (2008) might recognize as "spirited resistance." This complex instant held within it the simultaneities – a past, present and future – of the children and their educators in the midst of making meaning within a curricular change. They engaged educator peers in conversations that were both agential and inspiring. As I listened to them – they seemed ecstatic – I read their storying of this complex instant and co-construction as: "We are figuring it out. We are learning a lot and the children are engaged."

This is an example has not yet been allocated to a specific support document; it could fit within goal four, particularly within sustainable futures; and it would fit equally as well within goal three, literate communities, or within the documentation and assessment support document, or within curriculum planning for threes and fours. We have many implicit and explicit criteria when collecting and selecting examples: inclusion of as many educators as possible, recognition that the goals and the process of learning are highly integrative, and highlighting the local. We trust that these criteria will provide examples and inspiration to other educators while contributing to the valuing of the child care community, children's families, educators' learning, as well as care knowledge and know how across the province.

Place Pedagogies: Local, Storied, and Contested

> As centers of experience, places teach us about how the world works, and how our lives fit into the spaces we occupy. Further, places make us: As occupants of particular places with particular attributes, our identity and our possibilities are shaped. (Gruenwald as cited in Somerville, 2007, p. 151)

There was a moment in the midst of the *NBCF* project when I wanted to formally name the finished document *A Sense of Place*. I had been thinking of Te Whariki and the metaphorical meaning of woven mat.[14] I was imagining what metaphor might work for this

New Brunswick document. Place plays a critical role in the co-construction of the document; place is specific and yet at the same time could be metaphorical. I thought about what New Brunswick meant to me: a place my parents had left in the late 1940s to seek employment elsewhere, a place we returned to every summer, a place I held in my mind and heart as a place of magic. My childhood nostalgia and my own sense of belonging with/in/to the land of New Brunswick is what brought me back to New Brunswick in the mid-1970s. New Brunswick had been embodied within me since I was a very young child. If I trace my sense of place back beyond my memory to the 1800s my family histories makes explicit that when we came to this place, we intermarried with Acadians and First Nations. It is clear when I visit Northern New Brunswick that my Irish Catholic ancestors would not have survived this place if not for their relationships with the Mik'maq and Acadian peoples. In the closing section of this chapter, I begin to consider Margaret Somerville's theorizing of place pedagogies as local, storied, and contested and its place in the New Brunswick curriculum process.[15]

"Place Learning is Embodied and Local" (Somerville, 2007, p. 149)

> In what ways do you affirm families' connection to the centre? Think about how families see themselves reflected at the centre – through artifacts from home, favourite recipes, family pictures and stories. (*NBCF*, 2008, p. 86)

> I thought that incorporating pictures of the children and their families into my home room would be a good idea. I had made similar picture blocks in the past, but I had used pictures that were connected to certain themes that I was doing at the time. Making the blocks with the children's family pictures connects the centre with home. (Jennifer Curtis, Ashton, Hunt, & White, 2008, p. 22)

Jennifer Curtis worked as an early childhood educator at the Chatham day care in Miramichi, New Brunswick, when she wrote this reflection for the "Sense of Place" section in the *Well-Being* document.[16] One of the things that truly intrigued me about Jennifer's blocks was her kaleidoscopic curricular turn with these thoughtful homemade materials. She used many of the same materials (milk containers and paper) she has used previously and instead of focusing on theme, which may or may not have meaning for the very young children in her room, she focused on families and connected home with the centre in a very visual, emotionally meaningful way for children, educators, and families. Her reflective piece continues:

> Each child and educator in the room had their own individual block, when the children first saw their blocks; they took immediate ownership of them. They carried them around and would spend time looking at and studying the block. The blocks helped give children a sense of belonging in their new environment. The children often bring us their blocks and tell us who is on them. They also look at the educators' blocks and talk about their families too. Now the children always recognize our children and husbands when they come in to visit. The blocks have really connected the children's families with their daycare families.
>
> It is eight months later and the children still have an interest in the blocks. They now build more with them, they are not as possessive with them as they were at first, they share these blocks with their friends and we often see them together building towers. They will still carry them around sometimes and will sit and talk about the pictures. (Ashton, Hunt & White, 2008, p. 2)

After Jennifer presented her family blocks at a curriculum workshop, the UNB Curriculum team noticed similar blocks appearing at other centres around the province. These very personal blocks provide opportunities for comfort, conversations, and play. Jennifer's engagement with children and their families and hers are thoughtful, resourceful, handmade, and very personal materials that connect children's new place with a connection to many children's first place – their families.

"Our Relationship to Place is Communicated in Stories and Other Representations" (Somerville, 2007, p. 149)[17]

> It didn't take us long to realize that our perception of this "overall absence" challenged our focus on the use of professionally produced picture books as an accessible multimodal literacy practice. We realized we needed to put aside our own assumptions to better see, rather than judge, the literacy practices and events occurring within the childcare centres. (Whitty, Rose, Baisley, Comeau, and Thompson, 2008, p. 21)

Last year, Sherry Rose, one of the curriculum writers, and I had multiple opportunities to visit childcare centres. We were always welcomed and enlivened by our conversations with children, educators, and directors. At that time we were reading, writing, and researching goal three of the curriculum framework, communication and literacies. As former primary grade teachers and avid readers, we had a deep love of picture books in and of themselves and because of the pleasure, storying, and learning possibilities that picture books incite in young children. Once we were able to critique our focus on the absence of picture books, we became present to handmade texts that were occurring in many of rooms (See Whitty, Rose, Baisley, Comeau, & Thompson, 2008). Two of these stories, Angela Thompson's *Red Walk* and Leisa Comeau's *Vehicles,* took us into the author's and children's relationship with place and how this relationship is communicated in multimodal ways through the genre of handmade books. Just as Jennifer Curtis, above, had thoughtfully and resourcefully used materials at hand to help children negotiate their new place, and just as she had co-constructed curricula materials with them, so too Angela and Leisa also drew upon local materials and everyday events to story and represent place.

Angela's *Red Walk* book drew upon local landmarks representing objects such as post boxes, deer apples, and local landmarks that constitute the storying and conversations of their daily walks in their town. Leisa's *Vehicles* book began with her observation that on their daily walks the children were interested in vehicles. Their consistent interest lead to her retelling a story of her own that focused on the play-place of an abandoned vehicle on her property, one that occupied her own children for a long time. Their interest prompted her to invite families to share their vehicle stories, and they did! In a place like New Brunswick, where so much is rural, various kinds of vehicles play an enormous role in getting from place to place, in both our physical and imaginative worlds.

As a consequence of activities created by Anne Hunt and Kembubi Christie,[18] in the context of exploring goal three, handmade books have been taken up by hundreds of educators in the province. Some of these books are related directly to place, some are not. They all, however, say something about the place of handmade texts inside sites of children's early learning and care. As well, the sharing of handmade books at local cluster meetings seemed to serve as a kind of onsite breakthrough for educators in the co-constructing of curriculum and documenting of children's interests.

"Place Learning Involves a Contact Zone of Contested Place Stories" (Somerville, 2007, p. 149)

> The (place) framework offers three broad and interrelated principles that underpin critical place pedagogy: place learning is necessarily embodied and local; our relationship to place is communicated in stories and other representations; place learning involved a contact zone of contested place stories. (Somerville, 2007, p. 149)

Place as a way to teach us about how the world works and how we fit the spaces within which we live permeates New Brunswick curriculum documents in the form of sample narratives, photographs, children's mark making, curricular examples, and educators' reflections. We have provided many examples of how place is local and storied. We continue to collect place stories of landmarks, personal and official that children experience in their centres and within their communities for inclusion within forthcoming curriculum documents. For example, we have listened to stories of neighborhood walks that entail cruise ships in city harbors, the releasing of a whale from its entanglement in a fishing net, fir tipping for wreaths, a project on the circus emerging from a local juggler's interactions with children, and of walks along beaches, rivers in the woods, and in residential neighborhoods

As a sense of place is developed, questions concerning whose embodiment of the local is represented must be asked. Whose stories? What places, peoples, stories, and objects are absent or present? Who is represented and who is not? And why not? What might we do about absence? These questions may help us became aware of contested place stories and figure out with others how to make multiple stories of place visible, stories across peoples and place without resorting to defining people by their place and time only.

I read and re-read the words of Herménégilde Chiasson[19] "It is not the people that make the land – it is the land that makes them, that makes us. Living in New Brunswick has shaped the way we have of doing things, the way we have of taking out time and experiencing the environment around us." Is this how place shapes us, and if so, whose place, and when? What does time have to do with place? How do we illuminate place across time when both the First Nations and then Acadian populations were relegated to less desirable places by the British? What about more recent arrivals to New Brunswick? How do these multiple histories and multiple presences fit within a series of curriculum documents for young children and their educators?

Because we are still in the process of co-constructing documents, we have many possibilities to work with others to make visible multiple sites of place pedagogies and bring forward alternative stories of place. In particular, within goal three, one of the facets of learning addresses children's literate identities in communities recognizing that children co-construct a range of literate identities. To engage in this learning, suggested practices for educators include ensuring children's rights to participate in, create, and critique the range of products and practices within the classroom by connecting children's interests to local events and practices that they may not know about or could investigate deeply first hand (*NBCF*, 2008, p. 148-149). In goal four, diversity and social responsibility, there are at least two possibilities for the materialization of multiple local stories. These are within inclusiveness and equity and in particular the playing out of children appreciating their own distinctiveness and that of others. What is involved in learning includes learning about their cultural heritages and those of other families within the centre and the broader society, and learning about and engaging with communities representative of New Brunswick society (*NBCF*, 2008, p. 52)

In closing, and on the topic of communities, the work of Malta Gorodestsky and Judith Barak (2008), particularly the notion of participative edge communities, has been helpful in this articulation of deliberate and collective efforts of various learning communities within this project. I am struck by the hope and possibility that *participative edge communities* engage in the present and the future simultaneously. Defined as "critical zones of interactions between landscapes and habitats that influence the flux of energy and materials"(p. 1909), some features of the participative edge communities that resonate with my involvement inside this curriculum-making process include: deliberate knowledge production and change; encouragement of an egalitarian, democratic status of participation; and participation of different voices as points of departure for deliberations. In part, it is through the process of ongoing conversations in the co-construction of curriculum texts that the many writers of the New Brunswick Curriculum documents have contributed to the ongoing life of participative edge communities. In this curricular instance, edge communities might be thought of as interactive spaces where individuals and groups from modernist and postfoundational places come together, at least temporally, to engage in critical conversations, enact curricular change, and as part of this change, co-construct curriculum documents across and within the modernist-postfoundational spaces.[20]

Notes

[1] An earlier version of this paper was presented at *Honoring the Child, Honoring Equity: Young Citizen(s), New Citizenship(s)*, Centre for equity and innovation, University of Melbourne, Australia, November 2008.

[2] Since 2005, more than 220 presentations, publications, seminars, and workshops have been produced locally, regionally, provincially, nationally, and internationally from this project. The project was funded by the Department of Social Development, Government of New Brunswick, and carried out by The Early Childcare Centre at the University of New Brunswick

[3] Curriculum research team members during the making of the two documents presented in these chapter include: Pam Whitty, Pam Nason, Emily Ashton, Kembubi Christie, Anne Hunt, Sherry Rose, Kim Stewart, Tara-Lynn Scheffel, Jan Ashton, and Gillian Yeomans. Contributing pilot site participants whose thinking informs mine in this chapter are Linda Gould, Angela Little, Jennifer Curtis Leisa Comeau, Shawnda Farquhar, Kelly Trenholm, and Leanne Donavan.

[4] To respect the multiplicity of views expressed by those working within the curriculum project, I can only take responsibility for my own thinking. When I use the word *we* to describe our work as a group, I recognize that I am not speaking for the group and merely express my perception of our work as a whole.

[5] An extensive literature review was conducted prior to the development of the curriculum framework outline. As well, twenty-three research papers on various aspects of early learning and care curriculum were commissioned that inform/ed the process and content of curriculum materials.

[6] At the time of this writing there are 40 men and 1240 women enrolled in the thirty-six-hour Professional Learning Program for the New Brunswick Curriculum Framework for Early Learning and Child Care (English).

[7] Please see Emily Ashton's chapter in this volume on p. 63.

[8] For a listing of the presentations and publications, see the website http://www.unbf.ca/education/ecc/publications/documents/TeamWork-2005-2008.pdf

[9] This is a major debt we attribute to Reggio Emilia (Dahlberg & Moss, 2005; Gandini & Pope Edwards, 2001; Rinaldi 2006)

[10] Susan Fraser is an early childhood educator and researcher. When she was editor of *Canadian Children*, she introduced Reggio Emilia to many early childhood educators. She is the author *Authentic Childhood*.

[11] In 2006, an outline of the curriculum framework was shared at several consultation meetings in New Brunswick. In 2007, ten reviewers both internal and external to the project itself reviewed various drafts of the curriculum framework and lead to changes with the document prior to the publication of the *NBCF* in March 2008.

[12] Approximately 70% of licensed day cares are privately owned; 30% are not for profit. There are government subsidies in terms of day care fees and a wage enhancement program for licensed centres.

[13] She has given permission for me to write this up.

[14] Iris Duhn (2006) has critiqued the woven mat metaphor as having different connotations for Pakeha and Maori, the former more industrial, the later more organic.

[15] Emily Ashton introduced me to Margaret Somerville's critical place pedagogies.

[16] Sense of place is situated within sense of belonging in the well-being goal. In each of the aspects of learning such as sense of place, there are three double-page spreads; the first page is intended as an entry point with many ideas about the aspect of learning. The next double-page spread is a curricular idea conveyed/recorded by an educator and to close each learning aspect, there is an educator reflection story;in this case, the story is a reflection upon one of the questions.

[17] I focus upon handmade books in this section, while recognizing that storying occurs in many other materials, forms, and representations.

[18] Anne Hunt and Kembubi Christie are coordinators of Professional Learning Programme for the *NBCF*.

[19] Herménégilde Chiasson is the Lt-Gov of New Brunswick, a visual artist, writer, poet, and film-maker of Acadian background. These words were taken from a newspaper article I no longer can reference. They live on my office wall where I reread them frequently.

[20] Thank you to Sherry Rose, UNB for her suggestions concerning this work.

References

Ashton, E., & Whitty, P. (2007, November). *Shifting theoretical terrains in early learning and care.* Presentation at Works In Progress Series (WIPS), University of New Brunswick, Fredericton, NB.

Ashton, E., Hunt, A., & White, L. (2008). *Well-Being: Professional support document (English).* Fredericton, NB: Early Childhood Centre.

Bachelard, G. (1988). *The right to dream* (J. A. Underwood trans.). Dallas, TX: Dallas Institute of Humanities and Culture Publications.

Cannella, G. S., & Viruru, R. (2004). *Childhood and postcolonization: Power, education and contemporary practice.* New York: Routledge.

Carr, M. (2001). *Assessment in early childhood settings: Learning stories.* London: Sage Publications.

Carr, M., & Lee, W. (2004). *Assessment and Learning: Community Te Aromatawai me te Ako: Hapori. Kei Tua o te Pae, Assessment for Learning: Early Childhood Examplars.* Wellington, NZ: The Ministry of Education.

Dahlberg, G., & Moss, P. (2005). *Ethics and politics in early childhood education.* New York: Routledge.

Dahlberg, G., Moss, P., & Pence, A. (2007). *Beyond quality in early childhood education and care: Languages of evaluation* (2nd ed.). London: Falmer Press.

Department of Education, Tasmania. (2004). *Framework 1 and 2 overview, essential learnings framework. Key resource to support the essential learnings curriculum.* Tasmania: Department of Education. Retrieved from www.ltag.education.tas.gov.au/references.htm#ELresources.

Duhn, I. (2006) *Cartographies of childhood: Mapping the modern/global child.* Unpublished doctoral dissertation, University of Auckland: Aotearoa-New Zealand.

Dyson, A. H. (2003). Staying in the (curricular) lines: Practice constraints and possibilities in childhood writing. *Written Communication, 25*(1), 119-159.

Edmiston, B. (2008). *Forming ethical identities in early childhood play.* New York: Routledge.

Fraser, S. (2006). *Authentic childhood: Experiencing Reggio Emilia in the classroom* (2nd ed.). Toronto: Thomson/Nelson.

Gandini, L., & Pope Edwards, C. (2001). *Bambini: The Italian approach to infant/toddler care.* New York: Teacher College Press.

Gorodesky, M., & Barack, J. (2008). The educational-cultural edge: A participative learning environment for co-emergence of personal and institutional growth. *Teacher and Teacher Education, 24*(7), 1907-1918.

Katz, L. G., & Chard, S. C. (2000). *Engaging children's minds: The project approach* (2nd ed.). Stamford, CT: Ablex Publishing.

Kearney, R. (2008). Bachelard and the epiphanic instant. *Philosophy Today, 52*(Supplement), 38-45.

Martin, J. R. (1985). *Reclaiming a conversation: The ideal of the educated woman.* New Haven, CT: Yale University Press.

Martin, J. R. (1992). *The schoolhome.* Boston, MA: Harvard University Press.

McNaughton, G. (2006). *Doing Foucault in early childhood studies: Applying post structuralism ideas.* New York: Routledge.

Miller, J. (2005). *Sounds of silence breaking: Women, autobiography, curriculum.* New York: Peter Lang.

Moss, P. (2007). Meetings across the paradigmatic divide. *Educational Philosophy and Theory, 39*(3), 229-245.

Nason, P., & Whitty, P. (2007). Bringing action research to the curriculum development process. *Educational Action Research, 15*(2), 271-281.

New Zealand Ministry of Education. (1996). *Te Whariki: Early childhood curriculum.* Wellington, NZ: Learning Media Education. Retrieved from http://minedu.govt.nz/web/downloadable/dl3567_v1/whariki.pdf.

Pahl, K. (2009, February). *Ways of listening.* Seminar held at the University of New Brunswick, Fredericton.

Pence, A. (1998). Reconceptualizing ECCD in the majority world: a minority world view. *International Journal of Early Childhood, 30*(2), 19-30.

Pink, S. (2008). An urban tour: The sensory sociality of ethnographic place-making. *Ethnography, 9*(2), 175-196.

Rinaldi, C. (2006). *In dialogue with Reggio Emilia: Listening, researching, and learning.* New York: Routledge.

Rose, S. (2007, October). *Narrating learning – Opening possibilities.* Keynote at the Early Childhood Development Association (ECDA) Early Childhood Conference, Charlottetown, PE.

Somerville, M. (2007). Place literacies. *Australian Journal of Language and Literature, 30*(2), 149-164.

Taguchi, H. L. (2007). Deconstructing and transgressing the theory – Practice dichotomy in early childhood education. *Educational Philosophy and Theory, 39*(3), 275-290.

University of New Brunswick Early Childhood Research and Development Team. *New Brunswick Curriculum Framework for Early Learning and Child Care (English).* Fredericton, NB: Department in Social Development.

Walkerdine V. (2004). Developmental psychology and the study of childhood. In M. J. Kehily (Ed.), *An introduction to childhood studies.* Berkshire, UK: Open University Press.

Whitty, P. (1993). *A reclamation of the educational thought of Helen Keller: Her journey from "no-world to world-home".* Unpublished doctoral dissertation, University of Maine, Orono.

Whitty, P. (1995). Helen Keller: Words, worlds, and literacies. *Signal, 78*, 193-206.

Whitty, P. (2007). *Shifts in Practice, New Brunswick Curriculum Orientation.* Presentation at Curriculum Pilot Workshops, October, 2007, University of New Brunswick: Fredericton, NB.

Whitty, P., Rose, S., White, L., & Langille, G. (2006, November). *Across the waters: Learning stories – A New Zealand import.* Paper presented at the Atlantic Educators Conference, Fredericton, NB.

Whitty, P., Rose, S., Baisley, D., Comeau, L., & Thompson, A., (2008). Honouring educators' co-construction of picture books. *Canadian Children, 33*(2), 21-25.

Wien, C. A. (1995). *Developmentally appropriate practice in "real life": Stories of teacher practical knowledge.* New York: Teachers College Press.

Wien, C. A. (2008, October). *Emergent curriculum – What on earth do they mean by that?* Keynote address presented at Learning for Three, Four, and Five Year Olds, New Brunswick Curriculum Framework Institute, Fredericton, NB.

Wien, C. A., & Smith, K. S. (1998). Untiming the curriculum: A case study of removing clocks from the program. *Young Children, 53*(5), 8-13.

Young-Bruehl, E. (1987). The education of women as philosophers. *Signs, 12*(2), 35-49

3

Folding Ethical-Textual Tensions: Explorations in Curriculum Writing

Emily Ashton

In the spring of 2005, the University of New Brunswick (UNB) Early Childhood Centre was contracted by the Government of New Brunswick to develop a curriculum framework for infants, toddlers, and young children (Nason & Whitty, 2007). Four years later the *New Brunswick Curriculum Framework for Early Learning and Care – English* (subsequently referred to as *NBCF*) is mandated for all provincially "approved child care facilities" (Government of New Brunswick, 2008). In addition, members of Early Childhood Centre curriculum team are producing a series of curriculum support documents, similar in intent to New Zealand's *Kei Tua o te Pae* exemplars,[1] to extend the pedagogical principles, provisions, and practices introduced in the *NBCF* and accompanying implementation "program of professional learning" (Early Childhood Centre, 2007). As a member of the Early Childhood Centre team, one of the co-authors and co-editors of the support

document series, I present here a critical exploration of my participation in the construction and negotiation of curriculum writing.[2]
Reconceptualizing the Deleuzian image of the fold to represent curricular praxis, this chapter "folds both backward and
forward" (Lather, 2007, p. xvi). The first section reframes supposi-
tions from a past conference paper foreshadowing the possibilities
and constraints of author(iz)ing curriculum documents.[3] Critical
questions concerning the relationship between form, format, and
content are explored in, what was at the time, a folding forward.
Currently as the first support document, *Well-Being*, enters publication, I find myself moved to (re)reflect upon this textualizing of
tensions. In revisiting my theorizing, I am particularly troubled by
an earlier focus on textual design that seemingly overwrote the
lived pedagogy of educators. In latter sections of this chapter I fold
back on to my folding forward "in order to *reconstruct* something
new, which is dependent on the old for its new displaced meanings. And these new meanings, in turn, need to be deconstructed"
(Lenz Taguchi, 2007, p. 276). My hopes are that in folding the sections of this chapter together, I can "show a work in the
making . . . a sort of dialogue across texts, time and researching
selves" (Lather, 2007, p. 3).

Part 1: Folding Forward

> How we write has consequences for ourselves, our
> disciplines, and the public we serve. How we are
> expected to write affects what we can write about; the
> form in which we write shapes the content.
> (Richardson, 2002, p. 414)

Laurel Richardson's statement succinctly characterizes
lessons learned from early attempts at writing support documents
for the *NBCF*'s early learning and child care goals.[4] Like Richardson,
Elliot Eisner (2002) affirms, "form and content is most often inex-
tricable. How something is said is part and parcel of what is said.
The message is in the form-content relationship" (sec. 3).
Unspoken feelings of unease underwrote each possible design template, whereas symptoms of *postmodern paralysis* (Blake, Smeyers,
Smith, & Standish, 1998) sickened any attempts to fill in the hollow

spaces. With each new template (followed by another and yet another) a pattern slowly materialized: the support documents were literally boxing us in – we were entrapped by self-imposed linearity. Asking how closely the content, form, and format of the support document drafts reflected the values, goals, and principles espoused in the *NBCF* necessitated that we find *otherways* (Paul, 1998) to construct the documents. Reflecting on the original storyboards, three interrelated incongruities are especially problematic: the dominance of alphabetic print contradicted our curricular push for the recognition of multimodal literacies; the foregrounding of play as a curricular value and goal was challenged by the demanding work required to wade through the print-laden documents; and our reconceptualist sensibilities made the didactic inclusion of ethical responsibilities near heresy. Acknowledging the "gaps between our beliefs and actions" (Lather, 1991, p. 126) prompted us to seek new ways of "writing . . . traversed by becomings" (Deleuze & Guattari, 1987, p. 240), but "it was only by permitting ourselves to feel confused and a bit lost, were we eventually able to resituate ourselves in a different [writing] landscape" (Sumara, 1998, p. 37).

Theoretical Unfoldings

I position myself within and across critical feminist, reconceptualist, and *post* paradigms. These ways of being and becoming, thinking and acting, acknowledge the power and privilege attributable to writing in general and curriculum writing in particular. For example, feminist concerns include ethical questions of representation; continually asked is "not whether we will write the lives of people . . . but *how* and for *whom*" (Richardson, 1990, p. 9). Poststructuralists recognize the ambiguousness, situatedness, and multiple interpretiveness of language, and seek different ways "to articulate the multiplicity of our experiencing selves" (Davies, 2000, p. 41). Postmodern researchers challenge "claims to a singular, correct style for doing and presenting research" (Richardson, 1990, p. 11) in addition to positivistic claims of knowing, truth, validity, and objectivity. Postcolonial theorists deconstruct the hegemony of Anglo-American discourse (Dahlberg & Moss, 2005) and "cultural knowledge as it related to the material exigencies of marginalized subcultures and communities" (Dei & Doyle-Wood, 2006, p. 151). Reconceptualist early childhood educators are "variously immersed in feminist, post-structuralist, and postcolonial theorizing" and "actively experiment with different ways of representing 'data,' employing unconventional and unexpected genres, textual designs, and representations" (Jipson & Johnson, 2001, p. 8). These summaries are intended only as brief overviews; all the critical theories presented overlap, intersect, and collectively challenge dominant discourses of writing and representing.

Writing cannot be separated from power. As a curriculum writer, I am empowered by decisions of what *counts* as curricular content, but simultaneously constrained by academic, political, and publishing standards of presentation. Multiple power relations are always at play; power is unstable, often unspoken, and always shifting (Foucault, 1980; 1988). Maggie MacLure (2003) maintains:

> Writing is often considered, when it is considered at all, to be a merely technical business: a matter of finding the best words to convey, or to capture, the stuff that really counts – the meaning, the message, the ideas, the essence, the principles .... In this view, there's writing on the one hand and there's all that good stuff on the other. Writing is the subordinate partner in this dualism: it is the medium, vehicle or instrument ... that we need in order to capture those more important, extra textual phenomena. (p. 105)

MacLure's satirical renderings coincide with Michel Foucault's (1978) view of language as a constituting technology. "Writing is not simply a true representation of an objective reality, out there, waiting to be seen. Instead ... writing creates a particular view of reality" (Richardson, 1990, p. 9). My beliefs about children, childhood, and educators are reflected in my word choices, content selections, and page layouts. Dialectically, I construct and delimit subjectivities through these same means. All writing and representational forms are cultural constructions (Odin, 1997, p. 611). "No textual staging is ever innocent," Richardson (1990) affirms, "We are always enscribing values in our writing. It is unavoidable" (p. 12).

Multimodal Multiliteracies

Theorists of critical literacies (e.g. Fehring & Green, 2001; Muspratt, Luke & Freebody, 1997), New Literacy Studies (e.g. Pahl & Roswell, 2006; Street, 2003), and literary criticism (e.g. Derrida, 1997; Barthes, 1974) were instrumental in conceptualizing the *NBCF*'s third learning goal, Communication and Literacies. In turn, the learning principles of Communication and Literacies were vital in (re)shaping the support document designs. Central to the goal are multimodal literacies which recognize meaning as constructed through "multiple modes of image, print, gaze, gesture, movement, and speech" (Early Childhood Centre, 2008, p. 44). Gemma Moss (2003) explains that "from a multimodal perspective [how] text will be laid up on the surface of the page . . . determine[es] how these objects will be read and what we take them to mean" (p. 78). Required to publish the support documents in print, the multiple modes untenable on the printed page are conveyed by open spaces, words, and images. The draft documents combine print and image while alluding to other modes: for example, speech is expressed in callouts; gesture is represented by shifting fonts and typefaces; and movement is embodied by multidirectional text extensions. Such textual features symbolize "passwords" beneath the "order words" (Deleuze & Guattari, 1987, p. 110) of traditional curriculum guides.

Rejecting reductive definitions of literacy that conceive of writing as "a process of communication that uses a conventional graphic system to convey a message to a reader" (Lindemann, 1995, p. 11), the support documents are reconceptualized as writerly texts (Barthes, 1974). The documents "articulate an ecology of knowledges" which valorize meanings (re)made locally and contextually (Sousa Santos, 2004, p. 160). The co-constructed texts embody "a communication system in which all participants can contribute to and affect the content and direction of the conversation" (Gaggi, 1997, p. 103). Moving beyond the "death bound of deterministic and systematic curriculum planning" (Hwu, 2004, p. 181), the support documents encourage entry at any point. Meaning builds "as each layer of text is superimposed on the others, each layer contributes to the understanding of the other layers as well as to the overall picture of social life that the text conveys" (Ronai, 1999, p. 116). Spouting truths and generating lists of what to do Monday morning are replaced by invitations for multimodal meaning making; the "transformation of knowledge from one mode to another" (Early Childhood Centre, 2008, p. 44) is generated as textual allusions meet pedagogical practice.

Playful Texts

The current support document configurations "allow [me] to be playful" (Ball, 1995, p. 255). Considering the value the authors' of the NBCF attribute to play, we have found a means of performing what we profess to believe. While the support document (re)design process has been (re)invigorating, I do not wish to suggest that I have stopped dismantling my textual practices. I am habitually concerned about the power attributed to print in our page layouts. Following Gemma Moss (2003), I wonder if "the logic of the written text ... drives the reader's progress" (p. 79): Do photographs and images of children's mark making only "fill the space where the written text might have been" (p. 80)? Do "the illustrations follow the writing rather than vice versa" (p. 80)? We have started to use different shapes, such as ovals, banners, scrolls, and octagons, to offset text; image and print co-exist on the same page, one is not more privileged over the other. However, looking over the early versions of the revised documents the pages appear to be divided "into a series of ghost rectangular shapes" and, although intending otherwise, "a linear and vertical sense of order" has been imposed "on the potentially chaotic fluidity of the space. It is as if such [texts] cannot quite give up the old order, whilst simultaneously trying to adapt to the new" (p. 83). Efforts must now be taken to unlock the ghost boxes and remove the lines that bind. My technical design skills leave much to be desired, but I am playing my limits to blur the "distinction between texts that augur work, and texts that augur play" (p. 83).

Textual-Ethical Tensions

Intentions to write the documents otherways find theoretical impetus in the writings of Roland Barthes (1973; 1974). Following Barthes, the dichotomies of producer/consumer, owner/customer, and author/reader are resisted. Through curriculum workshops and onsite visits, co-authoring and co-researching practices, the support documents will be written and revised. The texts are intended to include voices, those oftentimes silenced by the exclusiveness of academia and political conceit, to be heard. This is not a pretentious proclamation of "giving voice" followed by a rewriting once safely back atop our university pedestals of privilege, but a genuine yearning for critique, ideas, and practices from educators who work with the *NBCF* daily. Iris Duhn (2006) contends that *Te Whariki*'s "effectiveness" as a "descriptive rather than a prescriptive model" of curriculum, hinges upon the "teachers' interpretation of it" (p. 183). Similar analyses can be levied against the *NBCF* and support documents; however, regardless of whether explicit, didactic instructions fill the pages or spaces for meaning making are provided, the ubiquitous possibility exists for every reading to be a misreading, every interpretation a misinterpretation (Bloom, 1975). Mikhail Bakhtin (1981) taught us long ago that "the word is only half ours, and half-someone elses" (p. 345), and "it is the interactions between participants in the literacy event that will both establish and steer what the text will mean" (G. Moss, 2004, p. 77).

A key event that provoked a crisis in the writing of the support documents was the stuttering (Deleuze, 1997) induced by attempts to write ethical guidelines for inclusion in the *Well-Being* support document. In researching other early childhood education and child care organizational codes of ethics (e.g. National Association for the Education of Young Children, 2005; Early Childhood Australia, 2006), I could not shake the unease of so-called ethics becoming moral metanarratives. Familiar with Drucilla Cornell's (1993) definition of morality as "any attempt to spell out how one determines a right way to behave" (p. 13), and its similarities to universalistic ethics "which treats ethics as a standard, norm or code – fixed, impartial, incontestable and generally applicable" (Dahlberg & Moss, 2005, p. 12), I could not believe what I had gotten myself into. While I shared many of the beliefs and values other codes outlined, my understanding of ethics as situational and contextual overrode attempts to designate "appropriate and expected behaviour" (Early Childhood Australia, 2007). My body remembers hours sitting at the computer waiting for some words I could live with to trespass the incessant delete key. Images of me and Moses standing atop mountain shouting out *thou shalt not's* haunted my waking, working dreams. After much discussion with team members the code of ethics was disbanded. If such a code is decided necessary for New Brunswick early childhood educators in the future, I hope such a framework would involve an intense consultation process whereby those living out the complexities of educative relations would be the individuals inscribing the principles.

Temporary Conclusions

Elinor Goldschmied and Sonia Jackson's (2004, p. 157) notion of a "framework of conformity" can be appropriated to theorize about the NBCF and support documents. How closely do our content, form, and format resemble other noted exemplary curricula?[5] Do we conform to what has been done before or do we seek new ways of thinking, writing, and representing. Our questions do not devalue the strides these other curricula have made, but keep us mindful that nothing is innocent (Foucault, 1980). To our knowledge, the support documents represent a shift from thinking otherways to doing otherways. We are in the process of creating mulitvocal, rhizomatic texts and, in doing so, we implicitly problematize the colonizing authority assumed by traditional curricular formats (Cannella & Viruru, 2004). We take up Ian Stronach's and Maggie MacLure's (1997) challenge of seeing "how far [we] can get by failing to deliver simple truths" (p. 6). The support documents aim to be about "engagement" and "possibilities," while not hiding the "limitations" (Rath, 2001, p. 117) inescapable in transitioning educative practices to textual representations. Cognizant of the critique that "post-modernists have seldom practised what they preach – their abstract, and often inaccessible, writings remain severed from the lived realities at their base" (Middleton, 1995, p. 87), we are doing differently. Incorporating multiple shapes, evocative content, educators' stories, varying fonts, and yet-filled spaces "*show* how openness and reflexivity *look* and *feel*, rather than simply talking about it" (Richardson, 1997, p. 2). The support documents do not dictate practice, but assemble possibilities. Exactly how these high hopes and collaborative processes will play out is unknown, but for now I take comfort in the possibilities.

Middles: Folding, Unfolding, Refolding

> What matters . . . is folding, unfolding and refolding
> in order to produce the new and strange out of the old
> and familiar. (Ansell-Pearson, 1997, p. 14)

This brief reprise "neither belongs to the inside, nor does it belong to the outside" (Weiskopf, 2002, p. 103), but is an in-between space of "folding, unfolding, and refolding" (Deleuze, 1993, p. 147). Through this middle spurts Deleuzian lines of flight: lines of contradiction, hope, doubt, and contestation. Mapping these lines of flight allows me to turn my text back on itself, to put "the authority of its own affirmations in doubt, an undercutting that causes a doubling of meanings that adds to a sense of multi-valence and fluidities. Such a practice makes space for returns, silence, interruptions, and self-criticism and points to its own incapacity" (Lather, 2007, p. 88). Biddy Martin (2001) uses the metaphoric fold to represent a way of thinking where old ideas are not thrown out but enfolded within newer ones; notions of succession are thereby severed from seductive themes of progress (as cited in Lather, 2007, p. 176). I have unfolded the previous piece in order to let "thought think its own history (the past), to free itself from what it thinks (the present), and be able finally to 'think otherwise' (the future)" (Deleuze, 1988, p. 119). Just as Michel Foucault (1991) stated, "I wouldn't want what I may have said or written to be seen as laying any claims to totality" (p. 90), so I refold what I have written into what I have learned throughout the processes of compiling the *Well-Being* curriculum support document (Ashton, Hunt, & White, 2008).

Part II: Folding Back

> How we write has consequences for ourselves, our
> disciplines, and the public we serve. How we are
> expected to write affects what we can write about; the
> form in which we write shapes the content.
> (Richardson, 2002, p. 414)

Reflecting now on my earlier interpretation of Laurel Richardson's words, I notice the foregrounding of the content-form dualism to the detriment of the lived relationships evoked in her first sentence. Decisions about "what should be learned" and "how it should be organized" (Petrina, 2004, p. 81) demand deconstruction, but not to the either/or of the real "consequences" for the early childhood educators whom we serve. Curriculum construction is "a matter of the politics of knowledge and the realpolitik of form" (Petrina, 2004, p. 82) – a politics of representation and the realpolitik of material positionings. Reconceptualizing the question "what *should* be learned" to ask instead "whose knowledge is of the most worth" (Apple, 2000) invites a problematization of the curriculum co-construction proclaimed in earlier sections. Face-to-face encounters with the educators whose stories fill the documents pages cause me to forefront the unbalanced power relations residing in the "tensioned place in the curricular landscape between the curriculum guide and the lived curricula" (Aoki, 2005, p. 211). Furthermore, examining the published pages of the *Well-Being* support document provokes me to revisit decrees of multimodal, playful textual designs. Whereas I earlier claimed to have acknowledged the "gaps between our beliefs and actions" (Lather, 1991, p. 126), I necessarily "[re]examine my own discourses and the practices they sanction[ed]" (Lather, 1991, p. 128) in order to trace "my own involvement in those regimes, and in so doing, I will attempt to find weak spots in them" (Gore, 1993, p. 139).

As a curriculum writer I am learning "to walk on two legs" (Dahlberg, Moss, & Pence, 1999, p. 139), to maintain footing across the paradigmatic postmodern/modern divide (P. Moss, 2007). This is not to deny that oftentimes I have wanted to lift my foot and hop solely in the postmodern realm, but I try "not to despair because change takes such a long time and is such hard work" (Dahlberg, Moss, & Pence, 1999, p. 139). The NBCF has shifted from the "normative-performative syndrome" (Whitty, 2006) characteristic of developmentalism to a values-based framework incorporating the local knowledges of New Brunswick educators. That being said, the NBCF has not completely shaken off curricula's modernist tendencies: words like *quality* are used without qualification, assessment technologies like ECERS are promoted without reference to their Anglo-American universalization, and values such as the distinctiveness of childhood seemingly deny learnings from the new sociology of childhood movement (James & Prout, 1990; Corsaro, 1997). Not meaning to diminish strides taken by the *NBCF*, this brief critique is offered as a reminder that "everything is dangerous" (Foucault, 1991, p. 46). The *NBCF* and support documents figuratively walk on two legs. In particular, the *Well-Being* support document contains many elements of postmodern, hypertextual design, but the content, for the most part, could be branded modernistic.

Well-Being extends the goal's three facets as introduced in the *NBCF*; extrapolated from these facets are an additional seven features.[6] These seven aspects are each elaborated in a series of three double-page spreads: the first spread sketches out in a rhizomatic fashion "what's involved in learning," for example, about one's sense of self; the second double-page spread presents an educator's story related to the pedagogy of sense of self; and the third spread includes a story of an educator's reflective practices in addition to the inclusion of questions for reflection. This brief overview makes apparent the educators' significant contributions to the support documents. Indeed, *Well-Being* would not have been possible in its current configuration without their participation and willingness to share their stories, images, and documentations. Foregrounding the stories and reflections of local educators challenges the discourse of the "always, already failing early childhood educator" (Novinger, O'Brien, & Sweigman, 2005) and affirms an image of the competent, capable pedagogue. *Well-Being* avoids the "mentioning" phenomenon Michael Apple (2001, p. 239) finds symptomatic of curricula portrayals of women and "minority" groups. The New Brunswick educators' stories are not "add-ons that have the status of afterthoughts" (Apple, p. 6) but are definitive.

Theoretical Refoldings

My academic influences – those representative critical educationalists (Apple, 2000) cited previously – form metaphorical "signposts in [my] intellectual journeys, significances from [my] academic biograph[y]" (Middleton, 1995, p. 95). Their teachings infuse my thinking and affect my decisions about curriculum construction. The forms that the support documents take imply my theoretical standpoints and makes apparent Petrina's (2004) assertion that "curriculum designs have theoretical orientations" (p. 83). I recall Morpheus's words to Neo in the film *The Matrix*: "There is a difference between knowing the path and walking the path" (Wachowski & Wachowski, 1999). But Morpheus's dichotomous view is perhaps too simple: what if knowingly *not* walking the path better fulfills responsibility to the other – in this instance, to those educators for whom the support documents are intended? This dilemma is related to what Deborah Britzman (1995) refers to as a "messy problem" (p. 236). Elizabeth Adams St. Pierre (2000) explains: the messy problem is "the paradox of a researcher who leans toward a poststructural feminism interpreting the lives of women who, if they had the words, would likely describe themselves as humanists" (p. 273). Continuing, St. Pierre (2000) outlines her ethical problemizations:

> How in the world can I presume to continue to interpret the lives of my participants, lives they have lived for decades within one theoretical description of the world, using another theoretical description that is committed to the persistent critique of all claims to truth, including the truth of their lives, the Truth of the logos? What does this mean? What kind of ethnographer am I? What kind of feminist am I? (p. 273)

What kind of curriculum writer am I? What kind of educational reconceptualist am I? What right do I have to (re)interpret and (re)write educators' stories for the curriculum documents? Twenty years ago Clifford Geertz (1988) wrote that "the burden of authorship cannot be evaded" (p. 140); I continue the struggle under that weighty admission.

I have been using the phrase *ethical editing* to denote the editing of educators' stories done behind the scenes. It has become my method of avoiding "'difficult knowledge' (Pitt & Britzman, 2003) sorts of questions about necessary complicities" (Lather, 2007, p. viii). Carolyn Ellis's (2004) concerns about incorporating her students' work in her methodological novel resonate with the unease I feel about my (re)actions in editing the work of others:

Sometimes I quoted directly from their work; other times, I edited it slightly better to fit my text. Then I wondered about what right I had to manipulate these words. Was it appropriate to edit them? I did, because I wanted to make the text the best it could be. Was I using students' words ethically? [...] I seemed to be more worried about all this than the participants were. They had no objection to my use of their work and seemed pleased to see it in the text. Still, considering the power inequality between them and me, I carefully deliberated on how best to present the students' words. (p. 345)

Educators graciously present us with their work and overtly share their excitement about the possibilities of being published. Their overwhelming appreciation induces in me a case of "front-pew-itis" (Lather, 2007, p. 11), remnant Catholic guilt which grows exponentially under the weight of ethical responsibility. I am treading dangerously here. I do not mean to imply that I have taken unleashed authorial license with the educators' stories; I have performed those same actions a professional editor would take to their client's text. I have edited, not editorialized – I think this distinction is important. But for some unpronounceable reason I stay fixated on this troubling tension. But what would be the ethical implications if I did nothing? The educators were sent back their stories before publication to obtain final consent, but critical conversations did not always accompany the consent forms: Did they notice I changed that word and combined this sentence? Were they curious about why all the photos they sent were not included? Did they wonder why I deleted this paragraph? Patti Lather (1991) speaks of an "ethic of risk" as based on an understanding of the "need for ethical conversations"(p. 31). Generating the time, space, courage, and relationships to have those conversations is something to work towards as the remaining support documents are produced.

Multimodal Hyperliteracies

"As we move from an industrial to a post-industrial information economy, one in which print literacy is not obsolete but certainly substantially transformed," Carmen Luke (1998) supposes, "then surely we need broader definition of knowledge, literacy, and pedagogy which will include study of the intertextuality of imageries, texts, icons and artefacts" (p. 27). The *NBCF* includes a thick description of literacies which is in turn reflected in *Well-Being*; meaning making and communication include social, cultural, affective, and multimodal elements (Heydon & Iannacci, 2004; Jewitt & Kress, 2003). As an interactive text, the first double page spreads in each section of the *Well-Being* support document make visible features of playful, hypertextual literacies. Dawnene Hassett (2006) explains:

> 'Hypertext' means that the text contains extensive cross-referencing elements, evocative graphics, various pathways to follow, links to other meanings, and/or parallel displays of information . . . .It is colorful, flashy, and full of cues for reading that extend beyond the letters and words on the page, demanding a sense of interpretation and interaction with the text beyond the decoding of print. To read these texts means to focus on symbols and signs and visual designs, cues often unrelated to the alphabetic writing system of language placed in print. To comprehend these texts means to assume there are multiple meanings, and no one shared reality. (p. 87-88)

Weary not to confine hypertext to electronic media, Eliza Dresang (1999) coined the term *handheld hypertext* to refer to page-bound books sharing characteristics of Hassett's outline. *Well-Being* tempts the reader to "voyage into other parts of the text for a bit of judicious cross-referencing" (G. Moss, 2003, p. 78). Select images and passages from the *NBCF* are repeated in the support document to summon connections; quotations are excerpted to prompt further discovery; picture books are suggested to incite further reading; blank spaces end bulleted lists to encourage participation. However, a label of hypertext does not necessarily signify that the critical theories referenced earlier have been put into play; to be critical, the *text* of hypertext must be constructed as such. While *Well-Being* may uphold many characteristics of the New Literacy Studies movement, if a core tenet of critical literacies is the deconstruction of power relations then, content-wise, *Well-Being*'s silences speak volumes.

Playful Hypertexts

Oscar Wilde wrote, "consistency is the last refuge of the unimaginative." As a handheld hypertext, *Well-Being* allots many "game openings" (Foucault, 1991, p. 91) for exploration and imagination. The design and organization of the *Well-Being* document instantiates elements of Barthes' theorizations laid out in the first part of this chapter. Hypertext requires "a particular kind of wakefulness" (Clandinin, Pushor, & Orr, 2007, p. 21), a textual openness to adventure not mandated by readerly texts. Returning to earlier questions raised about the support documents, I think we have effectively challenged certain rationalities about the "logic of the written text" (G. Moss, 2003, p. 79): the vibrant, colorful images that fill the pages are likely to initially grab the readers' attention; pictures tell their own stories without written prescriptions; and many of the ghost boxes have been unlocked leaving fluid text to roam the page space. The *Well-Being* document "is not only a product of technological possibilities with graphics and textual contexts, but also a product of different assumptions about what it is [educators] are capable of doing, knowing, and thinking" (Hassett, 2006, p. 95). Readers of hypertexts play at meaning making; they choose their "own center of investigation and experience. What this principle means is that the reader is not locked into any particular organization or hierarchy" (Landow, 2006, p. 38). The democratizing proclamations of hypertext are well documented (see Synder, 1998, for a critique), and although I find the utopian promises desirable, I join Nancy Kaplan (1995) in pointing out that all texts are "sites of struggle among competing interests and ideological forces" (p. 28). Whereas I hope the applied formatting of *Well-Being* conveys its constructedness and challenges the taken-for-grantedness of authorial conveyance, I do not believe any text can completely divorce itself from the power of Foucault's (1980) *author-function*.

Ethical-Textual Tensions

Glenda MacNaughton (2005) writes that "the politics of our time and place influence which stories are told, when and by whom . . . identifying the stories that are silenced or marginalized and then sharing them is a political act" (p. 4). Foregrounding educators' stories is a purposeful political act intended to counteract "negative assumptions of the academic value of their experiences and expectations" within "the climate of regulating and professionalizing that characterises a contemporary will to educate before school" (Gibbons, 2007, p. 516). However, after *Well-Being* has been published, many ethical-textual tensions remain unresolved. For example, I worry that these stories will be interpreted as the one-T "Truth" of *Well-Being*. I wonder if we should have risked lining up stories side by side to challenge each other, but what might that have meant to the educators who trusted us with their words? I worry that the stories presented will get taken up as best practice – as contextless, replicable activities. Resultant of curricular workshops, we have already seen much simulacra appear. I worry that the clean, technologized page layouts misrepresent the messiness and complexity of theory-practice. But how does one publish uncertainty in a curriculum document? I worry that in only including positive stories we have erased the ethical impasses that comprise everyday practice. But how could we have represented educators' otherwise than in the affirmative? These questions linger as work continues on the other support documents for the *NBCF* project.

Earlier I made passing reference to the rejection of the term *co-construction* as a descriptor of the support document writing processes. I did so in hopes of doing "something honest about what it means to negotiate that space" (Lather, 2007, p. 55). Lather continues, "I think there is a lot of bad faith, talk going on in the name of collaboration. What does it mean to negotiate the space more honestly, about who own what, who care about what, who is invested in what?" (p. 55). The prefix *co* always makes me pause, especially when the word construction follows; I always sense a slippage into romanticism whenever I hear the terms co-uttered. *Co* obscures the unequal power relations involved in the writing of the support documents; my power-imbued staging and assembling roles are hidden behind an alleged equality. *Well-Being* was compiled and edited within university walls; content was selected and organized with limited input from educators in the field. I believe that the document is collaborative and co-authored, but to name it *co-constructed* would demand that "I may be ethically obliged to change what I actually do" (Lenz Taguchi, 2006, p. 259), which might not be such a bad thing.

Tentative Conclusions

Looking up *fold* in the dictionary reveals two apparently con-trasting definitions: (1) "to lay one part over another; to become double or pleated", and (2) "to fail; to be unsuccessful" (Merriam-Webster Online, 2009). Both meanings fit my context. In this chapter, I attempted to "enact a text that both 'interrupts itself and gathers up its interruptions into its texture'" (Lather, 2007, p. 4); my "goal was a reading of my in-process work that produced rather than protected" (p. x). Simultaneously, this work is also about the textual impossibilities of representation. I have failed to account fully for the complexities of curriculum writing while cur-riculum documents fail to capture the lived experiences of educa-tors – this chapter is a folded doubled-failure. With regards to the ethics of representation, Rachel Heydon (2004) wonders, however, whether failure "is perhaps the only ethical route" (p. 3)?

Notes

[1] The following definition of exemplars was developed by advisers and co-ordinators of the New Zealand *Kei Tua o te Pae/Assessment for Learning: Early Childhood Exemplar* project: "Exemplars are examples of assessments that make visible learning that is valued so that the learning community (children, families, whanau, teachers, and others) can foster ongoing and diverse learning pathways" (New Zealand Ministry of Education, 2008). While the NB Framework support documents do not focus solely on assessment stories, the intent to make visible learning and practice is a shared thread.

[2] Throughout this chapter I struggle between the use of *I* and/or *we*. As a member of the Early Childhood Centre curriculum team much of what I say results from critical conversations with other people. Many individuals including the curriculum team, NB early childhood educators, centre directors, Department of Social Development representatives, editors, graphic designers, etc. have contributed to the NB Framework and support documents (see Acknowledgements pages of the NB Framework and Well-Being for more detailed listings). While some may share my thoughts, others would rightly disagree. In order to avoid, as much as possible, the colonialism invoked in speaking for, I try to use *I* as much as possible. As the pre-screening warnings flashed before any film plays state: the views expressed herein are my own and do not necessarily represent those of others.

[3] The first section will include theorizing undertaken in a paper originally presented at the Canadian Society for Studies in Education, University of Saskatchewan. The conference presentation also included a paper presented by Pam Whitty. See Ashton & Whitty (2007) for full reference.

[4] The *NBCF*'s four curricular goals are: Well-Being, Play and Playfulness, Communication and Literacies, and Diversity and Social Responsibility (Early Childhood Centre, 2008).

[5] Exemplary curricula as defined by the *NBCF* (Early Childhood Centre, 2008, p. 183-192) include: New Zealand, *Te Whariki*; Italy, Reggio Emilia; United States, *High Scope*; Flanders, *Experiential Education* (EXE); Sweden, *Curriculum for Preschool*; New South Wales, *The Practice of Relationships*; Tasmania, *Essential Connections: A Guide to Young Children's Learning*; Finland, *National Curriculum Guidelines on Early Childhood Education in Finland*.

[6] Embedded within the *NBCF*'s conception of Well-Being are (1) Emotional Health & Positive Identities (Sense of Self; Sense of Other), Belonging (Sense of Place; Respectful & Responsive Relationships), and Physical Health (Personal Care; Food & Nutrition; and Body & Movement).

References

Apple, M. (2000). *Official knowledge* (2nd ed.). New York: Routledge.

Apple, M. (2001). *Educating the "right" way: Markets, standards, and inequality.* New York: RoutledgeFalmer.

Ansell-Pearson, K. (1997). Deleuze outside/outside Deleuze: On the difference engineer. In K. Ansell-Pearson (Ed.), *Deleuze and philosophy: The difference engineer* (pp. 1-24). London: Routledge.

Aoki, T. (2005). *Curriculum in a new key: The collected works* (W. Pinar & R. Irwin, Eds.). Mahwah, NJ: Lawrence Erlbaum.

Ashton, E., Hunt, A., & White, L. (2008). *Well-Being: Support document.* Fredericton, NB: UNB Early Childhood Centre.

Ashton, E. & Whitty, P. (2007, May). *What counts as public knowledge in early learning and care: Shifting theoretical-textual-visual landscapes.* Paper presented at the Canadian Critical Pedagogy Association, Canadian Society for Studies in Education, University of Saskatchewan, Saskatoon, SK.

Ball, S. (1995). Intellectuals or technicians? The urgent role of theory in educational studies. *British Journal of Educational Studies, 43*(3), 255-271.

Bakhtin, M. (1981). *The dialogic imagination: Four essays.* (M. Holquist & C. Emerson, Trans.). Austin, TX: University of Texas Press.

Bakhtin, M. (1986). *Speech genres and other late essays.* (C. Emerson & M. Holquist, Trans.). Austin, TX: University of Texas Press.

Barthes, R. (1973). *The pleasure of the text.* (R. Miller, Trans.). New York: Hill.

Barthes, R. (1974). *S/Z.* (R. Miller, Trans.). London: Cape.

Blake, N., Smeyers, P., Smith, R., & Standish, P. (1998). *Thinking again: Education after postmodernism.* Portsmouth, NH: Bergin & Garvey.

Bloom, H. (1975). *Map of misreading.* New York: Oxford University Press.

Britzman, D. (1995). "The question of belief": Writing poststructural ethnography. *International Journal of Qualitative Studies in Education, 5*(3), 229-238.

Cannella, G., & Viruru, R. (2004). *Childhood and postcolonization: Power, education, and contemporary practice.* New York: RoutledgeFalmer.

Clandinin, D., Pushor, D., & Orr, A. (2007). Navigating sites for narrative inquiry. *Journal of Teacher Education, 58*(1), 21-35.

Corsaro, W. A. (1997). *The sociology of childhood.* Thousand Oaks, CA: Pine Forge Press.

Cornell, D. (1992). *The philosophy of the limit.* New York: Routledge.

Davies, B. (2000). *A body of writing, 1990-1999.* Walnut Creek, CA: AltaMira Press.

Dahlberg, G., & Moss, P. (2005). *Ethics and politics in early childhood education. Contesting early childhood series.* London: RoutledgeFalmer.

Dahlberg, G., Moss, P., & Pence, A. R. (1999). *Beyond quality in early childhood education and care: Postmodern perspectives.* London: Falmer Press.

Derrida, J. (1997). *Of grammatology.* (G. C. Spivak, Trans.). Baltimore, MD: John Hopkins University Press. (Original work published 1976).

Deleuze, G. (1988). *Foucault.* (S. Hand, Trans.). Minneapolis, MN: University of Minnesota Press.

Deleuze, G. (1993). *The fold: Leibniz and the Baroque.* Minneapolis, MN: University of Minnesota Press.

Deleuze, G. (1997). *Essays critical and clinical.* (D. Smith & M. Greco, Trans.). Minneapolis, MN: University of Minnesota Press.

Deleuze, G., & Guattari, F. (1987). *A thousand plateaus: Capitalism and schizophrenia.* Minneapolis, MN: University of Minnesota Press.

Dei, G., & Doyle-Wood, S. (2006). Critical ontology and indigenous ways of being: Forging a postcolonial curriculum In Y. Kanu (Ed.), *Curriculum as cultural practice: Postcolonial imaginations* (pp. 181-202). Toronto: University of Toronto Press.

Dresang, E. (1999). *Radical change: Books for youth in a digital age.* New York: Wilson.

Duhn, I. (2006). *Cartographies of childhood: Mapping the modern/global child.* Unpublished doctoral dissertation, University of Auckland, Auckland. Retrieved from http://researchspace.auckland.ac.nz/bitstream/2292/375/1/01front.pdf

Early Childhood Australia. (2006). *The Early Childhood Australia's code of ethics.* Watson, AU: Early Childhood Australia, Inc. Retrieved from http://earlychildhoodaustralia.org.au/pdf/code_of_ethics/code_of_ethics_web.pdf

Early Childhood Australia. (2007). *Code of ethics.* Watson, AU: Early Childhood Australia, Inc. Retrieved from www.earlychildhoodaustralia.org.au/code_of_ethics/code_of_ethics.html

Early Childhood Centre, UNB. (2007). *Early Childhood Centre: Program of professional learning.* Retrieved from http://www.eccenb-sepenb.com/en/download/curriculum/curriculumtraining.pdf

Early Childhood Centre, UNB. (2008). *New Brunswick curriculum framework for early learning and child care - English.* Fredericton, NB: Department of Social Development.

Eisner, E. (2002). What can education learn from the arts about the practice of education? *The Encyclopaedia of Informal Education.* Retrieved from: www.infed.org/biblio/eisner_arts_and_the_practice_or_education.htm

Ellis, C. (2004). *The ethnographic I: A methodological novel about autoenthnography.* Walnut Creek, CA: Altamira Press.

Fehring, H. & Green, P. (Eds). (2001). *Critical literacies: A collection of articles from the Australian Literacy Educators' Association.* Newark, DE: IRA.

Foucault, M. (1978). Discipline and punish: The birth of the prison. (A. Sheridan, Trans.). New York: Random House.

Foucault, M. (1980). Power/Knowledge: Selected interview and other writings, 1972-1977. (C. Gordon, Trans). New York: Pantheon.

Foucault, M. (1988). *Michel Foucault: Politics, philosophy and culture – interviews and other writings 1977-1984.* New York: Routledge.

Foucault, M. (1991). *The Foucault effect: Studies in governmentality: With two lectures by and an interview with Michel Foucault* (G. Burchell, C. Gordon, & P. Miller, Eds.). Chicago, IL: University of Chicago Press.

Gaggi, S. (1997). *From text to hypertext, decentering the subject in fiction, film, the visual arts, and electronic media.* Philadelphia, PA: University of Pennsylvania Press.

Geertz, C. (1988). *Works and lives: The anthropologist as author.* Stanford, CA: Stanford University Press.

Gibbons, A. (2007). Philosophers as children: Playing with style in the philosophy of education. *Educational Philosophy & Theory, 39*(5), 506-518.

Goldschmied, E., & Jackson, S. (2004). *People under three: Young children in day care* (2nd ed.). London: Routledge.

Gore, J. (1993). *The struggle for pedagogies: Critical and feminist discourses as regimes of truth.* New York: Routledge.

Government of New Brunswick. (2008). *Approved child care facilities.* Fredericton, NB: Department of Social Development. Retrieved from http://www1.gnb.ca/cnb/daycare/index-e.asp

Hassett, D. (2006). Signs of the times: The governance of alphabetic print over 'appropriate' and 'natural' reading development. *Journal of Early Childhood Literacy, 6*(1), 77-103.

Heydon, R. (2004). Writing Nonna: A consideration of ethical representation in narrative research. *Language & Literacy, 6*(1). Retrieved from http://www.langandlit.ualberta.ca/Spring2004/Heydon/Appraisal3.html

Heydon, R., & Iannacci, L. (2004). Learning how to "do": Creating spaces for the "missing" in language and literacy research. *Journal of the Canadian Association for Curriculum Studies, 2*(2), 1-6.

Hwu, W. (2004). Gilles Deleuze and Jacques Daignault: Understanding curriculum as difference and sense. In W. Reynolds & J. Webber (Eds.), *Expanding curriculum theory* (pp. 181-202). Mahwah, NJ: Lawrence Erlbaum.

James, A., & Prout, A. (1990). *Constructing and reconstructing childhood: Contemporary issues in the sociological study of childhood.* London: Falmer Press.

Jewitt, C., & Kress, G. (2003). *Multimodal literacy.* New York: Peter Lang.

Jipson, J., & Johnson, R. (2001). Resistance and representation: Rethinking childhood education. *Rethinking childhood* (vol. 12). New York: Peter Lang.

Kaplan, N. (1995). E-literacies: Politexts, hypertexts, and other cultural formations in the late age of print. *Computer-Mediated Communication Magazine, 2*(3), 3-35. Retrieved from http://www.ibiblio.org/cmc/mag/1995/mar/kaplan.html

Landow, G. (2006). *Hypertext 3.0: Critical theory and new media in an Era of Globalization*. Baltimore, MD: Johns Hopkins University Press.

Lather, P. (1991). Getting smart: Feminist research and pedagogy with/in the postmodern. New York: Routledge.

Lather, P. (2007). *Getting lost: Feminist efforts toward a double(d) science*. New York: State University of New York.

Lenz Taguchi, H. (2006). Reconceptualizing early childhood education: Challenging taken-for-granted ideas. In J. Einarsdottir & J. Wagner (Eds.), *Nordic childhood and early education* (pp. 257-287). Greenwich, CT: Information Age.

Lenz Taguchi, H. (2007). Deconstructing and transgressing the theory-practice dichotomy in early childhood education. *Educational Philosophy & Theory, 39*(3), 275-290.

Lindemann, E. (1995). *A rhetoric for writing teachers*. New York: Oxford University Press.

Luke, C. (1998). Pedagogy and authority: Lessons from feminist and cultural studies, postmodernism and feminist pedagogy. In D. Buckingham (Ed.), *Teaching popular culture: Beyond radical pedagogy* (pp. 18-41). London: Routledge.

MacNaughton, G. (2005). *Doing Foucault in early childhood studies*. London: RoutlegeFalmer Press.

Martin, B. (2001). Success and its failures. In E. Bronfen and M. Kavka (Eds.), *Feminist consequences: Theory for the New Century* (pp. 353-380). New York: Columbia University Press.

MacLure, M. (2003). *Discourse in educational and social research. Conducting educational research*. Buckingham, UK: Open University.

Middleton, S. (1995). Doing feminist educational theory: A post-modernist perspective. *Gender & Education, 7*(1), 87-100.

Merriam-Webster Online Dictionary. (2009). Fold. Retrieved from http://www.merriam-webster.com/dictionary/fold

Moss, G. (2003). Putting the text back into practice: Junior age non-fiction as objects of design. In C. Jewitt & G. Kress (Eds.), *Multimodal Literacy* (pp. 73-87). New York: Peter Lang.

Moss, P. (2007). Meetings across the paradigmatic divide. *Educational Philosophy & Theory, 39*(3), 229-245.

Muspratt, S., Luke, A., & Freebody, P. (Eds). (1997). *Constructing critical literacies: Teaching and learning textual practice*. Cresskill, NJ: Hampton Press.

Nason, P., & Whitty, P. (2007). Bringing action research to the curriculum development process. *Educational Action Research, 15*(2), 271-281.

National Association for the Education of Young Children (NAEYC). (2005). *Code of ethical conduct and statement of commitment*. Washington, DC: NAEYC. Retrieved from http://www.naeyc.org/about/positions/PSETH05.asp

New Zealand Ministry of Education. (2008). *What are the early childhood exemplars? Kei Tua o te Pae. Early childhood education: Teaching and learning.* Wellington, NZ: New Zealand Ministry of Education. Retrieved from http://www.educate.ece.govt.nz/Programmes/KeiTuaotePae/Introducti ontoAssessment/Whataretheearlychildhoodexemplars.aspx

Novinger, S., O'Brien, L. & Sweigman, L. (2005). Challenging the culture of expertise: Moving beyond training the always, already failing early childhood educator. In S. Ryan & S. Grieshaber (Eds.), *Practical transformations and transformational practices* (pp. 217-241). Amsterdam, NL: Elsevier.

Odin, J. (1997). The edge of difference: Negotiations between the hypertextual and the postcolonial. *Modern Fiction Studies, 43*(3), 598-630.

Pahl, K., & Rowsell, J. (Eds). (2006). *Travel notes from the New Literacy Studies: Instances of practice.* Clevedon, UK: Multilingual Matters.

Paul, L. (1998). *Reading otherways.* Portland, ME: Calendar Islands.

Petrina, S. (2004). The politics of curriculum and instructional design/theory/ form: Critical problems, projects, units, and modules. *Interchange, 35*(1), 81-126.

Rath, J. (2001). Representing feminist educational research with/in the postmodern: Stories of rape crisis training. *Gender & Education, 13*(2), 117-135.

Richardson, L. (2002). Writing sociology. *Cultural Studies/Critical Methodology, 2*(3), 414-422.

Richardson, L. (1997). *Fields of play: Constructing an academic life.* New Brunswick, NJ: Rutgers University Press.

Richardson, L. (1990). *Writing strategies: Reaching diverse audiences.* Thousand Oaks, CA: Sage.

Ronai, C. (1999). The next night sous rature: Wrestling with Derrida's mimesis. *Qualitative Inquiry, 5*(1), 114-129.

Sousa Santos, B. (2004). Interview with Boaventura de Sousa Santos, R. Dale & S. Robertson. *Globalisation, Societies & Education, 2*(2), 147-160.

St. Pierre, E. (2000). Nomadic inquiry in the smooth space of the field. In E. St. Pierre & W. Pillow (Eds.), *Working the ruins: Feminist poststructural theory and methods in education* (pp. 258-282). London: Routledge.

Street, B. (2003). What's 'new' in New Literacy Studies? Critical approaches to literacy in theory and practice. *Current Issues in Comparative Education, 5*(2), 77-91.

Stronach, I., & MacLure, M. (1997). *Educational research undone: The postmodern embrace.* Buckingham, UK: Open University Press.

Sumara, D. (1998). Action research as a postmodern practice. *Interchange, 29*(1), 33-45.

Synder, I. (1998). Beyond the hype: Reassessing hypertext. In E. Synder (Ed.), *Page to screen: Taking literacy into the electronic era* (pp. 125-144). London: Routledge.

Wachowski, A., & Wachowski, L. (2001). *The Matrix.* Burbank, CA: Warner Bros. Pictures.

Weiskopf, R. (2002). Deconstructing "The Iron Cage" – towards an aesthetic of folding. *Consumption, Markets & Culture, 5*(1), 79–97.

Whitty, P. (2006, November). *Across the waters: Learning stories – A New Zealand import.* Paper presented with S. Rose, L. White, & G. Langille at the Atlantic Educators Conference (AEC), University of New Brunswick, Fredericton, NB.

4

Rhizomatic Stories of Immanent Becomings and Intra-Activity:

Professional Development Reconceptualized

Veronica Pacini-Ketchabaw, Laurie Kocher,
Alejandra Sanchez, & Christine Chan

Many years ago Maxine Greene (1973) named the teacher 'as stranger'. She proposed the teacher as an incomplete project, as unfinished, as in the process of becoming a teacher with others. If the teacher chooses to become a critical subject, she supposed, what is critical only emerges when the teacher understands herself or himself as subject to uncertainty. Uncertainty resides within the acts of a self committed to becoming. Greene imagined teacher education happening not through debates on proper preparation but as philosophy in the making. Her address to learning links freedom to our courage: "If he can learn to do philosophy, he may liberate himself for understanding and choosing. He may liberate himself for reflective action as someone who knows who he is

as a historical being, acting on his freedom, trying
each day to be" (p. 7). The teacher's unfinished work
is to understand her representations of education as a
project of learning to live with others. Existentially,
development is uneven and uncertain because it is
always affected by the question of freedom.

Britzman, 2007, p. 3

O ne of the primary goals of professional development
programs in early childhood education is to engage educators in changing their knowledge, beliefs, skills, and practices to
ensure improvements in children's learning outcomes. The
emphasis is on the outcomes of change that occur in the educators
themselves and their practices in response to the implementation
of specific sources of change (e.g., programs, workshops, conferences, helpful books, etc.) (Smith & Gillespie, 2007). Much has been
written about effective models of professional development as
well as about effective evaluation models that promise successful
teacher change (Guskey, 2002; Smith & Gillespie, 2007). However,
this approach to thinking about professional development, with
its emphasis on external change agents, presupposes a static,
knowable teacher. The idea of professional development that
revolves around a change event moves the teacher we know to the
new and improved teacher *who will be known*. A definitive endpoint
is in mind. Thus, professional development diametrically opposes
the idea of "the teacher as an incomplete project, as unfinished, as
in the process of becoming," as Deborah Britzman (2007) suggests
in the introductory quote.

In this chapter, we engage with the *idea* of professional development as understood in the field of early childhood education
and interrogate it using postmodern critical analysis. Following
the critical engagements of the reconceptualist movement, we
address the possibilities of posthumanist theories for our own
understandings of change as we work with early childhood educators in professional development contexts. Specifically, the aims
of this chapter are: (a) to conceptualize change and transformation in professional development contexts from a posthumanist
standpoint through an ontology of becoming; and (b) to provide

an example of how understandings of change from a posthumanist perspective might take place within the context of professional
learning.

We begin the chapter with a brief outline of our position on
modernist understandings of professional development. We then
move on to critique the underpinnings and assumptions of modernist understandings of professional development. Based on this
critique, we argue that the change experienced by educators
within professional development can be best understood within a
posthumanist perspective, especially using the work of philosopher Gilles Deleuze and feminist physicist Karen Barad. We first
address the concepts that undergird this argument before presenting an example from our work with early childhood educators
in British Columbia concerning the transformation one educator
experienced to her image of the child. In our conclusion, we draw
together the concept of intra-activity with the experiences of this
educator to offer a vision of professional development that leads
towards multiplicities as opposed to closures – a conclusion
without endings.

Working in the Ruins of Professional Development

Based on the work of Jacques Derrida and Patti Lather, we
acknowledge the impossibility of working outside of the dominant
discourse and, hence, position our argument *within/against*
(Lather, 2001; Readings, 1996) this discourse. The task for those
working within/against the ruins of the idea of professional development is "to make the destruction . . . into an opportunity for
Thought rather than an occasion for denunciation or mourning"
(p. 179). Engaging in this work within/against is a way of moving
from the idea of professional development within the representation landscape (see next section of the chapter), addressing the
imperatives of the critique without paralysis (meaning the inability to engage in further action).

Working within/against the ruins of professional development as representation involves negotiating between "two build-
ings from heterogeneous historical periods [and contexts that are]
impossibly co-present" (Readings, 1996, p. 170). Therefore, as we
understand it, this work does not involve finding consensus
between two projects (modern and postmodern); rather, it is to

dwell in the dissensus that the ruined concept of professional development as representation leaves us.

Readings (1996) argues that on "the horizon of dissensus, no consensual answer can take away the question mark that the social bond (the fact of other people, of language) raises. No universal community can embody the answer; no rational consensus can decide simply to agree on an answer" (p. 170). By avoiding consensus on professional development, we do not work towards the construction of a mastery project of best and effective professional development, one that is ultimately accomplished. On the contrary, "the obligation becomes to read the unreadability of the impossible event" (Lather, 2001, p. 218) – to work towards the impossibility of professional development as representation, remaining conscious all the while that it is this difficulty (impossibility) that takes us toward true professional development. The impossibility of professional development means that "it always fails in the sense of complete certainty and final closure" (Mason, p. 517); it is future oriented as opposed to closure oriented. "The impossible is not simple logical contradiction of the possible, but the terminus of a hope beyond hope, of a hope against hope, of a faith in what we cannot imagine or in any way foresee beyond any present horizon of expectation" (Caputo, 2000, p. 263). In other words, working towards the impossible reminds us that "there is never any arrival or final destination" (Mason, p. 506). The impossible, then, is not a reason for despair. We can say that "the impossible constitutes the very possibility of ongoing" reflections on professional development (Mason, p. 507). According to Mason, Derrida argues that "it is in the act of breaking . . . of pushing up against the limits of the impossible that it is possible to get started on developing" an idea (p. 507).

The notion of impossibility has been used by Derrida as an alternative term for deconstruction in that "deconstruction is a passion for the impossible" (Mason, 2006, p. 207). Mason elaborates, saying, "This passion for the impossible, the desire to explore the impossible by running up against the limit of what can never be present, is the overarching aspiration that sets deconstruction in motion . . . to go where you cannot go" (p. 506). It is the passion for the impossible that keeps things open.

Further, Caputo (2000) explains that

> deconstruction is not out to deny that something
> exists but only to show ... the difficulty we have
> getting that claim nailed down in a definitive way.
> That is what it means to say that nothing exists
> outside of the text – viz, that existence claims cannot
> be disentangled from the web of discourse that makes
> them possible to begin with. Existential assertions
> cannot break out into the open with atomistic inde-
> pendence, seize upon the things themselves, and then
> vaporize, leaving a sighing and heaving in naked
> contact .... Deconstruction does not try to scatter
> existential claims to the four winds, but to heighten
> our appreciation for their difficulty. (p. 254)

It is the difficulty of the idea of professional development within a representation landscape that we attempt to work with in the next sections of this chapter.

Normative Discourses of Professional Development

How does the discourse of professional development acquire its unproblematic status? What are the *professional* and *developmental* processes that "allow it to take on the semblance of an 'already constituted entity'" (Chai, 1995, p. 595)? Chai (1995), writing about organizations, argues the importance of paying attention to the logic and organization of thought when conducting postmodern analyses:

> We cannot begin by assuming the unproblematic
> existence of social entities such as "individuals,"
> "organizations," "[professional development]" or
> "society." Instead, we should begin by assuming that
> all we have are actions, interactions and local orches-
> trations of relationships. From this we might then
> begin to ask how it is that some kinds of interactions
> appear to "succeed" in stabilizing and reproducing
> themselves, thus generating "effects" such as "indi-
> viduals," "[professionals]" or "organizations," whilst
> others disappear completely. (p. 595)

Our intent in this section is to interrogate three interrelated assumptions *always already* embedded in the idea of professional development: (1) Professional development is perceived as an innocent and passive event in educational processes. (2) The educator who participates in professional development is viewed as a stable and unchanging subject. (3) Change is seen as something exceptional, while stability and order are assumed as the norm. Professional development actively participates in generating the formations within which professionalism is possible. Our interrogations relate to "the crisis of representation in that the adequacy of language to capture experience is considered an effect of discourse rather than a reflection of that experience" (Pitt & Britzman, 2003, p. 756).

Within the idea of professional development, an ontology of *being* is privileged over an ontology of *becoming*. While an ontology of being concerns itself with the organized state of things – their unity, identity, essence, structure, discreteness; an ontology of becoming attends to plurality, dissonance, change, transience, and disparity (Chia, 1995). Bogue (2004) further draws out the implication of an ontology of being:

> Implicit in [the ontology of being] is the model of thought as a form of recognition, recognition being denned through "the harmonious exercise of all the faculties upon a supposed same object" (Deleuze, 1994, p. 133). Recognition in turn grounds the notion of thought as representation, every representation presuming a unifed perspective and stable objects governed by the complementary principles of "the Same and the Similar, the Analogous and the Opposed" (ibid., p. 167). *Thought's goal in a world of recognition and representation is to eliminate problems and find solutions, to pass from nonknowledge to knowledge.* [emphasis added] Learning in such a world is simply the passage from non-knowledge to knowledge, a process with a definite beginning and ending, in which thought, like a dutiful pupil, responds to pre-formulated questions and eventually arrives at pre-existing answers. (p. 333)

How is an ontology of being embedded in the idea of professional development that follows modern representational thinking? Let's begin with two related definitions of professional development:

> Professional development programs are systematic efforts to bring about change in the classroom practices of teachers, in their attitudes and beliefs, and in the learning outcomes of students .... Professional development programs are deliberate and purposeful endeavors, and the changes a professional development leader wishes to bring about can usually be well defined. (Guskey, 2002, pp. 381, 383)

Modern representational thinking works through language to deem objects, concepts, and events as real and as having a concrete entity onto themselves. For instance, professional development is primarily understood as a noun and object of study that can be applied in a limited time and space to produce an effect that can be measured. What is underprivileged in a modern understanding of professional development are "the micro-organizing processes which enact and re-enact [professional development] into existence" (Chia, 1995, p. 587). The definitions of professional development above reflect how language works to maintain control over meanings and understandings as they relate to professional development. The term professional development is "taken to be accurately representing an external world of discrete and identifiable objects, forces and generative mechanisms" (Chia, 1999, p. 215). Teachers are "required" to engage in professional development to maintain currency; necessitating an assumption that currency is in itself a humanly detached entity, and not necessarily a humanly constructed entity.

Because professional development is thought of as an already constituted entity, the processes that are often studied are those that privilege individuals and their actions, rather than those less obvious micro-practices which constitute the very idea of professional development (Chia, 1995), that is, the "systematic efforts" (Guskey, 2000, p. 381) that are clearly reflected in the first definition of professional development.

Guskey (2002) acknowledges that professional development involves different processes at different levels, but views them as purposeful endeavors that need to be carefully evaluated in order to determine whether they are achieving their purposes. Underlying this view is "an unshakeable assumption that reality is essentially discrete, substantial and enduring" (Chia, 1999, p. 215).

Figure 1, which depicts the effects of professional development, assumes that the learning that takes place in professional
development simply involves the passage from non-knowledge to
knowledge, from ignorance to enlightenment, responding "to pre-
formulated questions and eventually arriving at pre-existing
answers" (Bogue, 2004, p. 333):

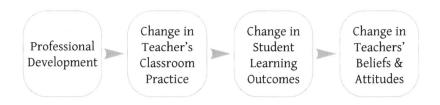

Figure 1: "A model of teacher change" (Guskey, 2002, p. 383)

Reflected in this model is an individual who can be known,
defined, and represented. Guattari (1995) explains that "traditionally, the subject was conceived as the ultimate essence of individ-
uation, as a pure, empty, prereflexive apprehension of the world,
a nucleous of sensibility, of expressivity – the unifier of states of
consciousness . . . " (p. 22). In this model, educators are seen as
psychological beings with internal characteristics which can be
shaped by the outside world.

Chia (1999) proposes that by giving priority to an ontology of
being and consequently to (re)presentation, change (seen as the
primary goal of professional development) is seen as something
exceptional that takes place under specific circumstances with the
help of certain people often referred to as *agents* of change – privileging outcomes and end-states. Through this lens, individuals
are viewed as primarily unchanging entities. For example, Michael
Fullan (2001), a leading scholar on educational change, suggests:

> Real change . . . represents a serious personal and col-
> lective experience characterized by ambivalence and
> uncertainty; and if the change works out it can result
> in a sense of mastery, accomplishment, and profes-

sional growth. The anxieties of uncertainty and the joys of mastery are central to the subjective meaning of educational change, and to success or failure thereof. (p. 32)

Tsoukas and Chia (2002) borrow from process-oriented philosophers Bergson and James to argue that change is not an exceptional capacity of individuals but rather a pervasive state of life: "Individuals are *reified entities* and are themselves tentative, and precariously balanced but relatively stabilized assemblages of actions and interactions" (Tsoukas & Chia, 2002, p. 592). Chia (1999) further states that

for Bergson, all real movement and change is indivisible and cannot be treated as a series of distinct states that form, as it were, a line in time. Bergson's main claim is that the temporal structure of our experience does not consist in putting together given discrete items. On the contrary, so-called discrete elements are only apparent when we have a need to pluck them from our continuing experience in order to represent them in spatial terms. (p. 216)

The model of change in professional development depicted by Guskell (2002) ignores the idea of change as the essence of life itself and treats change as a series of distinct phases.

Based on the arguments reviewed so far, we can say that professional development can be more accurately explained as an "attempt to order the intrinsic flux of human action, to channel it towards certain ends, to give it a particular shape, through generalizing and institutionalizing particular meanings and rules" (Tsoukas & Chia, 2002, p. 570). For instance, Fullan (2001) identifies *do's* and *don'ts* related to educational change that reflect the view of change as an exceptional process through which individuals need to be led, and as a process that needs to be carefully managed and orchestrated:

- Assume that people need pressure to change (even in directions that they desire) . . .

- Unrealistic or undefined time lines fail to recognize that implementation occurs developmentally. Significant change in the form of implementing specific innovations can be expected to take a minimum of 2 or 3 years . . .

- Do not expect all or even most people or groups to change . . .

- Assume that you will need a *plan* that is based on [specific] assumptions and that addresses the factors known to affect implementation . . . (p. 108-109)

As described here, professional development attempts to channel and tame the constant and unpredictable changing capacity of educators. It facilitates the manipulation of heterogeneous and multiple changes. We need to find an alternative idea to think about what we do with early childhood educators in practice, and this idea should free us from the representational aspect of the idea of professional development. In the next section, we propose that these events can be seen as rhizomatic stories of *immanent becomings*, as nomadic spaces where constant, heterogeneous, and surprising transformations are the norm.

Entering Rhizomic Planes of Immanent Becomings

How then can we re-imagine professional development through postmodern lenses? What postmodern theoretical tools can be useful for re-imagining professional development differently? How can we turn the idea of professional development on its head? In this section, we use poststructural writings to think of professional development differently. Specifically, we are resisting an ontology of being and juxtaposing an ontology of *becoming* that emphasizes a transient, ephemeral, and emergent reality.[1] From a Deleuzian perspective, "reality is deemed to be continuously in flux and transformation and hence unrepresentable in any static sense" (Chia, 1995, p. 579).

A re-imagined idea of professional development works with an ontology of *becoming*, characteristic of a postmodern style of thinking:

> A *becoming* style of thinking . . . strives to faithfully chart out the precarious, emergent assemblages of organizing with an eye towards processes of exclusion, negation and suppression which collectively contribute to the accomplishment of organization. It

> is to "identify the accidents, the minute deviations –
> or conversely, complete the reversals – the errors,
> the false appraisals, and the faulty calculations that
> gave birth to those things that continue to exist and
> have value for us". (Chia, 1995, p. 598)

From this perspective, professional development becomes the product of a heterogeneous project that involves the assemblage of micro-practices of inscription. Therefore, we need to look in further detail at the micro-practices involved in the processes of developing professionals and/or professionalizing.

Further, a *becoming* style of thinking refers to the educator as continuously produced, or as constituted – as opposed to a priori. Semetsky's (2004) words aptly reflects the becoming subject:

> For Deleuze, subjectivation is precisely the relation to
> oneself; it is a self-reference but of a slightly paradox-
> ical quality where one's self is always already in a
> process of becoming-other. As such, subjectivity does
> not presuppose what Taylor calls "my discovering my
> identity" (1991, p. 47): instead – and far from any pre-
> supposed return to identity – novelty as *difference*
> presents "life as a work of art" (Deleuze, 1995, p. 94).
> (p. 319)

If we accept that we are in a process of becoming, of constant change, then we must abandon our idea of a static, knowable educator and move on to a view of an educator in a state of constant change and becoming.

Change in an ontology of *becoming* is reconceptualized as the ultimate fact for every phenomenon, including individuals (Chia, 1999). Chia (1999) uses Deleuze and Guattari's concept of the rhizome to rethink the idea of change:

> Rhizomic change is *anti-genealogical* in the sense that
> it resists the linear retracting of a definite locatable
> originary point of initiation. Change ... is also multi-
> ple, unending and unexpectedly other. There is no
> unitary point to serve as a natural pivot for construct-
> ing subject and object, for drawing boundaries that
> define inside and outside and that distinguish
> "macro" from "micro" ... Multiplicities have only

> densities, determinations and lines of connections
> which ripple outwards. The idea of net-workings
> better encapsulates the transformative capacity ...
> of change .... Change, renewal and transformation
> develop along locally identified lines of least resist-
> ance rather than according to any pre-determined
> template. (p. 223)

According to this view, as we engage with educators in practice we
must pay less attention to what is institutionalized through a professional development program, and greater attention to the

> subterranean, microscopic changes that always go
> on ..., changes that may never acquire the status of
> formal organizational systems and routines .... Such
> change occurs naturally, incrementally, and inex-
> orably through "creep," "slippage," and "drift" as
> well as natural "spread" .... It spreads through a
> patch of oil ... takes place by adaptation, variations,
> restless expansion, and opportunistic conquests"
> (Tsoukas & Chia, 2002, p. 580).

Working from an ontology of *becoming*, as Tsoukas and Chia
(2002) suggest, professional development is seen in reference to
possibilities. We can't work on understanding the single (predetermined) trajectory that educators take through professional development; rather we need to work towards opening up to the
multiple trajectories of probabilistic processes through which
educators engage in: "A definitive quality of real change is its
unexpected and surprising, and hence unpredictable nature"
(Chia, 1999, p. 223). The task is not to provide *do's* and *don'ts* to educational change, but to *relax* these instructions and attend to the
surprising possibilities that emerge from the constant and unde-
termined nature of reality. Change in early childhood education is
not an exception; rather the exception is the manipulation of
change through professional development models.

Extending the rhizome metaphor further, change follows the
principle of immanence:

> According to this principle of *immanence*, the past is
> immanent in the present and this fact implies that
> each outcome, each situation or state, always neces-

sarily incorporates and absorbs the events of its past. Thus, the present is not merely the linear successor of the past but a novel outcome of it. Each moment of duration absorbs the preceding one, transforming it and with it the whole, constituting at each stage of the process a novel and never-to-be-repeated occasion necessarily grounded in its past, but always projected towards a not-yet-knowable future. (Chia, 1999, p. 220)

Given that it is naïve for us to talk about professional development as the unique direct cause that brings about change in educators' minds, we must consider that professional development programs are *made* to work through the experiences and always already-changing texture of educators:

Change programs trigger ongoing change; they provide the discursive resources for making certain things possible, although what exactly will happen remains uncertain when a change program is initiated – It must first be experienced before the possibilities it opens up are appreciated and taken up (if they are taken up). Change programs are *made* to work and, insofar as it happens, they are locally adapted, improvised, and elaborated by human agents; institutionalized categories are imaginatively extended when put into action. (Tsoukas & Chia, 2002, p. 578)

While we are stressing the idea that professional development programs are *made* to work, we also want to emphasize that we conceptualize change programs as important and key in the always already changing texture of educators. To explain this we draw on the work of feminist physicist Karen Barad.[2] Barad's (2007) agential realism, specifically her *intra-activity* framework, helps us to understand the entangled process of transformation that takes place through professional development. Her agential realism theory in fact resonates with the Deleuzian approach we have presented above. Barad (2007) provides us an innovative way of understanding matter (e.g., the physical world). Matter, Barad argues, cannot be thought of as passive. Rather, she says, matter is agentic, in constant *intra-action*. Further, it cannot be separated from discourse: discourse and matter matter, and thus she refers to discourse-matter. Barad (2007) speaks about intra-action as follows:

> "Intra-action" signifies the mutual constitution of entangled agencies. That is, in contrast to the usual "interaction," which assumes that there are separate individual agencies that precede their interaction, the notion of intra-action recognizes that distinct agencies do not precede, but rather emerge through, their intra-action. It is important to note that the "distinct" agencies are not only distinct in a relational, not an absolute, sense, that is, agencies are only distinct in relation to their mutual entanglement; they don't exist as individual elements. (p. 33)

Barad (2007) further notes:

> The notion of *intra-action* (in contrast to the usual "interaction," which assumes the prior existence of independent entities or relata) represents a profound conceptual shift. It is through specific agential intra-actions that the boundaries and properties of the components of phenomena become determinate and that particular concepts (that is, particular material articulations of the world) become meaningful. (p. 139)

We think of professional development as what Barad calls *apparatuses*, and, in turn, material-discursive phenomena, which materialize themselves "in intra-action with other material-discursive apparatuses" (Barad, 2007, p. 203). Barad (2007) explains that, from an agential realist position:

- apparatuses are specific material-discursive practices;
- apparatuses produce differences that matter – they are boundary-making practices that are formative of matter and meaning, productive of, and part of, the phenomena produced;
- apparatuses are material configurations/dynamic reconfigurings of the world;
- apparatuses are themselves phenomena (constituted and dynamically reconstituted as part of the ongoing intra-activity of the world);

- apparatuses are not located in the world but are material configurations or reconfigurings of the world that re(con)figure spatiality and temporality as well as . . . dynamics (i.e., they do not exist as static structures, nor do they merely unfold or evolve in space and time). (p. 146)

Change in professional development programs is constituted and reconstituted in intra-action (with educators, with practices, with children, with pedagogical narrations,[3] etc.), and therefore "perpetually open to rearrangements, rearticulations, and other re-workings" (Barad, 2007, p. 203). The educator participating in professional development programs does not change in time, but rather the change materializes *through* intra-action through time and space. The change that takes place is constituted. It is not a static relationality, it is a doing – Barad argues that the doing creates the enactment of boundaries, always constituting exclusions. The change cannot be dissociated from the knower and the known; it cannot be discussed as the object of the known.

Both the educator and the professional development program emerge from their intra-action. They are ontologically inseparable. Barad (2007) reminds us that "a phenomenon is a specific intra-action of an 'object' and the 'measuring agencies'; the object and the measuring agencies emerge from, rather than precede, the intra-action that produces them" (p. 127).

Immanent Becomings and the Image of Child

In this section of the chapter we present an example of how a postmodern conceptualization of change in professional development can be thought of. We draw from our experience of working with early childhood educators for the last five years in a large participatory action research project in British Columbia: The Investigating Quality Project. The project can be conceptualized as professional development activities.

The primary goal of the project is to engage with early childhood educators in discussions related to practices that produce crises or disrupt business as usual in the early childhood classroom. Together with educators, we engage in the ongoing process of deconstruction and reconstruction of our early childhood practices using poststructural, feminist, postcolonial, and anti-racist theoretical locations (also see Dahlberg, Moss & Pence, 2007; MacNaughton, 2003; Lenz Taguchi, forthcoming).

Since the beginning of the project, the participating educators have been collecting pedagogical documentation (Dahlberg & Moss, 2005; Dahlberg, Moss, & Pence, 2007) in their centres using journal writing, photography, video recording, and audio recording. The pedagogical documentations are shared with the project group. During our meetings, we reflect together critically on each educator's documentation and make visible how we might work with postfoundational theories (MacNaughton, 2001).

The data generated in the project by the researchers and educators are extensive and we do not report in this chapter the wide range of issues that emerged. For the purposes of this chapter, we show one moment in which we capture the way in which change took place during the project through the intra-actions of Christine, an early childhood educator with whom we have been working with for the last three years.

Christine was interested in challenging dominant ideas of thinking about the child, what educators in the early childhood programs of Reggio Emilia refer to as the image of the child. Discussions around the image of the child are a key component of our professional development programs (see McArdle & McWilliam, 2005; Moss & Petrie, 2002). The image of the child has been an important topic of discussion in the reconceptualist literature. The literature has challenged the image of the child advanced by developmental psychologists, this image being a child in need of intervention (Dahlberg & Moss, 2005; Dahlberg, Moss, & Pence, 2007; Moss & Petrie, 2002; Rinaldi, 2006). Reconceptualist scholars invite us to work with the idea of a child who is competent, rich, and full of potential (Dahlberg, Moss, & Pence, 2007; MacNaughton, 2003; Moss & Petrie, 2002). In fact, (as noted in the introduction of this volume), this 'alternative' image of the child is now emerging as a discourse in policy documents, training materials, and practices in some parts of Canada. One question that has emerged in our team conversations around in-service and pre-service professional development has been how change takes place from an image of the child in need of intervention to an image of the child who is competent, rich, and full of potential.

After being introduced to this competent and rich image of the child written about in the literature from Reggio Emilia, Christine became interested in challenging and unpacking the ways in which she viewed and worked with the children in her classroom. Moreover, she was troubled by the discursive-material meanings that were common place in her centre about Stephanie, the girl she portrays in her documentation.

Our example intends to show the intra-actions between the change program and Christine's always already changing texture. As we show this, our attention is focused on the additional intra-actions that take place in the classroom. We do this through the aids of pedagogical documentation. Before presenting the example, we want to clarify how we use pedagogical documentation in this example, following Lenz Taguchi (2008):

> "Pedagogical documentation materializes practice for us and makes it *a territory where intra-active phenomena can take place and can be "made visible" as processes of new becomings.* As such it temporarily "captures" an intra-active event that has happened, and in its materialization it becomes a territory for further intra-activity and processes of new learning . . . Any form of documentation can be understood as a *materializing apparatus of knowing* that produces different kinds of knowledge, as phenomena, depending on the onto-logical and/or epistemological perspectives we bring with us in our usage of it. Pedagogical documentation is a *material-discursive apparatus,* to speak with Barad (1998), that offers constraints on what is produced as knowledge and produces exclusions, depending on both the limits of our discursive understandings, and the limits and constraints of the material realities involved" (pp. 8-9).

In her new book, Lenz Taguchi (2009) says that "the actualization of the event in the documentation is simply a fragment or splinter of its dense mixture." Thus, our example reflects these characteristics. In order to show the change that takes place during a professional development program, we go to micro-spaces to highlight the dense mixture of one particular fragment.

Let's now look at some of the pedagogical documentation that Christine produced. Here we include a couple of moments, both involving a girl named Stephanie, that Christine brought to our meetings.

Stephanie and the Sticker Moment
(Christine Chan)

In the first moment, Stephanie has an encounter with another child over a much prized object, a sticker. Stephanie approaches Sally, taking her hand and walks across the room with her. Surprised by the gesture, Sally is even more taken aback when Stephanie removes Sally's sticker from her shirt, placing it on her own. Christine watches from a distance, carefully observing, as the situation resolves and generosity shines through.

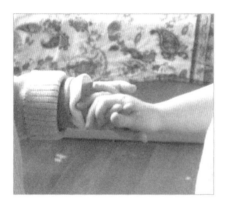

Stephanie approaches Sally and reaches for her. Stephanie laces her fingers into Sally's petite left hand. With fingers interlocking, hand in hand, a connection is made.

Stephanie leads and Sally follows, although a look of uncertainty is written on her face. My curiosity is piquing as I watch this unlikely pair. Where are they going? What does Stephanie have in mind? Better yet, I can't believe Sally is agreeing to follow ...

One step, two steps, STOP!

Abruptly, Stephanie turns towards Sally and peels her sticker off of her sweater.

With a look of slight panic, Sally shoots her gaze up, her eyes saying, "help me, she took my sticker!" Invisible behind the lens of the camera, Sally bypasses me and seeks intervention elsewhere. Stephanie studies the sticker and is transfixed by the characters of *Madagascar*. I am intrigued by the quick turn of events.

Stephanie places the sticker onto her own shirt and reveals a smile of contentment. Without any intervention, I wonder what Sally will do? Will she take the sticker back herself or will she choose to share it? I can tell she is busy thinking. I am curious to see how this unfolds.

Stephanie walks away and steals a few extended minutes alone with the sticker.

Not far behind, Sally stays close to her treasure from home, still quietly pondering what to do. Then suddenly, Stephanie approaches Sally with the sticker. Frozen in my step, my body clenched into a tight ball, I am hoping and praying for it . . . I am wishing in my head, "Please just give it back!" Like a hamster wheel in my head, my thoughts are running fast.

My balloon of hope makes a loud *POP!* as Stephanie pivots and walks in the opposite direction. At this point, grown-up hands gently enter the picture. What is Stephanie going to do? Will she protest loudly? Or has she spent enough time with the animals of *Madagascar* and willingly return the sticker back to its rightful owner?

With both hands, Stephanie pulls the sticker close to her face and observes intently, perhaps for one ... last ... look. Time seems to be elapsing and I am still holding my breath. Waiting stops time.

Quiet as can be, Sally stands still and is waiting. On her own, Stephanie positions the sticker up to Sally's chest. Sally's patience is astounding.

Stephanie pats down the sticker on Sally's sweater and then turns away. Ahhhhhh ... finally, I am breathing again, perhaps for both Sally and I.

... only to come back a millisecond later to have one last look. Paths may cross many times in one day, especially in our classrooms. What meaning can be made with this particular crossing? An unlikely pair meeting up for a short time over the shared interest of a sticker. Did time stand still for patience and generosity to shine through? Was an act of sharing repaid with trust that a beloved object would return? How will this crossing affect this "unlikely" pair in the future?

Stephanie and the Art Supply Cart (Christine Chan)

In the second encounter, Christine observes the gentle acts of kindness offered by several classmates as they make gestures of friendship to Stephanie while she works with supplies from the art cart, indicating intimately that they know their friend, utilizing their silent languages of the heart. Kindness, generosity, and connection are the focus of Christine's analysis.

Stephanie surveys the art supply cart, much like she does on most days. She stands over the area and surveys the assortment of pencil crayons and color markers. It is not unusual that she reaches over the clear glass jars and seizes handfuls of the markers and pencils. The drawing utensils are held captive in her tightly clenched fists as she walks away from the open art centre.

I pull up a chair at the open art table and guide her into the seat. To my surprise, Stephanie settles into the seat without any resistance. I ease her clenched fist free of the drawing tools. I place them in front of her on the table and hand one back to her. I simultaneously slip a piece of construction paper in front of her.

Minutes have gone by and she is still exploring the materials at the art table freely. Stephanie seems content and peaceful.

Danielle approaches the open art table. She chooses to sit next to Stephanie.

With uncertainty I prepare myself for Stephanie to make a move. Will she leave the table if Danielle gets too close? Will this closeness irritate her? I speculate and prepare to strategize to keep Stephanie at the table, in case she decides to leave. Will she or won't she?

I hear nothing and see nothing indicating Stephanie's desire to leave this post which was somewhat imposed on her. She doesn't seem to mind and I am ecstatic, yet I try to keep my energy calm. Danielle needs my assistance for writing a love letter to her parents. I am delighted to help but a bit distracted in absorbing Stephanie's experience at the open art table. Then suddenly . . .

Danielle approaches Stephanie and pats her on the shoulder without words, a soft gentle gesture. Stephanie reacts with a slight wince but more surprisingly, she does not reject the touch.

Unexpectedly, Ella approaches Stephanie and throws her arms around her. As quickly as Ella has come to hug Stephanie, she returns promptly back to her seat to continue with her own explorations. My heart feels full. Stephanie receives the hug by not rejecting the hug.

She returns to her exploration with the various Crayola markers. She evaluates the different caps and appraises the fit of each one.

Danielle and Ella are no longer at the table and their presence is replaced by Ryan. Stephanie reaches forward and grasps all the markers and colored pencils. She takes a few steps to the right and puts them all in a wicker basket and then returns to collect more.

Stephanie picks up the glue stick without its cap. Ryan gets up from his chair and positions his body in front of the wicker basket and gestures "Where?" Was Ryan watching Stephanie the whole time?

Ryan steps away and returns with a cap and places it on the table in front of Stephanie. I thank Ryan for helping Stephanie to find the cap for the glue stick. Once again, no words were spoken, just the glimmer in his eye.

Stephanie moves on to the natural collage materials where she continues her exploration.

Ryan dips his hand into one of the glass bowls and sprinkles a handful of beans on the table in front of Stephanie's collage. There are no words exchanged once again. "Are these for Stephanie?" He nods, "yes." What are these children conveying with their silent gestures? Were they just gentle acts of kindness? Did Danielle want Stephanie to simply know she was there? And was Ella's hug a gesture of encouragement, saying, "You're doing great, keep up the good work?" Did Ryan want to show Stephanie that he was helpful? Are the children expressing to Stephanie, "You're wonderful and I enjoy you being here with us"?

Regardless of the content and the meaning behind each gesture, only the children and Stephanie will truly know. Gestures of affection, care, and kindness occur in silence, and I continue to listen to them with my heart.

The Image of the Child

Christine's practices are agentive in that they play a role in producing the very phenomena (the image of the child) they set out to grasp (Barad, 2007). The observations Christine makes of Stephanie's engagement with art materials are part of the configuration of the image of the child in its intra-active becoming.

The image of the child is always shifting, always in the process of becoming. It doesn't exist as a priori but is made to matter through material-discursive practices – through the intra-actions she materializes in the moment as well as the intra-actions that materialize themselves in the process of writing/discussing the pedagogical documentation.

To read that Christine moved from an application of a deficient image of the child to a competent conceptualization is to assume: (a) an educator who can sit outside of her own practice, and (b) that the concept of the image of the child is an objective entity. The image of the child is constituted and constitutive. Its constitution is ongoing; it is always configuring and reconfiguring itself and also configures and reconfigures the educator (as well as the children, the environment, the intelligibility of practice, etc.).

The image of the child that we see in Christine's pedagogical narration is not a fixed essence that was directly transported from her readings during our meetings to her practice. Rather, she is actively entangled in the configuration and reconfiguration of the materiality and discursivity of the image of the child. "Reality is an ongoing dynamic of intra-activity" (Barad, 2007, p. 206).

In the documentation, Christine not only brings to us the intra-actions that are enacted between Stephanie, Sally, and the materials. She is also making visible the intra-actions in which she is herself entangled. She is not a mere observer that brings her image of the child to life in the moment. Rather, she is intra-actively configuring and reconfiguring herself in her configuring of the images of Sally and Stephanie. She is part *of* the image – of the ongoing articulation of the image of Stephanie and Sally.

The Sticker Moment:
(Re)Configuring Sally and Stephanie

Let's look at the intra-actions that were enacted in the images of Sally and Stephanie. Christine says: "Where are they going? What does Stephanie have in mind? Better yet, I can't believe *Sally is agreeing to*." Boundaries around the image of Sally are established in this intra-action and a specific representation of Sally is configured. A material meaning of the image of Sally is articulated and becomes meaningful. The image of the child discursively-materially emerges in this intra-action. But this is not a fixed image, as this intra-action is continuously entangled with others. Christine continues: "With a look of slight panic, Sally shoots her gaze up. Her eyes saying, 'help me, she took my sticker.'" Yet, the image of Sally is (re)configured as Christine writes: "Sally's patience is astounding."

And we cannot leave behind how these intra-actions also configure images of Stephanie: "Stephanie leads and Sally follows," Christine says, "although a look of uncertainty is written on her face." The boundaries placed here are entangled with the boundaries as well as the possibilities that the image of Sally enacts in its own intra-actions.

Moreover, the material-discursive intra-actions that Christine embodies are entangled in the configurings and reconfigurings of the image of the child: "Frozen in my step, my body clenched into a tight ball, I am hoping and praying for it"; "I am intrigued by the quick turn of events"; "I am curious to see how this unfolds"; "I'm wishing in my head, 'please just give it back.'" Christine's discursive-material practices are agentic in that they also make possible certain meanings about Sally and Stephanie.

The point is not that Christine's thinking about the child is changing over time. The point is not that the meanings of the images of Sally and Stephanie are achieved through the thoughts and actions of Christine. Rather, what we want to emphasize, is that the dynamics taking place are "what matters in the ongoing materializing of different spacetime topologies" (Barad, 2007, p. 141). Barad (2007) reminds us:

> The primary ontological units are not 'things' but phenomena-dynamic topological reconfigurings/entanglements/relationalities/(re)articulations of the world. And the primary semantic units are not 'words' but material discursive practices through which (ontic and semantic) boundaries are constituted. This dynamism is agency. Agency is not an attribute but the ongoing reconfigurings of the world. The universe is agential intra-activity in its becoming. (p. 141)

And the image of the child is not the only agentic phenomenon that is configured and reconfigured in this moment . . .

The Art Supplies, the Sticker, and the Image of the Child

> Barad (2007) says:
>
> Matter, like meaning, is not an individually articulated or static entity. It is not little bits of nature, or a blank slate, or a site passively awaiting signification; nor is it an uncontested ground for scientific, feminist, or economic theories. Matter is not immutable or passive. Nor is it fixed support, location, referent, or source of sustainability for discourse. It does not require the mark of an eternal force like culture or history to complete it. Matter is always already an ongoing historicity. (p. 150-1)

How do the art supply cart, the brush, the easel, the paints, the sticker (the material) becomes entangled in the configuration and reconfiguration of the image of the child?

We have to look at the art materials and the sticker that are included in these practices as being material-discursive. They are not ahistorical, nonhuman, or passive. Art materials as well as the sticker are enmeshed into early childhood histories as well as other kinds of histories. We have to, for example, ask how art materials and stickers have become an important tool in every early childhood classroom (Kind, 2008). We have to pay attention to "the material constraints and exclusions and the material dimensions of power . . . because 'materiality' refers to phenomena, which are explicitly not elements of nature-outside-of-culture" (p. 211).

The materials in these observations matter for the configurations and reconfigurations of Christine's image of Stephanie. The art materials and the sticker intra-act with Stephanie, with Christine, and with the other children. Furthermore, they are active agents in the intra-activity that constitutes the phenomenon (the image of the child); they are productive of the image of the child. The art materials and the sticker are also reinvented through intra-actions. They are not innocent aspects of the configuration of the image of the child, nor do they constrain the intelligibility of the image of the child. Rather, they are active agents as well as part of the image of the child that becomes configured. Therefore, they are also always open to rearrangements, rearticulations, and reworkings.

In short, the image of the child that becomes intelligible in the pedagogical narrations is entangled in intra-activity that involves Christine's and the children's constant becomings, but also the material's constant rearrangements.

Conclusions Without Endings

In this chapter, we have argued that professional development, as traditionally understood, embeds an ontology of being and therefore follows a representational style of thinking. We looked at three interrelated assumptions found in the professional development literature: (1) Professional development is perceived as an innocent and passive event in educational processes. (2) The educator who participates in professional development is viewed as a stable and unchanging subject. (3) Change is seen as something exceptional, while stability and order are assumed as the norm.

We have suggested that an alternative way of reconceptualizing professional development is through an ontology of *becoming*. Within this style of thinking, educators are viewed as *always already* in a process of becoming and *always already* in intra-activity with the world, and therefore professional development programs are *made* to work through the constant becomings and intra-activity of educators. As our example showed, however, we do not claim that it is only educators who make the professional development model work, but rather that the professional development model is an agentic part of Christine's intra-actions. Thus we claim that dense intra-activity between the professional development program and the educator make things work in uncertain and unpredictable ways. The consequences of this approach to professional development are complex, even overdetermined, but, as Roy states,

> What all this amounts to is a fervent invitation to see that there are no ready answers or values that we can seize upon and put to use in organizing learning. Our best bet here is to learn to think from within confusion as Deborah Britzman (2002) has noted, without demanding clarity. To pretend that we can clear out the messiness of life . . . and order education along the lines of a power plant run by effective communication of "high quality" performance data is naïve at best and deception at worst. (Roy, 2004, p. 311)

Using posthumanist theories requires that professional learning, as Haraway (2003) notes, recognizes "that one cannot *know* the other or the self, but must ask in respect for all of time who and what are emerging in relationship" (p. 50) – as we showed in Christine's example. Furthermore, we suggest that professional development cannot look for closure or the formation of an identity but "allow conflicting concepts to interact in order to see what might be produced" (Bastian, 2006, p. 1029).

Notes

1 An ontology of being and an ontology of becoming are not viewed here as opposite, but rather are conceived "in terms of a *logic of supplementary* whereby the presence of the Other is implicitly recognized as the very condition for the articulation of the One" (Chia, 1995, p. 580). Also, see previous discussion on "within/against" position.

2 We would like to thank Hillevi Lenz Taguchi for pointing us to the work of Karen Barad (see Lenz Taguchi, 2008, 2009).

3 The terms *pedagogical narration* and *pedagogical documentation* are used interchangeably in the chapter. The practice of pedagogical narrations has been inspired by pedagogical documentation (developed in the preschools and infant-toddler centres of Reggio Emilia, Italy) and learning stories (from New Zealand). See Berger (2008) for an analysis of pedagogical narrations.

References

Barad, K. M. (2007). *Meeting the universe halfway: Quantum physics and the entanglement of matter and meaning.* Durham, NC: Duke University Press.

Bastian, M. (2006). Haraway's lost cyborg and the possibilities of transversalism. *Signs: Journal of Women in Culture and Society, 31*(4), 1027-1049.

Berger, I. (2008). *Expanding the notion of pedagogical narration through engagement with Hanna Arendt's political thought: Implications and possibilities for early childhood in British Columbia.* Paper presented at the Reconceptualizing Early Childhood Education Conference, Victoria, British Columbia.

Bogue, R. (2004). Search, swim and see: Deleuze's apprenticeship in signs and pedagogy of images. *Educational Philosophy and Theory, 36*(3), 327-342.

Britzman, D. P. (2007). Teacher education as uneven development: toward a psychology of uncertainty. *International Journal of Leadership in Education, 10*(1), 1-12.

Caputo, J. D. (2000). *More radical hermeneutics: On not knowing who we are.* Bloomington, IN: Indiana University Press.

Chia, R. (1995). From modern to postmodern organizational analysis. *Organization Studies, 16*(4), 579.

Chia, R. (1999). A `rhizomic' model of organizational change and transformation: Perspective from a metaphysics of change. *British Journal of Management, 10*(3), 209-227.

Dahlberg, G., & Moss, P. (2005). *Ethics and politics in early childhood education.* London: RoutledgeFalmer.

Dahlberg, G., Moss, P., & Pence, A. R. (2007). *Beyond quality in early childhood education and care: Languages of evaluation.* London: Taylor and Francis.

Fullan, M. (2001). *The new meaning of educational change.* New York: Teachers College Press.

Guattari, F. (1995). *Chaosmosis: An ethico-aesthetic paradigm.* Bloomington, IN: Indiana University Press.

Guskey, T. R. (2002). Professional development and teacher change. *Teachers & Teaching, 8*(3/4), 381-391.

Haraway, D. (2003). *The companion species manifesto: Dogs, people, and significant otherness.* Chicago, IL: Prickly Paradigm.

Kind, S. (2008). *Encountering children's artistic languages.* Paper presented at the Reconceptualizing Early Childhood Education Conference, Victoria, British Columbia.

Lather, P. (2001). Postbook: Working the ruins of feminist ethnography. *Signs: Journal of Women in Culture and Society, 27*(1), 199-227.

Lather, P. (2000). Drawing the line at angels: Working the ruins of feminist ethnography. In E. St. Pierre & W. S. Pillow (Eds.), *Working the ruins: Feminist poststructural theory and methods in education* (pp. 284-311). New York: Routledge.

Lenz Taguchi, H. (2008). *Doing justice in early childhood education? Justice to whom and to what?* Paper presented at the European Early Childhood Education Research Association Conference, Stavanger, Norway.

Lenz Taguchi, H. (2009). *Going beyond the theory/practice divide in early childhood education: Introducing an intra-active pedagogy.* London: Routledge.

McArdle, F., & McWilliam, E. (2005). From balance to blasphemy: Shifting metaphors for researching early childhood education. *International Journal of Qualitative Studies in Education, 18*(3), 323-336.

MacNaughton, G. (2001) Action Research. In G. MacNaughton, S. A. Rolfe, & I. Siraj-Blatchford (Eds.), *Doing early childhood research: International perspectives on theory and practice* (pp. 208-223). Maidenhead, UK: Open University Press.

MacNaughton, G. (2003). *Shaping early childhood: Learners, curriculum and contexts.* Maidenhead, UK: Open University Press.

Mason, M. (2006). Exploring, "the impossible": Jacques Derrida, John Caputo and the philosophy of history. *Rethinking History, 10*(4), 501-522.

Moss, P., & Petrie, P. (2002). *From children's services to children's spaces: Public policy, children and childhood.* London: RoutledgeFalmer.

Pitt, A., & Britzman, D. (2003). Speculations on qualities of difficult knowledge in teaching and learning: An experiment in psychoanalytic research. *International Journal of Qualitative Studies in Education, 16*(6), 755-776.

Readings, B. (1996). *The university in ruins.* Cambridge, MA: Harvard University Press.

Rinaldi, C. (2006). *In dialogue with Reggio Emilia: Listening, researching and learning.* London: RoutledgeFalmer.

Roy, K. (2004). Overcoming nihilism: From communication to Deleuzian expression. *Educational Philosophy and Theory, 36*(3), 297-312.

Semetsky, I. (2004). Becoming-language/becoming-other: Whence ethics? *Educational Philosophy and Theory, 36*(3), 313-325.

Smith, C., & Gillespie, M. (2007). Research on professional development and teacher change: Implications for adult basic education. In John Comings, Barbara Garner, & Cristine Smith (Eds.), *Review of adult learning and literacy: Connecting research, policy, and practice* (pp. 205-244). New York: Routledge.

Tsoukas, H., & Chia, R. (2002). On organizational becoming: Rethinking organizational change. *Organization Science, 13*(5), 567-582.

5

Setting our Little Sails:
Pedagogical Documentation as a Phenomenological Act
Laurie Kocher

> I think we all put our boats out on a current, set our little sails, and when we hit something that impassions us, and our little boat begins to go there, the wind whistles through our hair, and we know we're on to something . . . You become alive as you're doing it, and you begin to develop gifts you just didn't know you had.
>
> Sister Helen Prejean as cited in Carter & Curtis, 1996, p. 62

When I was first introduced to the educational project of Reggio Emilia through viewing the travelling exhibition *The Hundred Languages of Children*,[1] I was overwhelmed by the depth and complexity of the children's work and by the multiple "languages" with which children expressed themselves – with words, movement, drawing, painting, building, sculpture, shadow play, collage, dramatic play, music, to name only a few. I was profoundly impressed with the reflective, sometimes metaphorical, text that accompanied these documentation displays. Transcribed recordings of children's conversations were paired with the reflective commentary of their teachers. These teachers seemed to *know* their children so intimately and to have such passion for their work with them. The image of the child as strong, resourceful, curious, and competent was everywhere evident in the exhibit. Indeed, children's thoughts and feelings were offered in such a deeply respectful way that I came away changed. Inspired by this experience, I was determined to attempt to document the work of children in my own classroom following the work of educators in Reggio Emilia. Some years later, I chose to focus my graduate research on the impact of the practice of pedagogical documentation on both the audience and on teachers themselves.

My research was located at a children's centre in Seattle, where I closely followed the work of a particular group of early childhood educators, Ann, Margie, and Sarah, and their practice of pedagogical documentation. I knew that I had become passionate about this way of working with children, and so I was curious to know what, if anything, sustained this passion in other teachers. After visiting Hilltop Children's Centre and spending time with some of the teachers there, I invited these three to be a part of my doctoral research project. The question I set out to follow as I worked with them was this: is there is a disposition to document?

Along the pathway of my doctoral journey, as I worked with these other teachers interested in the philosophies of Reggio Emilia, I encountered the work of Canadian phenomenologist Max van Manen. As I was immersed in reading his work, I identified some connections between my personal experiences of working with pedagogical documentation, the stories others told me about their practice of documentation, and the way that van Manen writes about phenomenology. Put simply, van Manen (1990) writes, "phenomenology aims at gaining a deeper understanding of the nature or meaning of our everyday experiences" (p. 9). This, in large part, is what Ann, Margie, and Sarah are doing as they use pedagogical documentation to make children's learning visible. It is these connections that I want to highlight throughout this chapter.

Pedagogical Documentation – A Brief Description

Pedagogical documentation is a way of making visible the otherwise invisible learning processes by which children and teachers work in early childhood settings.[2] It may include anecdotal observations, children's works, photographs that illustrate a process, audio and video tape recordings, and children's voiced ideas. A significant component is the teachers' reflective text, which is an integral part of the documentation. Pedagogical documentation can also be a focus for linking theory and practice, including evaluation, assessment, accountability, and dialogue among stakeholders (Dahlberg & Aasen, 1994). Most importantly, documentation provides a focus for concrete and meaningful adult and child reflection on children's learning processes.

Nowhere has the process of pedagogical documentation been so well understood and developed as in the early childhood programmes of Reggio Emilia. The influence of these documented moments on the school culture is significant. They represent children's construction of knowledge, demonstrate respect for children's work, validate the competencies of children, and communicate a socio-historical perspective to parents, teachers, and children of the school culture. The documentation reveals the teachers' ideas and understanding of young children, including the ways in which they co-construct knowledge. As teachers engage in "collaborative reflection . . . they socially construct new knowledge as they investigate, reflect, and represent children's construction of knowledge" (New, 1992, p. 17).

The educators of Reggio Emilia view pedagogical documentation as an instrument of communication and exchange of ideas. They especially try to communicate children's competence and power. To this end, the documentation of young children's work highlights their capabilities, as well as the capabilities of their teachers (Kocher, 1999).

Dahlberg, Moss, & Pence (2007) capture the essence of what it is to be a reflective practitioner when they write:

> Practicing a reflective and communicative pedagogy presupposes a reflective practitioner who, together with his or her colleagues, can create a space for a vivid and critical discussion about pedagogical practice and the conditions it needs . . . With inspiration

from the early childhood institutions in Reggio Emilia, in northern Italy, many pedagogues around the world have begun to use pedagogical documentation as a tool for reflecting on pedagogical practice. (pp. 144-145)

Along similar lines, Gandini and Goldhaber (2001) believe that documentation can be an agent of change in order to generate and accomplish a reconceptualization of early childhood education:

The process of documentation has the potential to change how early childhood educators see ourselves as professionals. It certainly requires that we expand our identity from nurturer and caregiver to include theoretician and researcher. We have found that documentation demands a high level of intellectual commitment and curiosity and a passionate engagement in our work. (pp. 143-144)

Rinaldi (1998), former pedagogical consultant for the pre-primary schools in Reggio Emilia, describes documentation as

a procedure that supports the educational processes and it is supported by the dynamic exchanges related to learning. Documentation is the process of reciprocal learning. Through documentation we leave traces that make it possible to share the ways children learn, and through documentation we can preserve the most interesting and advanced moments of teachers' professional growth. It is a process in which teachers generate hypotheses and interpretations of theories that can modify the initial, more general theories. Documentation makes it possible to create knowledge not only for teachers but also for researchers and scholars. (p. 121)

Documentation invites teachers to carefully and deliberately gather the children's stories and their own; to offer expansive opportunities for expression of those stories; to follow the tracks the children leave, and to present those stories of learning in more public ways. It offers a challenge to the research community to look carefully at the stories teachers uncover and to consider the ways in which teacher knowledge articulates a more complete picture of the teaching and learning process.

Phenomenology – A Brief Description

Phenomenology is an influential and complex philosophic tradition that has given rise to various related philosophical movements such as existentialism, poststructuralism, postmodernism, feminism, culture critique, and various forms of analytical and new theory. Major contemporary figures such as Foucault, Derrida, and Rorty find the impetus and sources of their writings in earlier phenomenological works by Husserl, Heidegger, Blanchot, Levinas, and others.

The term *phenomenology* is a compound of the Greek words *phainomenon* and *logos*. It signifies the activity of giving an account, giving a logos, of various phenomena, of the various ways in which things can appear (Sokolowski, 2000). In other words, the researcher tries to identify the lived experiences of participants directly involved with the phenomena. Creswell (2004) explains that "understanding the 'lived experiences' marks phenomenology as a philosophy as well as a method" (p. 15). Phenomenology has been applied in two ways; first, as a philosophical pursuit in which one tries to understand as a logical process of thinking about the world, and second as a methodology "that attempts to use the attitude of phenomenology to construct patterns of research that reveal lived formations of meaning" (Brown, 1991, p. 18). Van Manen suggests that phenomenology may also be considered a human science method: a profoundly reflective inquiry into human meaning. He explains:

> Lived experience is the starting and end point of phenomenological research. The aim of phenomenology is to transform lived experience into a textual expression of its essence – in such a way that the effect of the text is at once a reflexive re-living and a reflective appropriation of something meaningful: a notion by which a reader is powerfully animated in his or her own lived experience (1990, p. 36).

Phenomenology of Practice

Max van Manen is an example of a contemporary scholar who works with the contexts of phenomenology of practice, especially in education and pedagogy. Clarifying phenomenological research and phenomenological practice, van Manen (2002) explains that when exploring the nature of phenomenological research, it is helpful to distinguish between phenomenological research performed by professional philosophers and phenomenological research conducted by professional practitioners. The interest of the professional philosopher tends to lie with philosophical topics, themes, and issues emanating from the study of historical developments of philosophical systems and from the study of issues arising from the works of leading phenomenologists. On the other hand, professional practitioners tend to work within the applied domains of the human sciences such as education, clinical psychology, nursing, medicine, and specializations such as psychiatry or midwifery. For example, a practitioner in the health sciences may study concerns such as the nurse/doctor-patient relation, how young children experience pain, or how the body is experienced in illness and in health (van Manen, 2002).

Finding Connections

Phenomenological inquiry cannot be separated from the practice of writing. This is, to put it simply, where the primary connection between pedagogical documentation and the work of the phenomenological practitioner becomes evident. Despite its importance to phenomological inquiry, the practice of phenomenological writing is quite difficult to articulate. Writing is not the practice of some clever technique; "neither is writing restricted to the moment where one sets pen to paper, or the fingers to the keyboard. Writing has already begun, so to speak, when one has managed to enter the space of the text, the textorium" (Adams & van Manen, 2006). The space of the text is what we create in writing but it is also in some sense already there. In terms of pedagogical documentation, in the working of writing and reading text, we must always ask:

"how can we invent in the text a certain space, a perspective wherein the pedagogic voice which speaks for the child can let itself be heard?" (van Manen, 1990, p. 153).

For the teachers involved in my research study, it became very apparent that something moving and profound does happen in the act of phenomenological writing, particularly in the writing they do as documenters. Van Manen (2002) says that "phenomenological writing is the very act of making contact with the things of our world" (para. 4). Elsewhere he also says that phenomenological writing "encourages a certain attentive awareness to the details and seemingly trivial dimensions of our everyday educational lives. It makes us thoughtfully aware of the consequential in the inconsequential, the significant in the taken-for-granted" (van Manen, 1990, p. 8). Whether it's recording some of the "ordinary moments" that together create a picture of life lived in community within the children's centre, or the documentation that follows the unfolding of project work, it's this attentive awareness to detail that draw the reader/observer into the experience.

It's important to point out that the educators I researched with express comfort with the skill of writing. As one put it, "it's my natural language." Still, it is also helpful to be reminded that phenomenological writing is based on the idea that no text is ever perfect, no interpretation is ever complete, no explication of meaning is ever final, no insight is beyond challenge. It behooves us to remain as attentive as possible to the ways that all of us experience the world and to the infinite variety of possible human experiences and possible explications of those experiences.

Interweaving Ideas

In this section, I will develop these ideas further by focusing on Ann's experiences. By interweaving quotes from Max van Manen with selected quotes from Ann, who speaks eloquently of her experiences as a teacher-researcher, I will draw connections between the practice of pedagogical documentation and the orientation of the phenomenological researcher.

Ann describes her documentation work and how she finds it nourishing, on both intellectual and emotional levels.

> There's a poem by Mary Oliver that asks, "What is it you plan to do with your one wild and precious life?" That question lingers with me . . . My work with children and families fills a big piece of my life and my heart. I am deeply nourished by the relationships

with children, families, and co-workers that are at the
centre of my days at school, relationships full of joy,
honesty, belly laughter, and soulfulness. My writing
about teaching also feeds me; the act of articulating
the thinking and feeling that shapes my work deepens
my awareness and my practice.

Phenomenological research is, as described by van Manen
(1990), "the attentive practice of thoughtfulness. Indeed, if there is
one word that most aptly characterizes phenomenology itself,
then this word is "thoughtfulness" (p. 12). In the words of the
great phenomenologists, thoughtfulness is described as a minding,
a heeding, a caring attunement (Heidegger, 1962). The theoretical
practice of phenomenological research stands in the service of the
mundane practice of pedagogy: it is a ministering of thoughtfulness (van Manen, 1990, p. 12).

It is this attentive practice of thoughtfulness that emerges in
Ann's pedagogical documentation, but significantly also in the
way she relates to this experience, in a way she expresses as being
soulful. She continues:

> It's hard to even find words for it because it is such a
> heart-level experience ... I'd been exploring ideas
> and practices from Reggio for several years and I had
> a really similar experience of ... weeping both from
> being so deeply moved with this joy at what children
> and families and teachers were experiencing
> together, in Reggio, and weeping with this yearning
> for my own work, to continue to deepen in those sorts
> of ways of building relationships with children and
> families, and supporting children's thoughtful collab-
> orations – weeping out of the sense that I am so
> excited about it, and so overwhelmed by the 'bigness'
> of it. It's exactly what I want to be doing, and if I can't
> be doing that then I don't want to be doing this work

Clearly, there is a sense of resonance, a heart-felt connection
with Ann's perception of educators in Reggio Emilia living and
working with children in an authentic, intentional way. It is
almost as if she articulates an experience of coming home, of
arriving, metaphorically, in a place where the lived experience

meshes with the dream of what could be possible. Yet again, van Manen's seminal work, *Researching Lived Experience* (1990) comes to mind here again as he describes phenomenological research:

> From a phenomenological point of view, to do research is always to question the way we experience the world, to want to know the world in which we live as human beings. And since to know the world is to profoundly *be in the world* [emphasis added] in a certain way, the act of researching – questioning – theorizing is the intentional act of attaching ourselves to the world, to become fully part of it, or better, to become the world. Phenomenology calls this inseparable connection to the world the principle of "intentionality." (p. 5)

The vehicle of pedagogical documentation is what makes this principle of intentionality visible and sharable. As van Manen (1990) describes it, "a person who turns toward phenomenological reflection does so out of personal engagement" (p. 154), and clearly that is evident here for Ann. Further, van Manen (1990) captures the essence of Ann's presence as a teacher when he writes:

> A researcher who sees himself or herself as educator and who wants to arrive at better pedagogic understandings of questions concerning children's experiences needs to inquire (reflect, speak, and write) in a manner that is both oriented and strong in a pedagogic sense. In other words, as we speak or write (produce text), we need to see that the textuality of our text is also a demonstration of the way we stand pedagogically in life. It is a sign of our preoccupation with a certain question or notion, a demonstration of the strength of our exclusive commitment to the pedagogy that animates our interest in text (speaking and writing) in the first place. (p. 138).

Ann describes her documentation practice with passion and intensity, using expressive terms like it "feeds me," and "nourishes me." Her animation and engagement comes through in the following passages:

I feel the way it [documentation] feeds me, it's energizing, I love the way in which I pay attention to children as I'm writing, as I'm taking a photo, I feel the contact of it.

I felt that as this moment ... of recognition that this practice had become, like I'd absorbed it into my bones, into my understanding, in an utterly powerful way.

One way that I experience the power of this little being called documentation is finding myself invited to be nourished, to be challenged to be a close observer, and to be really present in the world.

That's sort of the heart of the whole relationship piece ... the whole heart of the beginning and sustaining piece for me of this work. Documentation is the practice that cultivates relationships, that reflects and cultivates relationships.

What that's all about for me is the practice of staying intimately present to the children, present with delight and curiosity, and readiness to reflect on what they're doing ... In large part, the reason I know them intimately, I think, is because of this practice.

Ann, as a documenter, writes as an educator who is oriented in a strong way to the world of real children, who has a fascination with real life. The meanings of the lived sense of phenomena are not exhausted in their immediate experience, but rather live on in her documentation:

The educator, as author, attempts to capture life experience in an anecdote or story, because the logic of story is precisely that story retrieves what is unique, particular, and irreplaceable. So, in textual terms, these epistemological considerations translate into an interest in the anecdotal, story, narrative, or phenomenological description. The dialogic quality of these devices is obvious, for they engage us, involve us, and require a response from us. (van Manen, 1990, p. 152)

More than merely capturing an episode or encounter, though, Ann seeks to draw the audience into the experience, to participate by standing alongside, *with* the documenter.

> A hope that I have is that documentation engages a reader on many levels, so it's not just watching something but getting curious side-by-side with the writer of this piece, or feeling my heart shift as I'm reading this, or a new understanding or a new opening or a new delight, some invitation to be engaged or to be in relationship with what happened.

> The process or way of being in the world, is really . . . a way of understanding our work, or understanding our relationships with children and with each other that is about mindful presence and authentic engagement and curiosity and delight. How that all gets lived out or made tangible is the form of this thing we call documentation, this paper we put up on the wall, this document we send out to the web-page, whatever form it takes, but that in fact documentation is an expression of a way of being with children.

> Documentation means a way of being with children – a habit of paying attention, watching and listening closely, reflecting together about what we see, planning from our reflections and understandings, and telling the stories in ways that enrich our communities.

This sense of living in relationship with children and families, this intimate way of *being* with children that Ann experiences (in large part through her pedagogical documentation), embodies a phenomenological perspective that

> helps us to bring to light that which presents itself as pedagogy in our lives with children. It is that kind of thinking which guides us back from theoretical abstractions to the reality of lived experiences – the lived experiences of the child's world, the lived experience of schools, curricula, etc. Phenomenology asks the simple question, what is it like to have a certain

experience, for example, an educational experience? (van Manen, 1990, p. 44-45)

Making the connection between the abstract and the reality, Ann frames documentation as both process and product, a very intentional practice.

> It's helpful for me to start with remembering that documentation is a process and a product, it's both things ... sometimes I write about practicing active documentation, to highlight the idea that ... documentation doesn't just mean something on the wall, that it's a conscious practice. I think that's true of the way someone, for example, practices Buddhism. There are times of day or week where you are actively giving it all of your focus, and the rest of the time you're sort of living in relation to it, you're living it the rest of the time even if you're not giving it a hundred percent of your focus to it ... I have this image of, it sounds too grand, to maybe align to documentation to a religious practice ... about mindful awareness or something.

A pedagogy that provokes such passion and makes space for intensity, energy, and honest engagement for the sake of understanding and meaning-making is described by Romano (2002) as "a gift of sustained discovery and potential transformation" (p. 376).

Concluding Thoughts

For the educators I have been working with, and for Ann whose thoughts are expressed here, pedagogical documentation has certainly had an impact on the way they see themselves as professionals and as researchers. As documenters, their written work puts into symbolic, textual form what they are seeing in the children's experiences. Van Manen (1990) expresses it thus: "My writing as a practice prepared me for an insightful praxis in the lifeworld – I can now see things I could not see before ... and so practice, in the lifeworld with children, can never be the same again" (p. 130). Viewing oneself as a theoretician and researcher fosters the intellectual commitment and curiosity and passionate engagement with one's work described earlier by Gandini and Goldhaber (2001).

Ultimately, phenomenological reflection effects a more direct contact with the experience as lived; as Ann said earlier, describing her documentation,"I feel the contact of it." This is, I believe, what van Manen (1990) refers to when he says:

> I want to grasp the meaning of teaching (of mothering, of fathering), so that I can live my pedagogic life with children more fully. Therefore, when I reflect on the experience of teaching I do not reflect on it as a professional philosopher or psychologist, as a sociologist, as an ethnographer, or even as a phenomenologist or critical theorist. Rather, I reflect phenomenologically on experiences of teaching and parenting as a teacher or as a parent. In other words, I attempt to grasp the pedagogical essence of a certain experience. (p. 78)

Pedagogical Documentation as a Phenomenological Act

As I have listened closely to educators speak of their experiences as teacher-researchers and documenters, I have been struck again and again at the similarities between the ways in which they describe their personal and individual orientations to this work and the way that Max van Manen writes about phenomenology as researching lived experience. Phenomenology is a certain mode of reflection done traditionally by scholars who write. The text engages the reader in a pedagogic reflection on how we live with children as parents, teachers, or educators. A certain form of consciousness is required, a consciousness that is created by the act of literacy: reading and writing. It is the "minded act of writing that orients itself pedagogically to a notion that is a feature of lived experience" (van Manen, 1990, p. 124).

The documented "ordinary moments" or anecdotes that these teachers have collected provide a launching point for thoughtful reflection and deconstruction. These anecdotes form, in van Manen's (1990) terms, "a concrete counterweight to abstract theoretical thought" (p. 119). Phenomenological description is not intended to develop theoretical abstractions that are separated from the reality of tangible, lived experience, but rather, "phenomenology tries to penetrate the layers of meanings of the concrete by tilling and turning over the soil of daily existence" (p. 119).

Van Manen (1990) describes phenomenological orientation as a kind of conversational relation that the researcher "develops with the notion he or she wishes to explore and understand" (p. 98). A conversation is structured as a triad. There is a conversational relation between the speakers, and the speakers are involved in a conversational relation with the notion or phenomenon that keeps the personal relation of the conversation intact. Gadamer (1976) has described this process as having a dialogic structure of questioning-answering. Every time a view is expressed, one can see the interpretation as an answer to a question that the object, the topic or notion, of the conversation asks of the persons who share the conversational relation. The conversation has a hermeneutic thrust: it is oriented to sense-making and interpreting of the notion that drives or stimulates the conversation. It is for this reason that the collaborative quality of the conversation lends itself especially well to the task of reflecting on the themes of the notion or phenomenon under study:

> In a phenomenological description the researcher/ writer must "pull" the reader into the question in such a way that the reader cannot help but wonder about the nature of the phenomenon. One might say that a phenomenological questioning teaches the reader to wonder, to question deeply the very thing that is being questioned by the question. (van Manen, 1990, p. 44)

It is often the commitment of an individual or small group of teachers to the rather arduous road of learning and innovation that makes a difference to their work. Pedagogical documentation, while being deceptively simple, is actually exceedingly challenging. The educators I speak of, including Ann, do manage to overcome the myriad of external and internal challenges in using pedagogical documentation, and report a renewed sense of commitment, energy, and joy in their teaching. Their stories reveal the intellectual rigor, engagement, and level of collaboration that creating documentation required (Clyde & Shepherd, 2006).

Their experience is mirrored in the words of Louise Cadwell (2003) as she describes how teachers at her school in St. Louis journeyed into this way of teaching:

> Now [documentation] is in the middle of everything, the centrepiece from which we move out, the hub of the wheel, the motor that drives the work. To say that it is in the middle of our work, however, is not to say that it has become easy to do. In the midst of our complex lives, we share many practices, one of which is observation and documentation. In our commitment to this practice, we move along together. We travel, pushing each other, pulling each other, going somewhere, making meaning ourselves, discovering, looking deeply at children. We are amazed and excited every single day. This is what catches us and won't let us go. (p. 97)

Ann, along with the others I've worked with, express a desire for their writing to serve pedagogy. Language is perhaps the only way by which the pedagogic experience can be brought into a symbolic form that creates by its very discursive nature a conversational relation. Writing and reading are the ways in which a conversational relation is sustained: a discourse about our pedagogic lives with children. Van Manen (1990) provokes one even to wonder whether the charge of pedagogy to address adequately its own nature is possibly too much to ask of ordinary conversational discourse. He asks, therefore, "what form of writing is needed to do justice to the fullness of pedagogy and pedagogic experience?" (p. 111). My response is that pedagogical documentation, as modeled after the early childhood project of Reggio Emilia and enacted by these educators, is just that form of writing.

Whatever approach we seek to develop, it always needs to be understood as an answer to the question of how an educator stands in life; how an educator needs to think about children; how an educator observes, listens, and relates to children; how an educator practices a form of speaking and writing that is pedagogically contagious. To say that our text needs to be oriented in a pedagogic way is to require of our orientation to research and writing an awareness of the relation between content and form, speaking and acting, text and textuality. To be oriented as researchers or theorists means that we do not separate theory from life, the public from the private. We are not simply being pedagogues here and researchers there – we are "researchers oriented to the world in a pedagogic way" (van Manen, 1990, p. 151).

A researcher who sees himself or herself as educator and who wants to arrive at better pedagogic understandings of children's experiences – through this practice of pedagogical documentation – aims to inquire (reflect, speak, and write) in a manner that is both oriented and strong in a pedagogic sense. In other words, as we speak or write, we come to see that the textuality of our text is also a demonstration of the way we stand pedagogically in life. "It is a sign of our preoccupation with a certain question or notion, a demonstration of the strength of our exclusive commitment to the pedagogy that animates our interest in text in the first place" (van Manen, 1990, p. 138).

What has emerged through my work with this cluster of early childhood teachers is that each has had a remarkable, intuitive response to the work of educators in Reggio Emilia, a response that resonates with a vision of great possibilities. The values, ideas, and ideals of the Reggio approach seem to be interwoven throughout their work. Having keen observational skills, delight in and curiosity about children, the ability to articulate and put into text their reflections, a commitment to nurturing relationships, and intellectual engagement that is fostered by the active role of researcher are all dispositions that these teachers bring to their work. It is also the description of the phenomenological researcher.

Van Manen (1990) writes, "when we raise questions, gather data, describe a phenomenon, we do so as researchers who stand in the world in a pedagogic way" (p. 1); this way of standing in the world is reflected in the way that Ann and her co-teachers speak of their experience both as educators and as documenters. As Heesoon Bai (2003) has said, "Any sustained practice conditions and forms a particular more of consciousness, or if you like, a way of seeing and being in the world" (p. 28). Ann describes how her practice of documentation changed her way of being in the world:

Documentation is an expression of a way of being with children. I think of documentation as growing out of deep listening and close observation . . . that's a core piece of documentation, really being present to what the children are experiencing, doing, saying, playing about, arguing about, collaborating about, feeling about. So, that is a central component of documentation, that mindful presence . . .

I find a strong parallel between phenomenology, particularly Max van Manen's description of human science research, and the experience of these educators as documenters. The way in which each of them stands in pedagogical relation to the world, and their abilities to write reflectively on the meanings of phenomena of daily life lived in this community, are echoed in these words of van Manen's (1990):

Pedagogy requires a phenomenological sensitivity to lived experience (children's realities and life-worlds). Pedagogy requires a hermeneutic ability to make interpretive sense of the phenomena of the life-world in order to see the pedagogic significance of situations and relations of living with children. And pedagogy requires a way with language in order to allow the research process of textual reflection to one's pedagogic thoughtfulness and tact. (p. 2)

What Ann and the others I worked with during this study, are doing in their everyday practice of pedagogical documentation appears to be, indeed, un-named phenomenological research of the lived experience of these teachers and children. Max van Manen (1990) suggests that "phenomenological research is often itself a form of deep learning, leading to a transformation of consciousness, heightened perceptiveness, and increased thoughtfulness and tact" (p. 163). Each embodies the disposition of a researcher who wonders, imagines, speculates, and thinks deeply about the nature of her work with children. Hearkening back to the quote from Sister Helen Prejean that opened this chapter, they have set their little sails, finding what impassions them, and developing gifts they didn't know they had. They are on to something.

Notes

[1] This refers to the preschools and infant toddler programmes of the municipality of Reggio Emilia, located in Northern Italy. These programmes are regarded by many as the best in the world for young children (Newsweek, 1991).

[2] In the Canadian context, this practice has also recently been termed "pedagogical narration".

References

Adams, C., & van Manen, M. (2006). *Embodiment, virtual space, temporality, and interpersonal relations in online writing.* Retrieved from http://www.senecac.on.ca/quarterly/2006-vol09-num04-fall/adams_van_manen.html

Bai, H. (2003). On the edge of chaos: Complexity and ethics. *Proceedings of the 2003 Complexity Science and Educational Research Conference, 19-30.* http:www.complexityandeducation.ca

Brown, R. (1991). *Toward a phenomenology of curriculum: The work of Max van Manen and T. Tetsuo Aoki.* Unpublished doctoral dissertation, Louisiana State University.

Cadwell, L. (2003). *Bringing learning to life.* New York: Teachers College Press.

Carter, M., & Curtis, D. (1996). *Spreading the news: Sharing the stories of early childhood education.* St. Paul, MN: Redleaf Press.

Clyde, M., & Shepherd, W. (2006). Response to part two: Beginnings. In A. Fleet, C. Patterson, & J. Robertson (Eds.), *Insights behind early childhood documentation* (pp. 163-169). Castle Hill, AU: Pademelon Press.

Creswell, J. (2004). *Research design: Qualitative, quantitative, and mixed methods approaches* (2nd ed.). Thousand Oaks, CA: Sage.

Dahlberg, G., & Aasen, G. (1994). Evaluation and regulation: A question of empowerment. In P. Moss & A. Pence (Eds.), *Valuing quality in early childhood services.* London: Paul Chapman.

Dahlberg, G., Moss, P., & Pence, A. (2007). Beyond quality in early childhood education and care: Languages of evaluation. London: Routledge..

Gandini, L., & Goldhaber, J. (2001). Two reflections about documentation. In L. Gandini and C. P. Edwards (Eds.), *Bambini: The Italian approach to infant/toddler care* (pp. 124-135). New York: Teachers College Press.

Gadamer, H.G. (1976). *Philosophical hermeneutics.* Berkeley, CA: University of California Press.

Heidegger, M. (1962). *Being and time* (J. Macquarrie & E. Robinson, Trans.). New York: Harper and Row. (Original work published 1927).

Kocher, L. (1999). *Butterfly transformations: Using the documentation process modeled in the schools of Reggio Emilia, Italy.* Unpublished master's thesis. Victoria, B.C.: University of Victoria.

New, R. (1992). The integrated early childhood curriculum: New interpretations based on research and practice. In C. Seefeldt (Ed.), *The early childhood curriculum: A review of current research* (pp. 286-322). New York: Teachers College Press.

Newsweek. (1991, December 2). The best schools in the world. pp. 60-64.

Rinaldi, C. (1998). Projected curriculum and documentation. In C. Edwards, L. Gandini & G. Forman (Eds.), *The hundred languages of children: The Reggio Emilia approach – Advanced reflections* (2nd ed., pp. 113-125). Norwich, CT: Ablex Publishing.

Romano, R. M. (2002). A pedagogy that presupposes passion. In E. Mirochnik & D. Sherman (Eds.), *Passion and pedagogy: Relation, creation, and transformation in teaching.* New York: Peter Lang.

Sokolowski, R. (2000). *Introduction to phenomenology.* Cambridge, UK: Cambridge University Press.

van Manen, M. (1990). Researching lived experience: Human action for an action sensitive pedagogy. Albany, Ny: SUNY Press.

van Manen, M. (2002). Phenomenology of practice. Retrieved from http://www.phenomenologyonline.com/inquiry/61.html

Reconceptualizing Children's Image and Agency

stories created and lived

substantially transformed

Discovery begins in the single that is singular in the blind street

to the child dancing to herself in a swirl of sunlight

6

Valuing Children's Roles in Research on Literacy Engagement

Tara-Lynn Scheffel

"what is the most interasing thing you learned from us?"
Spike, Age 7, Research Journal

As I begin this chapter, I am reminded of the above question by Spike, which prompted me to consider more deeply the ways in which we value children's roles in research. Spike asked me this question as I joined his classroom as a participant observer to study teacher and student perceptions of engagement during literacy learning. In this chapter, I highlight how Spike became engaged in the research process itself, as he shared his questions, curiosities, and interests with me, often with the goal of helping me learn more about what engaged him as a literacy learner. To set the stage for this discussion, I begin by outlining my journey through the literature, both in relation to studies specific to literacy engagement, and those more generally related to research with young children. I then offer Spike's narrative as a way of furthering the discussion of how we value children's roles in research. As part of this discussion, I share the feedback I received through the ethical review process as I raise questions about how children are perceived in research. In conclusion, I consider the assumptions we hold of learners and how we might move forward as researchers towards creating greater agency for young children.

Questions of Engagement

Questions of engagement were at the forefront as I began my research journey. I asked for example, what educators are looking for in their classroom when they try to gauge if they are engaging their students? And how did the students understand what it meant to be engaged or, perhaps, to show engagement? According to Vibert & Shields (2003):

> Student engagement is identified with both compliance and involvement. Hence if a child is following instructions, quietly completing a worksheet in math, (and especially if the child is attaining a high percent of correct answers), she or he is considered to be engaged. (p. 226)

Alternatively, student disengagement was often described in comparison to these same standards. For example, in the description of a young boy's reading and writing experiences below, constant movement and lack of time spent on-task were seen to indicate lack of engagement:

> He appeared to be unengaged much of the time when he should have been reading and writing. He flitted around during reading workshop. He began many books but often laid a book down before he had finished reading it." (Allen, Michalove, & Shockley, 1993, p. 89)

While this outward appearance does perhaps denote disengagement, I reflected on Greene's (1988) notion that human freedom lies "in the capacity to surpass the given and look at things as if they could be otherwise" (1988, p. 3). As such, I wondered if there was more to the story?

Beyond conceptual concerns with the term engagement, I began to notice that while some researchers made an attempt to work with younger children, children's perspectives were often not sought. For example, while Bryan, Fawson, and Reutzel (2003) promoted discussion in order to engage students in reading, their observations appeared to be little more than records of time spent on-task, or perhaps more accurately, time spent *not* on task. They failed to question the reasons for students' lack of pleasure in reading and even suggested that individual factors such as ethnicity fell outside the realm of study. Though the authors suggested "a need to look at student background to establish factors contributing to student non-engagement during independent reading" (p. 68), they failed to consider this question more deeply.

On the other hand, Hicks' (2002) research on the literate engagements of children growing up in poor and working-class white families, highlighted the stories of two students, Jake and Laurie, offering a much richer and in-depth look at moments of engagement that went beyond a checklist of time-on-task behavior. Consider the following observation of Jake during a read-aloud lesson:

> . . . typically distant and disengaged during such book discussions, (Jake) was alert and engaged. Some of the text and pictures depicted the construction of heating and air conditioning systems in the new building. At one point, Jake raised his hand and commented that his father worked as a heating and air conditioning repairman. (p. 119)

In this example, the combination of engaging pictures and text, as well as a personal connection to his life, appeared to draw Jake into the story. The uncovering of these moments helped to shed light on the *how* and *why* of engagement, by getting to know more about the learner.

The role of the teacher becomes an important consideration here as well. Harkening back to Dewey's (1938) progressive education, Dewey too, saw the role of the teacher as significant to the promotion of a child's interests. He proposed a project-based approach that bridged the gap between the curriculum and children's interests. In Early Childhood Education, especially in my work in New Brunswick, I see a return to similar notions in the newly outlined Early Childhood curriculum for the province. The influence of researchers such as Katz and Chard (1992) and Helm and Katz (2000) offer concrete ways for teachers to build upon the strengths and interests of their students. Interestingly, what I have come to see throughout the implementation of the framework is that for the teachers who take up this practice, their own engagement in teaching seems rejuvenated. It very well may be that teachers need an engaging curriculum as much as students do.

In studies of engagement specific to literacy learning, Pflaum and Bishop (2004) offered one example of how engagement could be explored separately from quantitative, behavioral approaches. Having asked students to complete drawings about a time when they were both deeply engaged in learning, as well as a time when they felt detached, they interviewed students with the goal of hearing them describe and explain their drawings. Though limited in scope and requiring further elaboration as to how students interpreted the term, this study brought forward students' voices in an attempt to understand what it meant to be engaged. The importance of this attempt is suggested in Devine's (2003) conclusion that

> there is a fundamental contradiction in a school system that seeks to empower children through education and learning but does not recognize the importance of their voices in that process of empowerment. (p. 143)

Having found that many teachers "surveilled the bodily position of children to judge how effectively they were concentrating on the task in hand" (p. 59), Devine interviewed children with the purpose of helping them articulate what school meant to them. This was fitting given Samuelsson and Sheridan's (2003) finding that researchers have a tendency to "think that children must be 'close to becoming adults' in order to be allowed to be heard and to express their perspectives" (as cited in Samuelsson, 2004, p. 5).

Another example is provided by Allen, Michalove and Shockley (1993). Using a combination of observations and interviews, these researchers studied the literacy learning experiences of six African American students (five male, one female) over a period of three years, from grade one to grade three. Though the theme of engagement was general, the narratives were powerful, revealing the need to take a closer look at engagement in connection with lived experience in the classroom.

The generality of engagement is also found in educational teacher resources. For example, Lyons (2002) included engagement as one of ten generic aspects of teaching. She posed the following two questions for teachers to consider: Are all the students engaged in the lesson? Does she/he hold every child's attention? Given the discussion thus far, these vague questions do not do justice to the question of engagement. The second question for example is little more than a visible determinant. Moreover, if teachers are being evaluated on how well they can hold a student's attention, they may attempt to hold a student's attention out of routine or fear, which is very different from holding attention out of interest and active involvement. While not intended to be content specific, such generic characteristics may limit teachers who are unsure of what engagement means and how to determine its presence and value in the classroom.

Therefore, while researchers such as Taylor, Pearson, Clark, and Walpole (2000) proposed that more accomplished teachers elicit higher levels of engagement, and Pressley, Allington, Wharton-McDonald, Block, and Morrow (2001) described effective teachers as actively engaging students in reading and writing, my search through the literature revealed a need for more in-depth studies that take the time to explore what is meant by engagement and how it is viewed by both educators and students. I questioned how researchers consider children's perspectives in relation to literacy engagement and how they go about doing research with young children. I explore these questions throughout this chapter.

How Do We Value Children In Research?

Referring to Bronfenbrenner's (1979) claim that "a child's perspective is always subject to an adult's interpretation," Samuelsson (2004) looked at how adults, including researchers, attempt to make sense of what they hear children tell them. She stressed the role of the adult in Bronfenbrenner's work as someone who creates possibilities for expression in the first place, and then attempts to interpret what takes place. Sharing an example of misinterpretation related to issues of gender,

Samuelsson (2004) reinforced how researchers can become occupied with their own questions and risk missing what a child is actually saying. How then can we as researchers value the voices of the children we work with?

First, I am reminded of the *United Nation's Convention of the Rights of the Child* (UNCRC, 1989), which outlines three categories of rights pertaining to provision, protection, and participation. In addition, four principles guide our interpretation of the treaty: (1) the best interests of the child; (2) the right to protection from discrimination; (3) the right to life, survival, and optimum development; and, (4) the need for opportunities for participation in matters of concern (Canadian Coalition for the Rights of Children, 2002). A poignant example of "participation that matters" is provided by Soto (2005) as she shared children's responsive drawings to the World Trade Center tragedy on September 11th, 2001. Soto presents these drawings as a means of moving towards participatory democracy, for they give visual expression to the often disregarded insight of children. Soto explained,

> Our ability to visualize children's voice, children's wisdom, and children's theory can be an integral part of participatory democracy. Children's representations, voices, and wisdom can guide our democratic dreams as we listen for what children intend to say. (p. 18)

The power of the children's drawings and words is evident throughout her work, demonstrating that children do indeed have a voice to share.

Drawing on Bakhtin (1981) and his notion of dialogism, Graue and Hawkins (2005) described interviews as, "conversations – interactions that ebb and flow and that represent opportunities given and taken by participants" (p. 51). Interviews can also be read in multiple ways, as Graue and Hawkins (2005) demonstrated as they responded and asked questions of each of their participants. What they found was that they each authored the interactions taking place with the knowledge, purpose and intentions they held for the interview. They concluded that children "were anything but passive in their conversations with us, enacting ways of thinking about the world and their relationship to us in a context of us thinking about the world and our relation to them"

(p. 54). The power of this last statement lies in its recognition that each set of researcher/participant brings a unique combination to the interview. In this way, interviews cannot be predicted for their sets of questions but require openness for dialogue to take place. It is in the analysis that researchers frame their understandings of children and the techniques used. Graue and Hawkins' (2005) discovery that they "learned as much about [them]selves through the interview responses as [they] did about the children [they] interviewed" (p. 50) is a testament to this unpredictability.

Kay, Cree, Tisdall and Wallace (2003) called for a continuous negotiation, or reflexive approach, between researchers and participants. In a study of children and young people dealing with parental HIV in Scotland, Kay and her colleagues (2003) negotiated the context of interviews and who would be present, and also incorporated multiple tools within the interview such as drawing, simple games, writing, and puppets. In all instances, the goal was to ensure sufficient time and space so as not to create expectations for responding. Importantly, the researchers spent time creating conditions that situated what was a taboo and secretive topic within the context of their life experiences. They were respectful of any reluctance, silence, or change of topics demonstrated by the participants. In their conclusion, Kay and her colleagues (2003) noted that when discussing such emotional experiences with children, there can be little objectivity. For this reason, the researchers foregrounded reflexivity when they began the project by reviewing their own positionality by writing and sharing personal histories of parental illness with one another. This teamwork, they argued, also created a more transparent research process.

One question researchers of children often worry about is whether children will participate regardless of a desire to be involved. Graue (Graue & Hawkins, 2005) admitted that the researcher side of her was disappointed when two students opted out of an interview about home-school relations. On the other hand, the methodologist in her was pleased that these students were able to make non-participation their statement (p. 48). In order to encourage this form of participant autonomy, Kay and her associates (2003) provided participants with a red stop sign card so that they could terminate the interview at any time. They were also shown where to stop the tape-recorder if they did not want to continue. None used the card but one child turned the tape recorder off momentarily to discuss a personal issue.

In an attempt to uncover students' perceptions and understandings of research, Edwards and Alldred (1999) spoke with seventy primary and secondary students (ages ten to fourteen), on the topic of home-school relations. Five themes emerged from the feedback: (a) research as a confirmation of links between home and school, (b) research as educational, (c) research as fun rather than educational, (d) research as being like therapy where you have conversations and are listened to, (e) research as empowerment. Though the themes overlap and sometimes contradict each other, they provide insight into the various ways in which children perceive research. In addition, these themes offer a starting place for methodological issues related to researching children. Many of these issues fall under the larger question of power, including questions of truth, interpretation, control, and voice.

Sleeter (2001) cautioned that unacknowledged power can lead to unintentional silencing. For this reason, I knew I would need to continually remind myself of the power I held as both a researcher and an adult working with children throughout my study. The issue of consent in research with children is raised by Edwards and Alldred (1999) who concluded that "underlying much of the discussion of consent for childhood researchers is a concern with issues of power – to treat children as active subjects of research rather than passive objects, to hear their voices, and to respect and empower them" (p. 266). When children are viewed as passive objects, the question of their consent is put aside. However, recognizing children as knowledgeable learners with a voice to share highlights the need for shared power.

In a conversation between mother and daughter, Jipson and Jipson (2005) asked themselves and various colleagues the following question: "In doing research with young children how can we be confident that our understandings represent their thoughts/behaviours/experience?" (p. 36). Although one of the researchers approached this question from an education background and the other from psychology, both agreed that both perspectives inscribe power and privilege. They cautioned that we all bring notions of childhood into our experiences. Their work highlights several important notions for researchers working with children to consider. The first consideration is the belief that it is possible for researchers to represent the thoughts, behaviors, and experiences of young children through the information they collect. In keeping this in mind, the researcher acknowledges that "our confidence should be tempered with skepticism so that we look for weaknesses in the methods we use and the interpretations that we render about young children" (p. 38). Second, it is very important for researchers to recognize of relational issues implicit in their work. As one of the respondents wrote,

> I find it necessary for children to know me, in some ways, if I want to know them in more than superficial ways. It requires risk taking, of sorts – and the sharing of vulnerability. What I ask, how I ask it, and later representations are all informed by a relationship that is at first, humane and caring – at least I hope so. (p. 39)

The authors discuss the importance of continued participation and rapport building to help the children feel more comfortable engaging in the research. The third notion is the understanding that we must challenge ourselves as researchers to ground our work in the interpretations of the children. Despite our attempts, however, what is captured will always be a representation of what the researcher considers to be a child's reality.

To address issues of power in our interactions with children, Punch (2002) supported the use of participatory research tasks that combine visual, written, and traditional methods of research. This combination, she felt, allowed for differing techniques to address differing preferences of children. In particular, she used a combination of drawing, taking photographs, journaling, spider webs, and worksheets in her work with children in Bolivia. Punch's approach produced some encouraging results, but it also raised new problems that once again bring to fore the difficulty of negotiating this power dynamic between researchers and children and the children's community. Punch observed that the children enjoyed the novelty of the camera, and also noted that taking photos did not depend on ability to depict an image, as with the drawings. However, the community was concerned that such an expensive activity would instill in the children unrealistic ideas about future careers. Moreover, Punch found that the need to ask open-ended questions was also crucial so as to correctly interpret the drawings from the children's viewpoints and give them the opportunity to control their own expression.

Grover (2004) also argues for collaborative research efforts that recognize children's rights and believes that "such an approach has the potential to lead to social policy which more accurately and compassionately reflects the concerns of children" (p. 83). When children are viewed as collaborators in the research process, they are no longer *objects* but rather active *participants* permitted to share their own stories. As researchers negotiate boundaries of communication, we must make a conscious effort to listen to the voices of children by involving them as collaborative and active participants who are respected for the knowledge and lived experience they have to share. Achieving this collaborative process is not an easy one. Fielding (2001) and Rudduck and Demetriou (2003) named three stages of student involvement in research. They argue that schools are just beginning to contemplate the first stage where students are viewed as sources of data and therefore subsequent stages where students are active respondents, and later co-researchers, have yet to be realized.

Valuing Children's Roles

Reading through the literature furnished me with a theoretical and methodological framework from which to situate my research. I chose to conduct my research from socio-cultural approach. Although it is difficult to provide an all-encompassing definition, socio-cultural approaches tend to "emphasize the interdependence of social and individual processes in the co-construction of knowledge" (John-Steiner & Mahn, 1996, p. 191). This understanding leads to a view of learning that moves beyond a sole focus on the learner to a greater consideration of the content and context surrounding engagement. It is an approach that allows for opportunities to hear the voices of the participants in more open-ended ways. Applied to the study of engagement in literacy, this involves highlighting "the important relationships between language, culture, and development" (Razfar & Gutierrez, 2003, p. 34) as they are evidenced in children's learning. Questions of purpose, power, and exclusion must therefore be examined (Butler-Kisber & Portelli, 2003) along with a closer look at the role of gender, ethnicity, and socio-economic status. Finally, I saw this as an approach that would allow me to consider conceptions of engagement with respect to the various educational philosophies and paradigms represented in the literature. Viewing my study as emergent, I understood that the application of specific theories could not be determined prior to the research, but must rather occur afterwards in order that the data speak first and inform possibilities for understanding links to relevant theory.

In forwarding this type of research, an ethnographic approach to studying engagement was applied. Adhering to Miller and Goodnow's (1995) approach of studying a "person-participating in-a-practice," my goal became to draw upon such influential ethnographic studies as Heath (1983) and Dyson (2003), in an attempt

> to make visible the often invisible patterns and practices of life, to understand who has access to knowledge of these patterns and practices, and to identify the consequences for particular members of knowing (or not knowing) and understanding (or not understanding) these patterns. (Dixon, Frank, & Green, 1999, p. 5)

By making the everyday visible, my goal was to share a greater understanding of classroom life in relation to engagement. I proceeded upon the conviction that the worth of ethnography is in its commitment to people, understanding, learning, and advocating for others (Noblit, 1999). Ethnography through participant observation permitted a more collaborative approach to be taken when researching children – one that would build upon the need for empowerment and reciprocity suggested by researchers such as Lather (1990), and Fine, Weis, Weseen and Wong (2000). Moreover, I was encouraged to adapt this approach because it offered the potential to view children as collaborators in the research process (Grover, 2004). In this way, the children that I studied were no longer objects but, rather, active participants permitted to share their own stories.

Joining a grade two classroom as a participant observer, I asked the following research question: From the subjective viewpoints of teacher(s) and student(s), what constitutes engagement for primary-aged students in literacy learning? Four complementary research methods were drawn upon as part of this approach: (1) participant observation, (2) informal conversational interviews and picture talks, (3) formal teacher interviews/questionnaires, and (4) journaling. In total, fifty-three classroom observation days occurred from February to June of 2007.

Children as Collaborators

As I documented classroom events, one of the ways I sought to invite all students within the classroom into the joint role of researcher was to provide them with their own field notebook to share their drawings/thoughts pertaining to our interactions. Negotiating this process with the classroom teacher, I included both structured and unstructured times for journal responses. Structured journal response times included specific, scheduled moments of journal writing where I provided a prompt for the students (e.g., Tell me about today's activity). These questions were based on the informal conversational interviews and field notes collected during participant observation. Unstructured journal response times were described to the students as moments when they had finished any required work and had something they would like to share with me. As a lead-up to using the journals, I showed the students my own field notebook and shared some of the general, nonconfidential observations I had included. I then talked with them about confidentiality and the research process as related to this study.

While some of the students at first commented that my tape recorder looked like an MP3 player, they understood that its purpose was to "remember what we've said" (Sarah, Observation Day 23). In response to a question about whether they could listen to the tape, Chloe ventured a guess that confidentiality meant, "once you play something you can't play it again" (Chloe, Observation Day 23). Explaining the private nature of what they would share with me, I added,

> If I write about some of the things that I've seen in your classroom I won't actually use your name. I would use a different name so that nobody would know it was you. That's what it means to be confidential . . . so if I was to talk about something that someone shared with me, I might say it was Susie

that told me that, so nobody knows that it was actually someone in this classroom.

As the discussion continued we talked about the use of real names as opposed to nicknames, which was a concern of one student who worried over being called a silly nickname. When another student started to share a possible nickname I could use for him, I invited everyone to tell me a name in their journals. At the conclusion of the study, six students selected their own pseudonyms, with one negotiating the process with me in his research journal by (1) asking if he should be Jetfire, (2) offering his initials in response to my request for a regular name, (3) agreeing to the name PJ, which stood for a combination of the initials in his name and his teacher's name, and (4) using contextual knowledge to suggest that he would like to call me Western because that was in the name of the university where I worked.

Elsewhere, I discuss the process of negotiating a researcher identity with the students and classroom teacher but for the purposes of this discussion, I focus on one student, Spike, who took the greatest visible interest in participating in the research. Spike instantly wanted to share his curiosities, questions, and involvement in the research project as the following narrative written from field notes demonstrates. I begin on the 23rd day of observation following my introduction of the research journals as discussed above. All words are presented as Spike wrote them with prompts provided in brackets when unclear.

Spike's Journal

Before leaving for the day, Spike asks, "When will we get to write in the journals?" Knowing I need to first clear this with the classroom teacher, I suggest, "Maybe tomorrow." Spike goes on to explain his rationale for wanting to begin writing by sharing that he already knows the name he wants me to use for him. The next day, his first research journal entry reads:

> I really like ready [reading] books and drawing. I want my name to be Spike. I name every thing Spike it is just a cool name . . .

Also written on the front inside page of Spike's journal is a series of nondescript x's to represent his address and telephone number, as well as the words "no tresspassin."

Not only was Spike the first person to offer a pseudonym in the research journal but his understanding of confidentiality is also conveyed in this first entry.

As Spike continued to write in his journal, he would ask me questions in response to the questions I asked of him. For example, explaining that Pokémon books were his favorite to read, he inquired about my favorite books to read. Another time, sharing his favorite things to do at school, he wrote, "what is the most interasing thing you learned from us?" I admit that I was taken aback when he asked me this question. He held me accountable for what I was asking of both him and his classmates – to respond to a question asked of them about the classroom. I wondered whether this was how some of the students felt when answering my questions. Part of my reason for pausing stemmed from and ethical concern. What could I share of my observations with Spike? I attempted to select something from that morning that would give a concrete example. I referred to the chanting of the Word Wall words and followed by asking Spike what he thought I should know about his class.

Shortly after it was introduced, Spike and I had already written back several times in the journal. To illustrate his written text, Spike often drew images of new Pokémon creatures that he had created. This use of pictures differed from the classroom journal, which did not include the option to draw pictures along with the text. Yet, for Spike, this was central to his interests. Following my 26th day of observation Spike explained, "I am very interested in drawing because my gramie is an artist." Without the research journal, I may not have known the importance or origin of Spike's interest in drawing. The journal became a space for him to share who he was with me.

Spike's desire to continue our written discussion was highlighted during the 32nd day of observation when, in a moment of transition, I suggested the students take out their research journals and tell me about what I had missed that morning. As the teacher returned to the classroom, however, she asked the students to first complete an entry in their classroom journal. When they had written enough in their regular classroom journal, she explained, they could move onto the research journals. I observed Spike switch to his classroom journal and reluctantly begin to write. Although he checked with his teacher several times throughout the period, he had evidently not written enough yet to move onto the research journal. Though he barely said a word, each time he went to his teacher's desk, the look in his eyes suggested a plea, "Please tell me I can write in the research journal now?"

This was not the first time I had observed Spike struggle to complete the expected amount of writing in his classroom journal. He often wrote in large letters to use up space and would be sent back to his desk to write more. With the research journal, I offered no specific expectations on how much was to be written and it may be this lack of expectation, the accepted use of illustrations, and the shared conversation that held Spike's intrigue to write and share information about himself.

In our final discussion, Spike highlighted the shared interaction of the journals as he described the research journal as a private space akin to the trading of sticky notes, a habit that had begun in the classroom when he and some other students received a prize pack of sticky notes for not watching television during "Turn Off the Screens Week." The following is an excerpt from our taped discussion on the 53rd day of observation.

> Tara-Lynn: So I'm just kind of wondering what you thought about the whole journal writing where we wrote in the journal together?
>
> Spike: I thought it was kind of fun, I thought it was kind of like writing sticky notes back and forth.
>
> Tara-Lynn: Oh cool, I can see how it would be like that.
>
> Spike: It was really fun because when I was passing sticky notes I know I wasn't supposed to, but like, when I got the thing [the research journal] I knew we were going to kind of do it, pass them back and forth, and I was really excited to pass them back and forth so I really thought it would be fun.

Though Spike also had choice in what to write in his classroom journal, the interactive nature of the research journal seemed to be what prompted him towards increased engagement with writing. Perhaps the greater sense of control in asking questions and drawing pictures also created an avenue for him to share his knowledge and curiosity in a more engaging way, one that was initiated by him rather than presented to him as an expectation.

Spike's Path To Engagement

Baker, Dreher, and Guthrie (2000) proposed that "engaged children read widely for a variety of purposes and create situations that extend opportunities for literacy" (p. 1). Similarly, Spike initiated literacy tasks on his own time that focussed on his popular culture interests (e.g., Pokémon). His engagement is fitting of the following observations from Baker and her colleagues (2000):

> The heart of engagement is the desire to gain new knowledge of a topic, to follow the excitement of a narrative, to expand one's experience through print. Engaged readers can find books of personal significance and make time for reading them. The investment of time is rewarded by the experience of immersion in the text itself. Engaged readers draw on knowledge gained from previous experiences to construct new understandings, and they use cognitive strategies to regulate comprehension so that goals are met and interests are satisfied. Benefits to readers may also occur through their satisfaction in possessing valued information about a topic that plays a central role in their sense of self. Engaged readers are curious and involved in a literate lifestyle. (p. 2)

Spike found spaces within the school day and at home to follow self-initiated literacy activities. His literate lifestyle included making trading cards, writing his own stories and even researching animal reports. His curiosity drove him towards discovery, which may also explain his desire to contribute to the research. The research process enabled him to participate and write about his interests during the structured school day. In many ways, it was clear that Spike followed his own path to literacy engagement.

Valuing Spike

So what can we learn from Spike about the way we value and invite children into the research we conduct for and about them? As an instructor of pre-service students who observe and participate within UNB's Early Childhood Classroom, I often hear the comment that four years olds are capable of so much more than what was believed to be possible. This is also true of the way we view research with young children. To elaborate, I will offer some responses from my department ethics committee to my proposed research. Although I understand the need for caution with respect to research with young children, the committee's responses raise questions and uncover a view of children that is important to early childhood researchers and educators to consider.

First, the committee wanted to know how I would explain confidentiality to the students because they "were concerned that young children may not fully understand the meaning of *confidentiality*." Yet, Spike demonstrated that he fully understood what confidentiality meant. Further, the committee did not understand that I could share the process of doing research with the students without compromising confidentiality. I explained that the sharing of my field notebook would be used as a lead-up to using the journal. The intent would be to "share some of the general observations I have included." I did not plan to reveal my field notebook but I would be open about what I was doing by showing students where I talk about the classroom set-up or descriptions of what was taking place in an activity without revealing names.

The committees concerns were unwarranted as students very quickly realized that if they were writing a spelling test for example, I was writing the words down too so that I would remember them. As Spike noted in response to the class discussion about doing research, "I think you're doing things that we're doing so you're writing that . . . what we're doing."

The committee also wondered how I would explain the research process to six-to-eight-year-old students, cautioning me to be alert to cues of refusal. Perhaps it is because I have always worked with young children that I have come to know that if children do not want to participate, they will most often tell you. Being alert is crucial, but getting to know the children first is what helps you become alert to their responses. When I asked a student if I could tape record our discussion throughout the study, they responded, "no," and I kept it turned off as we continued to talk. I did not devalue their input but I respected their choice to not be recorded, just as I would with an adult.

The committee also expressed concern over the use of participant observation and the "possibility of coercion of students" if I assumed a role of "helping out" within the classroom. They reasoned that,

> If the researcher is perceived as a teacher, can students be expected to refuse any request for information? When they are asked about the degree of their engagement with the lesson, can they reasonably be expected to distinguish this from a teacher asking why they are not paying attention? If they interpret the query as criticism of their in-class behavior, is there possible risk of some emotional damage?

Although the committee ultimately suggested that I reconsider my role in the classroom, I did not because I knew it was central to building their trust and interacting with them on a daily basis. Instead, I explained to the committee that I would tell students that I was looking at how they participated in activities in the classroom because I had questions about what would improve teaching. I also explained that I was aware and sensitive to issues of consent. To ensure students understood they were being interviewed for research purposes, I clarified that I would express that I wanted to talk to them about how they work and play in the classroom, and that I was interested in writing about how children learn.

It seemed that the committee did not understand that there are often many adults in most primary classrooms (e.g., parents, volunteers to teaching assistants) and that none of these adults have the same authority as the teacher. Grade two students understand this and can distinguish between the teacher and assistants in a classroom. Students do not just accept someone into the classroom space without a curiosity about who they are either, and it is for that reason that I sought to be upfront with them despite the constraints of an ethical protocol that would not allow me to talk with them about who I was until all the consent forms were returned.

Discussion

I have come to see that how we value children as research participants has much to do with the notions and beliefs we hold about children as learners. Bruner (1996), for example, high-lighted five possible assumptions that have a potentially enormous impact on teaching. These assumptions view children

> as willful and needing correction; as innocent and to be protected from a vulgar society; as needing skills to be developed only through practice; as empty vessels to be filled with knowledge that only adults can provide; as egocentric and in need of socialization. (p. 49)

In the case of my ethical review committee, the assumption taken appears to be one of children as innocent and in need of being protected from a vulgar society. Yet, this view, along with the others, reinforces a view of children as passive learners who are unable to take an active role in research. Such views have had a definite impact on literacy research involving children. Gillen and Hall (2003), for example, have outlined the predominance of psychology-based research approaches during the early-to-mid nineteenth century. These approaches have focused on sound/symbol relationships and the notion of *readiness*. Noting an emphasis on measurable behavior, they suggested the inherent assumptions such behaviorist approaches have historically rein-forced:

> That children's agency was insignificant, that children could learn nothing for themselves, that they were objects to be manipulated by teachers, and that reading and writing were individual acts involving sets of discrete perceptual skills. (p. 4)

A major consequence for twentieth century researchers, they concluded, was the belief "that there was simply no point in investigating or even considering very young children's thinking about, understanding of and use of reading and writing..." (p. 4). Children, especially young children, were not viewed as capable of offering valuable insight into their own literacy development.

It was not until after the Second World War, Gillen and Hall (2003) noted, that literacy was seen to be functional in relation to everyday lives. This understanding led to the recognition of a social element in literacy development that went beyond a simple process of decoding and began to acknowledge the role of writing. Thus, for the first time, children were seen as agents capable of meaning making. This emphasis on children's understanding led to a view of the literacy learner as an active meaning maker, as well as a redefinition of literacy that moved beyond a focus on reading and writing skills. However, as this study on literacy engagement demonstrates, children are not passive learners unaware or uninterested in research taking place in their classrooms. To not value their desire to participate and ask questions is to return to a behaviorist view of children as passive recipients rather than curious and knowledgeable participants. One of the final shifts noted by Gillen and Hall (2003) problematizes the instructional space of the classroom. This more critical look at the context of the learner helps to reveal the ways in which learners, for example, negotiate behavior and construct identity during literacy sessions (McDermott, 1979). It also raises questions about positioning within early childhood discourses and ideologies (Cannella, 2002). It is this questioning and observing that helps researchers reconceptualize how they conduct research with children.

References

Allen, J., Michalove, B., Shockley, B. (1993). *Engaging children: Community and chaos in the lives of young literacy learners.* Portsmouth, NH: Heinemann Portsmouth.

Baker, L., Dreher, M. J., & Guthrie, J. T. (2000). *Engaging young readers: Promoting achievement and motivation.* New York: The Guilford Press.

Bakhtin, M. M. (1981). *The dialogic imagination.* Austin, TX: University of Texas Press.

Bronfenbrenner, U. (1979). *The ecology of human development: Experiments by nature and design.* Cambridge, MA: Harvard University Press.

Bruner, J. (1996). *The culture of education.* Cambridge: Harvard University Press.

Bryan, G., Fawson, P. C., & Reutzel, D. R. (2003). Sustained silent reading: Exploring the value of literature discussion with three non-engaged readers. *Reading Research and Instruction, 43*(1), 47-73.

Butler-Kisber, L., & Portelli, J. (2003). The challenge of student engagement: Beyond mainstream conceptions and practices. *McGill Journal of Education, 38*(2), 207-212.

Canadian Coalition for the Rights of Children. (2002). *Education and the United Nations convention on the rights of children.* Retrieved May 14, 2005, from http://www.rightsofchildren.ca/pdf/ed.pdf

Cannella, G. (2002). *Deconstructing early childhood education: Social justice and revolution.* New York: Lang.

Devine, D. (2003). *Children, power and schooling: How childhood is structured in the primary school.* Stoke on Trent, UK: Trentham Books.

Dewey, J. (1938). *Experience and education.* New York: Macmillan.

Dixon, C. N., Frank, C. R., & Green, J. L. (1999). Classrooms as cultures: Understanding the constructed nature of life in classrooms. *Primary Voices K-6, 7*(3), 4-8.

Dyson, A. H. (2003). *The brothers and sisters learn to write – Popular literacies in childhood and school culture.* New York: Teachers College Press.

Edwards, R., & Alldred, P. (1999). Children and young people's views of social research: The case of research on home-school relations. *Childhood, 6*(2), 261-281.

Fielding, M. (2001, September). Slide used in paper given as part of the Consulting Pupils Network Project Symposium. BERA Annual Conference, University of Leeds, UK.

Fine, M., Weis, L., Weseen, S., & Wong, L. (2000). For whom? Qualitative research, representations, and social responsibilities. In N. K. Denzin, & Y. S. Lincoln (Eds.), *Handbook of qualitative research* (2nd ed., pp. 107-131). Thousand Oaks, CA: Sage.

Gillen, J., & Hall. N. (2003). The emergence of early childhood literacy. In N. Hall, J. Larson, and J. Marsh (Eds.), *Handbook of early childhood literacy* (pp. 3-12). Thousand Oaks, CA: Sage Publications.

Graue, E., & Hawkins, M. (2005). *Relations, refractions, and reflections in research with children.* In L. D. Soto & B. B. Swadener (Eds.), Power and voice in research with children (pp. 46-54). New York: Peter Lang.

Greene, M. (1988). *The dialectic of freedom.* New York: Teachers College Press.

Grover, S. (2004). Why won't they listen to us? *Childhood, 11*(1), 81-93.

Heath, S. B. (1983). *Ways with words – Language, life and work in communities and classrooms.* New York: Cambridge University Press.

Helm, J. H., & Katz, L. (2000). *Young investigators: The project approach in the early years.* New York: Teachers College Press

Hicks, D. (2002). *Reading lives: Working-class children and literacy learning.* New York: Teachers College Press.

Jipson, J., & Jipson, J. (2005). Confidence intervals: Doing research with young children. In L. D. Soto and B. B. Swadener (Eds.), *Power and voice in research with children* (pp. 35-43). New York: Peter Lang.

John-Steiner, V., & Mahn, H. (1996). Sociocultural approaches to learning and development: A Vygotskian framework. *Educational Psychologist, 31*(3/4), 191 206.

Katz, L. G., & Chard, S. C. (1992). *Engaging minds: The project approach.* Norwood, NJ: Ablex Publishing Corporation.

Kay, H., Cree, V., Tisdall, K., & Wallace, J. (2003). At the edge: Negotiating boundaries in research with children and young people. *Forum: Qualitative Social Research, 4*(2). Retrieved May, 2008, from http://www.qualitative-research.net/ggs/

Lather, P. (1990). Research as praxis. *Harvard Educational Review, 65*(30), 257-277.

Lyons, C. A. (2002). Becoming an effective literacy coach: What does it take? In E. M. Rodgers & G. S. Pinell (Eds.), *Learning from teaching in literacy education: New perspectives on professional development* (pp. 93-118). Portsmouth, NH: Heinemann.

McDermott, R. P. (1979). *Kids make sense: An ethnographic account of the interactional management of success and failure in one first-grade classroom.* Unpublished doctoral dissertation, Stanford University, CA.

Miller, P., & Goodnow, J. J. (1995). Cultural practices: Toward an integration of culture and development. In J. J. Goodnow, P. J. Miller, & F. Kessel (Eds.), *Cultural practices as contexts for development* (pp. 5-16). San Francisco, CA: Jossey-Bass.

Noblit, G. W. (1999). *Particularities: Collected essays on ethnography and education.* New York: Peter Lang.

Pflaum, S. W., & Bishop, P. A. (2004). Student perceptions of reading engagement: Learning from the learners. *Journal of Adolescent & Adult Literacy, 48*(3), 202-213).

Pressley, M., Allington, R., Wharton-McDonald, R., Block, C. C., & Morrow, L. M. (2001). Learning to read: Lessons from exemplary first-grade classrooms New York: Guilford Press.

Punch, S. (2002). Research with young children: The same or different from research with adults? *Childhood, 9*(3) 321-341.

Razfar, A., & Gutierrez, K. (2003). Reconceptualizing early childhood literacy: The sociocultural influence. In N. Hall, J. Larson, & J. Marsh (Eds.), *Handbook of early childhood literacy* (pp. 34-50). Thousand Oaks, CA: Sage Publications.

Rudduck, J., & Demetriou, H. (2003). Student perspectives and teacher practices: The transformative potential. *McGill Journal of Education, 38*(2), 274-288.

Samuelsson, I. P. (2004). How do children tell us about their childhoods? *Early Childhood Research and Practice, 6*(1). Retrieved October 22, 2004, from http://ecrp.uiuc.edu/v6n1/pramling.html

Sleeter, C. (2001). Epistemological diversity in research on pre-service teacher preparation for historically underserved children. In W. G. Secada (Ed.), *Review of research in education* (pp. 209-250). Washington, DC: American Educational Research Association.

Soto, L. D. (2005). Children make the best theorists. In L. D. Soto & B. B. Swadener (Eds.), *Power and voice in research with children* (pp. 9-19). New York: Peter Lang.

Taylor, B. M., Pearson, P. D., Clark, K., & Walpole, S. (2000). Effective schools and accomplished teachers: Lessons about primary grade reading instruction in low-income schools. *Elementary School Journal, 101,* 121-166.

UNCRC (1989). *United Nations convention of the rights of the child.* Retrieved April, 21st, 2008 from: http://www.everychildmatters.gov.uk/strategy/uncrc/articles/

Vibert, A. B., & Shields, C. (2003). Approaches to student engagement: Does ideology matter? *McGill Journal of Education, 38*(2), 221-240.

7

Lion and Landscaper:
Embracing Multiplicities Inside Schooled Spaces
Sherry Rose

> To emphasize narrative is to keep alive a spirit of ten-
> tativeness, pluralism, inclusiveness, otherness, and
> contingency in the face of encroachment by regula-
> tory, outcomes-based, or market paradigms that
> neither emphasizes nor provide for self-critical
> expression.
> Farquhar & Fitzsimons, 2008, p. 4

Children, families, and educators are *storied* in a multitude of ways both inside and outside of schools. These stories created, told, and recounted play an essential and often lasting role in producing and altering our identities. In this paper I fold forward "old storylines, to sound them again in new contexts and times," (Miller, 2005, p. 1) to complicate normalizing forms of individuality that limit children's subjective experiences and relationships inside *schooled* spaces. As an early childhood educator, I retell, rewrite, and rethink critical contradictory moments embodied with tensions, as a way to fulfill my responsibility to others (Dahlberg & Moss, 2005, p. 75). Inside these storied – sometimes disobedient – encounters, I "address issues of identity construction, subjectivit[ies], and power relations that circulate through language as well as human interactions" (Miller, 2005, p. 50). My aim is to understand "the processes by which subjectivities are produced, explore subjectivity as a locus of social change, and examine how emerging subjectivities remake our social worlds" (Blackman, Cromby, Hook, Papadopoulos, & Walkerdine, 2008, p. 1).

As a normalized/resisting subject, my desire is to cultivate a "deconstructive ethic that takes the wor(l)d very seriously in tracing and troubling signs of meaning, by way of absences and the otherness of what we think we know and believe" (Lenz Taguchi, 2007, p. 286). My retelling reconstitutes my fumbling grasp of "an attitude of indeterminacy and paradox, as conditions of what Lather writes as 'affirmative power by undoing fixities and mapping new possibilities for playing out relations between identity and difference, margins and centres'" (Lenz Taguchi, 2007, p. 286). As ceremonies of belief (Chamberlin, 2003), my stories represent my patient resistance to politics that grant higher status to stories of assessment scores. Embracing an ethics of care and encounter, they describe "relational complexit[ies]" (Somers, 1994, p. 631) that are unrecognizable, silenced, or put at risk by schooled evaluation practices. They sustained my hope that it may be possible to penetrate the incommensurate discourses[1] (Babich as cited in Moss 2007, p. 233) that limited the scope of communication and debate between democratic visions for learning and evaluation and hegemonic normative teaching and assessment practices (Lenz Taguchi, 2005). They represent a search for "a contrary-wise praxis that enables the working through that allows one to go on" (Lather, 2007, p. 60); "They ask for your consideration" (Pelais, 2004, p. 11).

> Identity is a relational and relative concept, always open for change and where the meaning of what the child is, could be and should be, cannot be established once and for all.
>
> Dahlberg, Moss & Pence, 1999, p. 134

Fragment of an urgent conversation:

"Do you have cross country skis?" I asked a boy who spent far too much time in detention.

"No."

"Have you every cross country skied?"

"No."

"Well I am going to try and get you a pair of skis so you can join our ski club. Would you ski with us?"

"I'll give it a try."

Authoring the self – a conversational glimpse:

"You know what . . . I'm smart . . . I bet I can learn to knit just like they can." the boy states nodding his head toward two grade five girls who were knitting away.

"I bet you can. What would you like to knit?"

"A dish cloth for my mother for her birthday."

"What color of yarn would you like?" as I handed knitting needles to him.

"Green. Green is her favorite color."

"How come whenever I am in detention with you I learn something?" asked this boy who spent too much time in my office.

I am unable to recall my answer to him or even if I did answer him beyond a smile, but what I do remember is my surprise at his assessment.

Necessity demanded that I combine my supervisory duties and extra curricular commitments by including this boy in each club I organized. His reflective questions and comments offer his assessment of himself as a learner, the learning he valued, and my attempts to include him, which unfolded in part out of necessity.

Rewriting these rhizomatic incitements, I reach for the contradictory heart of teaching and learning. I resist writing the troublesome episodes of conflict that I shared with this student, as
they would diminish our identities and our relationship. Instead,
years later, I choose to revisit his penetrating question, "How
come whenever I am in detention with you I learn something?"
Where do children see learning taking place? How do I value children's time, their relationships, and their lives inside institutional
spaces? Where are the spaces for their contributions? "What do I
notice and recognize about each child's personal goals, interests
and working theories? What social roles and culturally valued literacies [do] I recognize in [my] assessments? How do children contribute to their own assessments?" (New Zealand Ministry of
Education, 2004, p. 24) How do I respond to "children who challenge" (MacNaughton, Hughes, & Smith, 2007) my embodiment of
schooled norms? How might I rethink educational discourses and
practices that function to position of some children as permanently other, knowing that I am always caught up in and by the
very languages and resulting practices that I wish to challenge"
(Miller, 2005, p. 232-233)?

As a classroom teacher, I resist(ed) exclusionary practices
such as detentions, school suspensions, and sending children to
the principal's office. Inspired by educators who "value children as
participants in honest conversations where they share both difficult and positive feelings while discussing content and consequences" (Edmiston, 2008, p. 66; Holland, 2003; Katch, 2001; Paley,
1992; Silin, 1995), I believe these schooled practices crystallize
socially constructed identities of bully, child at risk, or many other
schooled labels that limit experiences, relationships, and learning.
However, positioned as principal, my participation in these practices was expected in support of relational challenges faced by
school bus drivers, classroom teachers, and parents. I struggled to
rethink these and many other constitutive practices even as I participated in them.

Rhizomatic Shoots

We can judge a narrative, if judge we must, in terms of
the consequences it produces – the new stories it
arouses, the possibilities for reforming and reshaping

a life it introduces. (Bochner as cited in Santoro & Boylorn, 2008, p. 202)

Choosing to excavate these rhizomatic incitements provokes troubling questions. How do I give admission to the "rhizomatic shoots" (Gough, 2006, p.xi) that challenge my habits of belief and lead me to construct different understandings, "understandings that may mean I will be ethically obliged to change what I do" (Lenz Taguchi, 2006, p. 260)? How do I deconstruct my participation in discourses that construct blame and exclusionary practices inside current social contexts of learning and teaching (Berlinger & Biddle, 1995)? How do I hear the conflict that is at the heart of language and stories, to learn to watch out for dangerous stories "that celebrate habits of belief" (Chamberlin, 2003, p. 30)? How do I negotiate my subjective positioning(s) as I am "identified with the context, the possibility of my being outside the system becomes unthinkable?" (Rose, 1989, p. 208). In what ways can power circulate productively "when people are not equally located" (Eyre, 2007, p. 99)? How do I "learn to be vulnerable enough to allow [my] world to turn upside down in order to allow the realities of others to edge themselves into [my] consciousness" (Delpit cited in Cannella, 1997, p. 1)?

Writing with "a profound uncertainty about what constitutes an adequate depiction of social 'reality'" (Lather, 1991, p. 21) can be terrifying. Working class insecurities and anxieties, amplified by my reverberating history of school failures (Sparkes, 2007; hooks, 1994), threaten to silence my stories. Recognizing that I cannot "see the whole or sing the whole, . . . that all perspectives are contingent, that no one's picture is complete" (Greene, 1995), I fold forward on these past rhizomatic shoots, story my experiences as an "examination of the various things that present themselves for admission to my soul or mind" (Ransom as cited in Dahlberg, Moss, & Pence, 1999, p. 34). I confront the possibilities and challenges for living "different worlds that might, perhaps, not be so cruel to so many people" (St. Pierre & Pillow, 2000, p. 1). By framing "the multiplicity, ambivalence and uncertainty of life, . . . as sources of rich possibilities rather than obstacles to be overcome to arrive at the truth" (Dahlberg, Moss, & Pence, 1999, p. 25), I am able "to find and relate to the unpredictable, incorrigible, uncontrollable, unmanageable and disobedient aspect that is also part of pedagogic relationship" (Ellsworth as cited in Lenz Taguchi, 2007, pp. 246-247), an aspect that can provoke ethical challenges and new kinds of action (Lenz Taguchi, 2007).

Ethically Answerable Actions

> Constructing and disrupting fixed meanings of differ-
> ence is profoundly situational, and often tedious. It is
> also personal and social at the same time, risky, never
> predictable, and requires imagination and courage of
> the intellect as well as of the heart.... And as
> [Patricia] Williams reminds us, working difference is
> life work. "Nothing is simple. Each Day is a new
> labor". (Ellsworth & Miller as cited in Pinar, 2005,
> p. xxviii)

I recognize that "the social is the site for the production of discursive practices which produce the possibility of being a subject (Butler, 2005). My challenge is "to understand how people of particular ages become subjects within specific, local practices and to understand how those subject positions and practices operate within complex circuits of exchange" (Castenada as cited in Walkerdine, 2004, p. 103). Encountering and valuing the other, whether it is "the Otherness of my reformulated thinking, recon-stituted performative practices, or the Other as in Other human being" (Lenz Taguchi, 2007, p. 287) requires that I recognize "we are all constructed within and constructive of relations of power (Novinger & O'Brien 2003, p. 15). In these shifting relations of power in which "we are each caught up, we are always at risk of negating the other in the task of managing our own vulnerabili-ties – to each other, and to the normative discourses and practices through which we are made, in any particular moment and place, to make sense" (Davies, 2008, p. xvi). The story of Lion and Landscaper confronts such vulnerabilities and exposes how I transgressed of the normalized boundaries of *teacher* to use power in productive ways to expand possibilities for students to remake themselves (Butin, 2001).

Lion and Landscaper, retold out of context, out of community, may provoke ethical questions in readers. It certainly provoked ethical questions as I lived it. But Brian Edmiston's theorizing alleviates some of my ethical burdens. Drawing on Bakhtin's work on ethics, Edmiston (2008) writes, "A person's actions are ethical when they are answerable: to anyone who "addresses" them about the consequences of those particular actions" (p. 27). "Being answerable is more than responsible: 'when people are answerable their ethical understandings are affected and transformed because they allow themselves to be addressed by another person's ideas that dialogically affects or shapes the framework they use to make meaning" (Dahlberg and Moss as cited in Edmiston, 2008, p viii). Being answerable to Lion and Landscaper certainly transformed my ethical understandings, for it showed me that fostering the visibility, inclusion, and active participation of thirty-five children meant that I had "to seek . . . potentially in every situation, in relation to *every body,* not in relation to *everybody*" (Olson, 2009, p. 5). To this end, I had to cultivate a commitment to becomings, relationships, desires, and disruptions.

In an effort to narrate their transformative influences, I reinterpret the story of two extraordinary students. What do I mean when I write *extraordinary students?* Specific to this telling, these two students had internalized the gaze of the "official teacher" and using that gaze they challenged my "unorthodox ways." They were confident enough to question decisions, act as advocates for other children, and co-author themselves against the grain of school norms. I codename these students "Lion" and "Landscaper" in order to characterize their positions to the politics of classroom space. As archetypes, their positioning as "bad boy" and "class brain" will be familiar to many educators.

As an early childhood educator, I work at "acknowledging children . . . as being capable and fully human, curious and able to investigate their places in the world, to be critically able to analyze the systems of oppression that shape and constrain their lives and learning" (Novinger & O'Brien, 2003, pp. 13-14). It is difficult work inside a system that enforces sameness. But by embracing conflict as productive, a source of curriculum, and by interrogating conflict with "a faithful attention to the discursive detail that we are made from" (Davies, 2000, p. 11), I deepen my understandings experiencing "an opening up to multiple movements" (p. 11). These movements, or ethically answerable actions, involved "adopt[ing] the stance of an artist to challenge the taken-

for-granted values and culture that one shares with others"
(Grumet, 1988, p. 81). What pushed me deeper into challenging the
values and culture of school life was my struggle to meet the individual educational goals of these extraordinary students, Lion and
Landscaper, whom I see as the "bright particulars."

In the green and silver chorus of the grass
they lose themselves, the bright particulars.
Discovery begins
in the single that is singular,
the one stem your eyes are suddenly unsealed to see,
jointed with the latest, fragile, golden light.

Go hand in hand with generalities,
you will never be surprised,
you will never cross over

to the child dancing to herself
in a swirl of sunlight in the blind street,
to the travelling star in the running stream,
or the lucky clover.

You will never reach that tall one
talking with clouds as he mends a roof.
or the naiad rising from birth waters in the stone fountain,
or under birds crossing the air, your voice will never carry
to the old saint sweeping leaves and frost jewels in
the autumn morning.

Kay Smith, (1978, p. 35)

Lion

My recent move to upper elementary was shadowed with
other troublesome worries. I worried about learning new curriculum content, negotiating the landscape of a new school and
forming new staff relationships. In spite of my anxieties our first
day of school arrived. Thirty-two grade-four children introduced
themselves as a collective, as a group: "We are the worst class. We
have lots of bad kids." Their depiction of themselves silenced their

multiple subjectivities. How would I disrupt this schooled identity to come to know their individual and collective contributions, questions, and passions?

This class was framed in a discourse of difficult illuminated by their own comments and those of administrators and parents. Administrators informed me, "They are great kids but there are many slow readers – a challenging group, the kind of readers who would benefit from your integrative approach to learning." On that first day, two parents told me they felt sorry for me. These comments did little to settle the anxiety I was experiencing as I carried my early childhood practices into an upper elementary space.

Lion is a boy without a desk; he refused to be geographically confined. He is a boy who is economically poor, academically unsuccessful, rebellious, and violent, but also expressive, artistic, a dramatist, with an ability to think, question, and create.

Lion first challenged me the day I met him. I was wearing a harmony pendant. Reaching to touch the metal ball, he asked me, "What is this?"

I took it from his fingers, gently shook it to sound the chimes and explained, "It's called a harmony ball. It contains small chimes that ring bringing peace to anyone who wears it."

Lion looked directly into my eyes, gave a small chuckle and stated, "There is no peace for anyone with me in their life."

Lion epitomized Karen Gallas's (19940) Bad Boys: "These boys . . . work to control the dynamics of a classroom, determining its discourse style, teacher management strategies, and hidden agendas. . . . they resist any efforts to make learning routine and disciplined" (p. 55). Like Gallas's bad boys, Lion enjoyed meaty conversations with adults. He was sensitive, artistic, and articulate and he could be rude and aggressive to others. Frequently he would make fun of other children through racist or sexist comments. Many times he lost his temper, destroying their work while, at the same time, he was deeply hurt if his hard work met the same end. He was sensitive and insightful. As we worked together, he studied me. On one occasion as he and I jogged to the Saint John River to conduct our river study, he commented, "You aren't like other adults I know." I asked him to explain. His answer rattled me, "You run, laugh and have fun."

Several months later, as we rested from our jog to the pool, he climbed up on a bolder I was leaning on and philosophically stated. "You know what, I have come to a decision about you. You are not a grown up at all. You're a twelve-year-old girl trapped in a women's body."

As we worked together he also studied other children. He defended their right to complete projects and to speak out. He could be heard arguing social issues. Once I interrupted a huge argument in the hallway where Lion was crying and being accused of calling another child spoiled rotten. I tried to diffuse the situation. I asked him what he meant by spoiled rotten?

He explained, "He is spoiled because he has his own bedroom and his own backyard."

His definition of spoiled stopped the children in their tracks.

In spite of his strengths, I recognized he was trapped in a negative public persona, a reputation he had co-constructed inside school discourses. Every teacher knew who he was. The first days of school rolled into the first week, I became increasingly frustrated with Lion. It seemed together we were in constant conflict.

I recall reading parodies of fairy tales to the class. As I read, he challenged my choice, stating loudly, "These are girly stories. Just wait, next she'll be reading Barbie stories."

When I ignored him, maintaining my focus on reading to the other children, he used bathroom humour and curse words to drown me out. I immediately thought of Valerie Walkerdine's (1990) chapter about five year old boys exerting power over their kindergarten teacher. "The very practice which is suppose to liberate produces the possibility of this discursive power in the children. There is no counter discourse and the children know it" (p. 8). I was living the reality of how my teaching philosophy set me up. This boy saw the space to challenge and I had no effective counter discourse. I was trapped inside my philosophy and my desire to be a maternal educator (Ruddick, 1989) who valued every child. He was trapped inside a public bad boy image, enjoying the control and public attention he was receiving from some of the other boys. His power in the face of school authority was very provocative.

As weeks rolled by he would openly predict, "You'll lose it. All teachers lose it with me. Eventually you will yell."

I knew this was the response he most wanted, and I was stubborn enough not to give in. But each night I cried, then talked and wrote my frustrations in an attempt to work out strategies. Each day, teachers in the staff room, aware of my struggles, asked, how I was doing. Some were supportive telling me, "Your classroom is just what he needs," while others followed this question of concern with the statement, "You are letting him walk all over you." Instructing or helping me, they would state, "In the past he was sent home when he got like this."

I didn't want to send him home. But I didn't know what to do. Sara Ruddick's (1989) work offered a helpful theoretical frame. Because I was applying Ruddick's maternal thought and practice in the classroom, the contradictions and differences between mothering and teaching became apparent. Ruddick was right. I could kick him out. However, my maternal thinking made me desire another solution. Madeleine Grumet's (1988) point:

> Few of us would excuse our own children from their
> futures with the grace and understanding we extend
> to other people's children. Other people's children are
> abstract. They are reading scores, FTE's, last year's
> graduating class, last week's body count. (p. 173)

I aimed to embrace their challenge – I would not reject this boy.

Our struggles reached a peak in early October when Lion, frustrated by my persistence, lashed out at me. The vice principal and principal intervened and decided to send him home for three days. Upset, I felt we performed exactly as he predicted. This boy would view me as he did all adults. My power had been displaced by administration; my concern now was that he would not trust me.

How could I show that it was his behavior and not him we were rejecting? I decided to go to his house each night to take him books and the work we had covered in school. My primary goal was not to deliver his schoolwork but to maintain contact in acknowledgement of our relationship.

During these early days, provocative events revealed to me Lion's intelligence and talent. I saw no school evidence of reading or writing but an abundance of evidence of his television literacy. In particular, he loved nature programs. He would often spend recess or noon hour sharing his wealth of animal information with me. Eager to enter his conversations, I shared stories of how a family friend in Nova Scotia was establishing a lion pride on his property. Lion and I would spend endless conversations sharing our knowledge of lions. Eventually this led to a critical analysis of Disney's movie *The Lion King*.

This analysis of *The Lion King*, represented a shift in Lion's thinking. *The Lion King* was a significant theme in his dramatic play and family fantasy as well as his reading, singing, and body movement. I recall being struck by the beauty of his body as he moved throughout the classroom imitating a lion's posture and gestures. He was a lion! When I shared my friend's experiences of the lion matriarchy, Lion became very upset, informing me I did not know what I was talking about. Clearly, he fully believed Disney's construction of the lion patriarchy.

His first piece of writing occurred when he set up a lion's den in the back of the classroom. He wrote and posted ten rules for entry into the den. I was thrilled he used writing in a functional way. While he prowled around the classroom like a lion, I wondered how other adults visiting the room would view him and me. However, my commitment to provide him with this space came from my belief that at some level, his imagination, his ability to invite others into his play was key to obtaining success in friendship and academic work. Soon his skill at orchestrating dramatic play episodes during choice time took over. More and more students joined his play. He was recognized as a dramatist.

Evidence of his learning was quick to follow, as his artistic representations were now a blend of words and models or drawings. I strategically placed science books about animals in the art and science centres. I took advantage of incidental teaching moments to refer directly to these reference texts in his presence when he asked questions so he could see me actively researching. In time, he took over this research, disrupting the school's construction of him as a nonreader.

Early in the fall he came into the classroom with a cricket in his hands. Together we set up a jar for his cricket. As we did, I was unsure, concerned about the violent way he might treat the cricket. My courage to forge ahead came from my belief it was better to provide the opportunity to witness this behavior and deal with it than to leave it outside the classroom.

That day he wouldn't leave the school until he had completed a scientifically accurate enlarged colored image of the cricket as a gift to me. Again his persistence, focus and visual literacy intrigued me – all this ability lay outside the domain of official school curriculum. Here was a child, an artistic scientist, who clearly made his passion for *outside* space and his contempt for *inside* space visible. If I not been watching and listening carefully to those outside spaces or if I'd controlled his access to materials, I would have missed his talents and gifts completely.

I discovered his passion for plasticine as he left the classroom one day with a large bundle under his shirt. "What do you have hidden under your shirt?"

"Nothing."

Smiling, I persisted, "Come on Lion, tell me. I can see the big bulge. What is it?" Lifting his shirt he revealed a large ball of plasticine.

Searching for a way to reframe this incident, I explained, "You know, if you would like to borrow the plasticine all you have to do is sign it out. Then if we need it I will know where it is."

As he walked away I found myself wondering how many other children would like this kind of opportunity. Is this possibly a more interesting medium for homework?

Lion lived with plasticine in his hands. When his confidence to read grew, he never abandoned the plasticine. I would watch him crouched on the floor reading factual picture books while his hands busily modeled the subject of his reading.

My strategy for negotiating between Lion and some sense of control inside the classroom was to ignore him publicly. Refusing to participate in the subjective positioning we were embroiled in, I avoided public confrontation. This freed him to be productive as he worked independently within the classroom studios/areas that held accessible materials which structured and invited learning. In these areas students made meaning, representing and communicated their experiences and questions in a range of ways that authored and co-authored new identities. Lion spent much of the day working as a visual artist in drawing, painting, and constructing works from his life experiences and creatures in the science centre or resource books. This was true even during times that the rest of us pulled together as a class to work on official curriculum.

I would talk, work, and listen to Lion during choice time when children engaged in a variety of individual and small group activities. This responsive interaction with Lion proved to be more productive. In these private educative spaces we were less inclined to enter into power struggles – a power he gained through public performances. As Gallas (1994) concludes her chapter Bad Boys in the Classroom:

> By paying close attention to the stories they tell, draw, dance, and enact, I am more able to include their divergent world-view in the culture of the classroom. My hope, as they see that school is not a battleground, is that they will begin to alter their picture of where their own personal power lies. In the end, I want these boys to experience how powerful it is to belong and fully commit oneself to the creation of a dynamic learning community, where, rather than struggling continuously to assert their superiority and control, they work to fuel the intensity and excitement of everyone's participation. (p. 70)

In spite of some successes I struggled daily with my actions. On a good day I was struck by his ability to work on his own agendas, and participate in whole class discussions simultaneously. His industrious, self-directed work allowed me to teach the other children. On a bad day, I was frustrated by how he interrupted the lessons, silenced children, and devalued himself. His co-authoring of himself disturbed me. More troubling was how his peers reinforced his authoring.

A turning point occurred one day during a math workshop. Students were demonstrating their solutions to problems on the board. They explained their strategies while their classmates offered feedback, asked questions, or demonstrated their own routes to the solutions.

Balancing a paper constructed cricket house with multiple rooms on his head, Lion paraded around each child's desk interrupting the lesson. Giggles filled the air. I was angry! My anger was directed at the class and not simply at Lion. In a violent act, I slammed my hand down on the desk so hard it hurt for several hours. Lion dropped to the floor where he was standing; his classmates were shocked into silence.

What followed was my lecture on their unfairness toward Lion. I explained that he was just as smart as any of them. Publicly I stated they all knew he was not successful in school. I challenged them:

> One reason I believed he is unsuccessful is because you all help him to be unsuccessful by giving him attention for actions you yourselves would not do in school. You know why you don't do these things. You want to do well in school, you're afraid you will be punished or you want to please your parents or you recognzse they are wrong to do. What I don't understand is why you are not afraid for him? Why don't you think he deserves the same opportunity?" I continued . . . "Each one of you in here knows what is appropriate and inappropriate behavior. You can feel it inside your body. So from now on when you laugh at him or give him attention for doing something you know you would never do, you will be punished! (Teaching notes)

Desperately, I needed their help. I interrupted their power as *recognizable students* (Davies, 2000) by questioning their subjectification of Lion. I had to break this cycle. I wondered if the freedoms I offered Lion reinforced their belief that he was unworthy of an equitable educational experience. I worried all night. Had I gone too far? Would the children accept my call for help? What had Lion thought as he dropped to the floor listening to my subjectification of him and the others? Did he and the other children recognize that I was attempting to value him? them?

There were other perceived freedoms that contributed to his difference in the class. They evolved out of my attempts to negotiate his participation in school life in a more positive way.

Lion refused to stay seated in his desk during whole class teaching. His vacant seat seemed to scream out, "Look what I don't have to do!" Lion stuffed items he valued into his desk and it overflowed onto the floor. Students complained he never kept it clean. One day I insisted he clean his desk. He raised it high over his head, walked across the room and plopped it on top of the garbage can. "There . . . are you happy?"

"No, not yet," I calmly responded disguising my inner turmoil.

I saw that Lion's desk was a physical symbol of his inability or refusal to function as the other students could. His desk was a fixed territorial space offering little movement, limiting the breadth of subjective positions available to him. He was unrecognizable as a student in his bad boy positioning and this desk kept him unrecognizable (Davies, 2000). To the children his vacant seat seem to scream difference and unfairness. Why didn't he have to do what they had to? As the children's complaints got louder so did my feelings about my failure to make this student mind.

I recognized the crux of the problem lay deeper than oppositional behavior. I suspected that this desk, this enclosed space, represented the controls and restrictions he wanted to be rid of. It was wildness, the space to move, create, and build that he most desired. Trying to find a solution, I asked Lion if he really needed a desk. He responded no and so I removed his desk.

I wanted to accept not reject this boy. I knew expelling or sending him into the hall reinforced the established hierarchy of the class. These actions stated, "You are not good enough to be with us." My decision to keep him in the room left me with the problem of what to do when his behavior became so disruptive we couldn't function. I decided to take the other students out. Subsequently, we went to the library or the gym to continue our work and left him alone in the room.

Soon students modeled my behaviors. During a math workshop as I stood behind the class watching them conduct the group interrogation of math strategies, Lion made a similar attempt to disrupt the lesson. Not a word or snicker was breathed. He gave up and returned to his own work. The rest of the class seemed to know I was serious about their role in his disruptive behavior.

One day as the children gathered in the story corner, I noticed a boy stand up and get a chair. I asked where he was going. He whispered to me that he was going to invite Lion to join us. Eventually Lion did. He asked for his desk back. He read to the class conducting a book talk using many of my own discussion strategies.

As the children and I implemented the strategies of ignoring inappropriate behaviour, removing ourselves from the classroom, and inviting Lion in, the children questioned me, echoing my fears and challenging my practices. "Why don't you just send him home?" or "Why don't you just make him do it?" or "Why do we have to leave?" or "Why can't I do what he is doing?"

In order for the children and I to come to terms with my actions I had to expose my thinking and practices. Beneath my practices was my belief that in life we meet, work with, and (sometimes discover to our surprise) live with people who are challenging. Would these lessons help all of us in our future lives? We would all be losing by accepting his exclusion. bell hooks (1994) theory on radical pedagogy helped me see that I must insist that everyone's presence is acknowledged; everyone influences the classroom dynamic and everyone contributes (p. 8). I spoke frankly to the children's questions, making my practice explicit and public and inviting them to participate in my practice.

Evaluating Lion was an ethical dilemma. Attempting to complete Lion's report cards honestly, I did not grant him grades in subject areas I felt unable to evaluate due to his low level of participation in the official curriculum. However, I spent the end of each day collecting his self-initiated projects from various table-tops, to inform my record of his efforts. It was my practice to type an anecdotal letter to individual children highlighting their strengths and contributions while also offering suggestions for further focus. In this narrated space, I was able to validate Lion's efforts out side the official curriculum. Unfortunately, this was prior to my current knowledge on narrative documentation and I only went public with this kind of assessment during official reporting periods. On the last day of school, I handed him a garbage bag containing the work he completed over the year (much of it three dimensional); he said with surprise, "Wow, I guess I passed! Look at all the work I did!" Lion had not completed the expectation of a grade four student by New Brunswick's standards. In spite of his deep intelligence, he was a *social promotion*.

I carry my challenging experiences with Lion into each new classroom to "use them strategically" (Miller, 2005, p. 1). They remind me that inclusion is a complex goal that may come in the guise of the chaotic. As Jane Roland Martin (1992) writes "inclusion is not a recipe for sameness" (p. 181) and "the Schoolhome can be united by their shared knowledge of one another while cherishing each person's individuality" (1992, p. 181). I want to value my own subjectivities, to author that young girl he saw. It is critical to be playful, joyous and curious when working with children. This takes effort inside a system where being an adult is loaded with power and where teaching young children "is historically grounded in social expectation and school structures that rely on women's accustomed roles as subservient, genteel and docile reinforcers of the status quo" (Miller, 2005).

My experiences with Lion speak to the significant relational work we as teachers can do on behalf of individuals inside a community – transforming teaching (hooks, 1994) and communities. "Children, too, can be given access to an understanding of the constitutive force of language and of the possibility of refusing the old subject positions of old discourses. They, too, can participate in the creative constitution of new discourses that open up new possibilities, that encourage the multiplicity that comes so easily to them and the adults generally work so hard to constrain" (Davies, 2000, p. 53).

I recognize that the privacy of the classroom isolates teachers and their complex practices leaving all of us victims to individuality and complicit in hegemonic practices. I now believe it is important to disrupt comments like 'Your room is the perfect place for him' or 'You are the perfect teacher to work with him'. Exalted status that maintains my/our isolation and devalues and even dismisses my/our critical questions and reflections that may contribute to educational debate and the possibilities such debate might open up for individual learners. As Grumet (1988) writes:

> We teachers hide the work we care about in our own classrooms just as artists stack it in their attics (1988, p. 91). The danger is that a room of one's own becomes a bunker . . . where we quietly sabotage the skills program without releasing the methods and meaning that we have devised so that they may attract attention, stir comment, ultimately influence textbook selection, state requirements, and the in-service program. Terrible vulnerability accompanies aesthetic practice. (p. 93)

Landscaper

While my pedagogy provided room for Lion, I believe it's openness initially challenged Landscaper. Landscaper enjoyed the security of defined borders. She occupied a desk tied off by yarn to keep others out! She is a girl who is middle class, academically successful, dramatic, artistic, inventive, and poetic. Quiet often she could be seen under the trees reading during breaks.

One day as we walked back from the pool, Landscaper, asked me pointedly, "Why don't you just make him do things like other teachers do?"

I explained that I believed he would join us. I thought it would be better if he decided to join instead of me forcing him. I explained that I believed he needed to make these decisions now before he got any older.

"Who will make him do things when he is twenty?" I asked.

"I think you're right. This way it would be him doing it. But what will you do if he doesn't join in?"

I didn't have an answer.

Landscaper made attempts to protect her desk, a private space from our interactive and dynamic public space. For weeks she tied her desk area off with yarn. She would forbid other students to cross into her territory. Her valued privacy challenged my communal use of materials and space. In school where students have very little privacy, I had disrupted the only privacy they had: ownership of materials and space. Landscaper was claiming her right to a private space within a space I designated as public.

Landscaper was a loner, an obsessive reader, and she enjoyed the conversation of adult company. She didn't seem to make or keep friends easily. She often was frustrated to tears when a friend joined the play of others. She challenged my instructions for collaborative work by consistently choosing to work alone. Co-constructed by her peers as a "brain" she was often left out when small groups formed for project work or recess play. I never felt sure if this was her choice or theirs. There seemed to be a "tension between her access to specificity, with its attendant right to be different, and her access to group membership, which assumes and achieves sameness" (Davies, 2000, p. 24). At times, I felt I had deeply upset her school world.

Like Lion, Landscaper was very industrious. I was always surprised by her ability to build or create while participating in whole class workshops. I recall my amazement when I discovered her knitting on two sharpened pencils during a book talk. Publicly, in the face of student complaints, I acknowledged her ability to do two things at the same time: to knit and listen. Over the year she knit several inventions, including a pencil holder for me.

Ironically, I suspected the children viewed her industriousness as disruptive to school rules and the spaces of official school business. This first occurred to me when as a class we were getting ready to catch a bus to a local landfill site. As we gathered at the door, several of the girls called out to me, "Teacher, Landscaper has a book. She's taking a book on the bus." The tone of their voices was recognizable; make her stop, they seemed to say. Did I misunderstand them? A passion for reading is a disposition I value, that schools value. But her reading passion was clearly defined by the girls as unacceptable school bus behavior. The reinforcement of schooled conformity reared its ugly head again. Landscaper stood, holding her novel, looking at me, surrounded by girls, anticipating my response.

"That's a great idea. It's about a twenty minute drive." Other children ran to select their books.

Over time Landscaper began to incorporate many of the artistic materials of the room into her desk site. She received peer attention for plasticine miniatures she created and put on the corner of her desk. They usually represented the characters and/or setting of a novel she was reading or writing. These realistic miniature figurines became very attractive to other children. Soon characters appeared on other desktops. This troubled Landscaper. She complained to me they were copying her ideas. Did she sense a loss of her own defined space? I assured her, her ideas were so good that they wanted to give it a try. Their response was a compliment and, in this way, she was a teacher in our room.

Her peers continued to struggle with her. One day when I returned to the classroom, I found a group of students gasping around Landscaper's desk. "Look what you did! Wait 'till the teacher sees this!"

"Sees what?" I asked.

The crowd parted and I saw that Landscaper had painted a wonderful watercolor landscape on her desktop. It was stunning! Its beauty and her talent struck me. (In the future I would support her talent by inviting a series of painters to paint with her and five other students). As I was engaged with her remarkable landscape I was aware of the student's gaze upon me, anticipating my "teacher" response.

"In this school, you are not allowed to mark on the desks!" a girl informed me. Her comment reminded me I was new on the block, I needed to learn and reinforce the rules. This desk painting was wrong! I was struck that what seemed more important to the children were the rules not the artistic talent before them or the feelings of the artist. The rules that governed the public space, the protection of school property, silenced their recognition of this individual artist, circumscribed their critical thinking on whether this was a serious transgression, and stunted their curiosity about why she was painting her desk or how she had come to possess such skill in painting landscapes.

Jane Roland Martin's (1992) critique of schoolhouses gives further support to what I was witnessing:

> our school houses inure children to disconnection. Labeling speaking to friends, [painting the desk, reading on the bus] misbehaviours and defining helping others as the cardinal sin of cheating, they treat our young as separated and isolated beings . . . schools typically deny the value of individuality. (p. 180)

I knew I had to be very careful in my response to validate both the students' concern about rules and Landscaper's initiative inside her precarious position with her peers. I asked, "What do you plan to do with your painting?

She responded, "Oh I'll wash the desk when I am through with it. I did a little test to see if the paint would come off before I did the whole thing. Don't worry, I'll clean it completely." Following her reassurance, I entered a discussion on her artistic techniques, aware of the shifting student glances around me.

As soon as possible, I met with the custodian to assure him of her plan. This proved to be a wise decision because soon her peers solicited Landscaper to paint their desk surfaces. Landscaper was in great demand and valued publicly for her talents. And like many episodes in the classroom, this desk painting came to pass.

Martin (1992) writes, "It is one thing for school to provide integrative activities that unite the mind and body, thought and actions, reason and emotion, it is quite another for it to teach each child to interact with every child and adult too – as one fully human being to another" (p. 104). Landscaper's challenge to negotiate her individual spaces contributed to our community space as a place of "sustained human relationships of sufficient intimacy that support" (Grumet, 1988, p. 56). This involved the negotiation of dialogic spaces where the official and unofficial curriculums, where public and private worlds, could meet through rich, passionate negotiations; spaces of freedoms where rights and responsibilities had to be openly discussed. It involves attempts to offer "more space and recognition of the various actions and 'selves' performed daily in a social landscape blinded and hostile to variety" (Butler as cited in Miller, 2005, p. xiii).

Lust for Certainty

> In light of the current assessment obsession, educators need to question and combat the ways in which practices have become technologies of contemporary colonization that are more about surveillance and monitoring than about teaching and learning. (Cannella & Viruru as cited in Iannacci, 2008, p. 141)

A rise in large-scale testing emphasizes modernist tree-like logic (MacNaughton, 2004). A cause and effect logic – tree logic – perpetuates the dangerous belief that if you begin at the roots, give it the right nutrients (curricular content, childhood experiences, lessons, motivations, tests, and teacher responses) you will progress up the stem of development to produce a completed, autonomous, flexible, self-governing, book-literate, life-long-learning adult. Tree logic leaves little room for accepting doubts, reflecting on mistakes and negotiating the unruly, realities of experience (MacNaughton, 2004). This dominance of tree logic silences critical conversations, creating an "absence of dialogue and debate that impoverishes early childhood and weakens democratic practices" (Moss, 2007, p. 229). When educational debate is reduced to a monologue, what are the consequences for children, their families, and educators?

As an educator/student/parent, I know the paralysis that this logic – this monologue – inflicts. Leaving no room to "comprehend and accommodate human diversity, complexity and contingency" (Dahlberg, Moss, & Pence, 1999, p. 22), this logic orders them out of existence, silencing our "capacity to become reflexively and critically literate, to catch ourselves in the act of constituting worlds in particular ways" (Davies, 2000, p . 73). As two of many educational *classificatory practices* (Popkewitz, 1993), "standardized tests and developmental assessments are dividing practices (Foucault, 1977), methods of manipulation that combine the mediation of science and the practice of exclusion" (Dahlberg, Moss, & Pence, 1999, p. 37) to objectify and create hierarchies among children, their families, and educators. Exercising power through close monitoring, increased assessments and a range of interventions, testing divides "children from each other [and] divides children within themselves, . . . while cultivating a diagnostic, assessment and therapeutic culture where normative judgments about the child enter in and take over" (Dahlberg & Lenz Taguchi as cited in Dahlberg, Moss, & Pence, 1999, p. 37). Destructively, these divisive, normative practices reduce pedagogical practices, policy actions, and communications to a preoccupation of "correcting and preventing deviations from the norm" (Dahlberg, Moss & Pence, 1999, p. 37). This regulatory, modernist lust for certainty, this measuring and determination of how children should be, incites a blaming culture while also dangerously constructing identities of underperforming schools, uninvolved, or disinterested parents, poorly educated mothers, disengaged students, and poorly prepared educators (Berlinger & Biddle, 1995; Moss, 2007; MacNaughton, 2004). And Bronwyn Davies (2000) warns that being positioned as one who belongs in or is defined in terms of the negative can lock people into repeated patterns of powerlessness render(ing) them unrecognizable in other subjective positions.

Keeping in mind that "everyone is being subjected to disempowering, regulatory (and potentially punitive) gaze in the name of higher standards" (Novinger & O'Brien, 2003, p. 1), it is imperative that educators, (and others) publicly, "critically analyze the systems of oppression that shape and constrain our lives and learning" (Novinger & O'Brien 2003 p. 13-14). To this aim, feminist, poststructurally inspired educators (among others) situate normalizing categories, theories of identities, knowledge, and learning, and educational concepts and practices as "permanently contested sites of meaning" (Elam as cited in Lenz Taguchi, 2008,

p. 52). In this way they reconceptualize education as a pursuit of social justice (Cannella, 1997; Dahlberg, Moss, & Pence, 1999; Grumet, 1988; MacNaughton, 2004; Martin, 1992; Thorne, 1993; Virura, 2005; Walkerdine, 2004).

Vital to a rereading of Lion and Landscaper is the reconceptualization of assessment as meaning making. With the aim to make meaning, educators document and evaluate children's learning through dialogue, observational notes, narrative texts, videos, and annotated photographs. These daily processes provide an alternative to the modernist concept of quality, where evaluation is understood as conformity to the norm through the application of universal and stable criteria (Dahlberg & Moss, 2005). Valuing knowledge as partial, perspectival, provisional, and communal (Moss, 2007) educators interpret and reinterpret children's learning seeking participation from children and their families in daily assessment processes. Meaning making informs curricular planning while creating a shared public space for the participation of children, their families, multiple educators, and community members. In this way narrative "documentation has great potential for . . . creating a space for critical thinking, for taking responsibility and for developing new types of conversations and practices" (Dahlberg, Moss, & Pence, 1999, p. 17). What difference might such a public narration of our learning make to Lion, to Landscaper, to their families, to their classmates, to the school community, and to teachers like me?

Whose Stories and Who Benefits?

The politics of our time and place influence which stories (of individuals and societies) are told, when and by whom, which is why some stories are heard more often and given greater status than others. Consequently, identifying the stories (of individuals or societies) that are silenced or marginalized and then sharing them is a political act. (MacNaughton, 2005, p. 4)

The incidents that I story in this chapter are ones that "opened up the possibility of a new storyline that unhooked the old story of lack and put another, more abundant, enabling story in its place" (Davies, 2000, pp. 28-29). They are stories that document "pedagogy as a social relationship that gets right in to your brain, your body, your heart, in your sense of self, of the world, of others, and documents possibilities and impossibilities in all these realms" (Dahlberg, Moss, & Pence, 1999, p. 18).[2] They "acknowledge that a pedagogical mode of address is where the social construction of knowledge and learning gets deeply personal. It's a relationship whose subtleties can shape and misshape lives, passions for learning and broader social dynamics" (Ellsworth 1997, p. 6). Patrick Shannon (1999) writes "Whose stories get told? What can these stories mean? Who benefits from their telling? . . . are political questions because they address the ways in which people's identities – their beliefs, attitudes, and values – are created and maintained" (p. 397). Stories are central to subjectivities; "All of us come to be who we are (however ephemeral, multiple and changing) by being located or locating ourselves (usually unconsciously) in social narratives rarely of our own making" (Somers, 1994, p. 606).

In choosing stories, we can "disturb the status quo, re-route feelings that were thought to be central and allow peripheral imaginings to take root" (Doll, 2000, p. 178). The story of Lion and Landscaper disrupts individualization (child blaming) as it attempts to analyze the socially constructed worlds of the classroom. Davies (2006) writes "our responsibility . . . is to understand, to the extent that is possible, the complex conditions of our mutual formation. We must understand our own contributions to creating and withholding the conditions of possibility of particular lives" (p. 435). I am all too aware of how easily I can fall into the conforming nature of school life, how difficult it is to open up the possibility of new storylines that unhooked the old stories of lack and put another, more abundant, enabling story in its place (Davies, 2000). Yet the difficulty of living, abundant, enabling storylines inside schooled spaces is made easier if "[we] take up [our] personal stories and troubles as symbols of larger social issues" (Shannon, 1999, p. 407) By critically contextualizing our stories, we crack open the possibilities so that we can take up the responsibility of being answerable to those whom we relate to daily. For, as Novinger and O'Brien write, "The stories we tell, the stories our students tell, the stories *all* teachers tell have the potential to become the means through which we [support each other as we] examine and expose how disciplinary practices function" (p. 16). The cost of silencing our stories that unfold in messy, hard to resolve issues of freedom, democracy, and difference, the contradictory nature of teaching and learning remains glazed over, bubbling beneath the surface, never to be engage with, while we trick ourselves and others into believing that more testing, more interventions, more regulation, more surveillance will improve learning and teaching.

Notes

[1] *Incommensurate discourses* limit the scope for communication: statements that are clear and coherent within one discursive formation may not be intelligible within another (Foucault, 1977). So communications get dismissed by the other as invalid, unintelligible, uninteresting, or incredible and mainstream policies and practices become isolated from important sources of new and different thought giving a dominant discourse too much uncritical space and increasingly undermining democracy. Soon dominant discourses are seen as the only true account instead of socially constructed perspective that privileges certain interests.

[2] Dahlberg, Moss, and Pence, 1999 deepen my understanding of "pedagogy and pedagogical work as terms that communicate a way of relating to the world and other human beings which is value-based and complex, and view knowledge as produced through co-construction." (18) They draw upon Patti Lathers (1991) work: "[Pedagogy] denies the teacher as neutral transmitter, the student as passive and knowledge as immutable material to impart...[instead focusing] attention on the knowledge and means by which knowledge is produced" (p. 15).

References

Berliner, D., & Biddle, B. (1995). *The manufactured crisis: Myths, frauds, and the attack on American public schools.* New York: Perseus Books.

Blackman, L., Cromby, J., Hook, D., Papadopoulos, D., & Walkerdine, V. (2008). Creating subjectivities. *Subjectivity, 22,* 1-27.

Butin, D. (2001). If this is resistance I would hate to see domination: Retrieving Foucault's notion of resistance within educational research. *Educational Studies, 32*(2), 157–176

Butler, J. (2005). *Giving an account of oneself.* New York: Fordham University Press.

Cannella, G. (1997). *Deconstructing early childhood education.* New York: Peter Lang.

Chamberlin, E. J. (2003). *If this is your land, where are your stories? Finding common ground.* Toronto: Random House.

Dahlberg, G., & Moss, P. (2005). *Ethics and politics in early childhood education.* New York: RoutledgeFalmer.

Dahlberg, G., Moss, P., & Pence, A. (1999). *Beyond quality in early childhood education and care: Postmodern perspectives.* London: Falmer Press.

Davies, B. (2000). *A body of writing: 1990-1999.* Walnut Creek, CA: AltaMira Press.

Davies, B. (2006). Subjectification: The relevance of Butler's analysis for education. *British Journal of Sociology of Education. 27*(4), 425-438.

Davies, B. (Ed.) (2008). *Judith Butler in conversation: Analyzing the texts and talk of everyday life.* New York: Routledge.

Doll, M. A. (2000). *Like letters in running water: A mythopoetics of curriculum.* Mahwah, NJ: Lawrence Erlbaum.

Edmiston, B. (2008). *Forming ethical identities in early childhood play.* New York: Routledge.

Ellsworth, E. (1997). *Teaching positions: Difference, pedagogy, and the power of address.* New York: Teachers College Press.

Eyre, L. (2007). Whose ethics? Whose interests? The Tri-Council Policy and feminist research. *Journal of Curriculum Theorizing, 23,* 91-102.

Farquhar, S., & Fitzsimons, P. (Eds.) (2008). *Philosophy of early childhood education: Transforming narratives.* Malden, MA: Blackwell Publishing

Foucault, M. (1977). *Discipline and Punish: The birth of the prison.* Harmondsworth, UK: Penguin.

Gallas, K. (1994). *The languages of learning: How children talk, write, dance, draw and sing their understanding of the world.* New York: Teachers College Press.

Greene, M. (1995). *Releasing the imagination: essays on education, the arts, and social change.* San Francisco, CA: Jossey-Bass.

Grumet, M. R. (1988). *Bitter milk – Women and teaching.* Amherst, MA: University of Massachusetts Press.

Gough, N. (2006). Forward. In I. Semetsky (Ed.), *Deleuze, education and becoming*. Rotterdam, NL: Sense Publishers.

hooks, b. (1994). *Teaching to transgress - Education as the practice of freedom*. New York: Routledge.

Holland, P. (2003). *We don't play with guns here: War, weapon, and superhero play in the early years*. Philadelphia, PA: Open University Press.

Iannacci, L. (2008). A case study of asset-oriented approaches to cultural and linguistic diversity in early childhood education. In L. Iannacci & R. Heydon (Eds.), *Early childhood curricula and the de-pathologizing of childhood*. (pp. 130-153) Toronto: University of Toronto Press.

Katch, J. (2001). *Under deadman's skin: Discovering the meaning of children's violent play*. Boston, MA: Beacon Press.

Lather, P. (1991). *Getting smart: Feminist research and pedagogy within/in the postmodern*. New York: Routledge.

Lather, P. (2007). *Getting lost: feminist efforts toward a double(d) science*. Albany, NY: State University of New York Press.

Lenz Taguchi, H. (2005). Getting personal: How early childhood teacher education troubles students' and teacher educators' identities regarding subjectivity and feminism. *Contemporary Issues in Early Childhood, 6*(3), 244-255.

Lenz Taguchi, H. (2006). Reconceptualizing early childhood education: Challenging taken for granted ideas. In J. Einarsdottir & J. Wagner (Eds.), *Nordic childhoods and early education* (pp. 257-287). Greenwich, CT: Information Age Publishing.

Lenz Taguchi, H. (2007). Deconstructing and Transgressing the theory-practice dichotomy in early childhood education. *Educational Philosophy and Theory, 39*(3), 275-290.

Lenz Taguchi, H. (2008). Deconstructing and transgressing the theory-practice dichotomy in early childhood education. In S. Farquhar & P. FitzSimons (Eds.), *Philosophy of early childhood education* (pp. 52-67). Malden, MA: Blackwell Publishing.

MacNaughton, G. (2004). The politics of logic in early childhood research: A case of the brain, hard facts, trees and rhizomes. *The Australian Educational Researcher, 31*(3), 87-103.

MacNaughton, G. (2005). *Doing Foucault in early childhood studies*. New York: Routledge.

MacNaughton, G., Hughes, P., & Smith, K. (2007). Rethinking approaches to working with children who challenge: Action learning for emancipatory practice. *International Journal of Early Childhood, 39*(1), 39-57.

Martin, J. R. (1992). *The schoolhome - Rethinking schools for changing families*. Boston, MA: Harvard University Press.

Miller, J. L. (2005). *Sounds of silence breaking*. New York: Peter Lang.

Moss, P. (2007). Meetings across the paradigmatic divide. *Educational Philosophy and Theory,. 39*(3), 229-245.

New Zealand Ministry of Education. (2004). He aha nga hua a nga tamariki ki to ratou Aromatawi Children Contributing to their own Assessment. In *Kei tau o te pae Assessment for learning: Early childhood exemplars*. Wellington, NZ: Learning Media Ltd.

Novinger, S., & O'Brien, L. (2003). Beyond 'boring, meaningless shit' in the academy: Early childhood teacher educators under the regulatory gaze. *Contemporary Issues in Early Childhood, 4*(1), 1-31.

Pelais, R. J., (2004) *A methodology of the heart: Evoking academic and daily life*. Walnut Creek, CA: AltaMira Press.

Pinar, W. F. (2005). What should be and what might be. In J. L. Miller, *Sounds of silence breaking*. New York: Peter Lang.

Paley, V. G. (1992). *You can't say you can't play*. Cambridge, MA: Harvard University Press.

Popkewitz, T. (Ed.) (1993) *Changing patterns of power: Social regulation and teacher education reform*. Albany, NY: State University of New York.

Rose, N. (1989). *Governing the soul: The shaping of the private self*. London: Routledge.

Ruddick, S. (1989). *Maternal thinking toward a politics of peace*. Boston, MA: Beacon Press.

Santoro, P., & Boylorn, R. (2008). Re-imagining possibilities: Honoring the work of Carolyn Ellis and Art Bochner. *Qualitative Inquiry, 14*, 195-211.

Shannon, P. (1999). Sociological imagination, stories and learning to be literate. *Theory and Research in Social Education, 27*(3), 396-407.

Silin, J. (1995). Sex, death, and the education of children: Our passion for ignorance in the age of AIDS. New York: Teacher's College Press.

Smith, K. (1978). *When a girl looks down*. Fredericton, NB: Fiddlehead Poetry Books.

Somers, M. R. (1994). The narrative constitution of identity: A relational and network approach. *Theory and Society, 23*, 605-649.

Sparks, A. C. (2007). Embodiment, academics, and the audit culture: A story seeking consideration. *Qualitative Research, 7*, 521-550.

St. Pierre, E. A., & Pillow, W. S. (Eds.), (2000). *Working the ruins: Feminist poststructural theory and methods in education*. New York: Routledge.

Thorne, B. (1993). *Gender play: Girls and boys in school*. Piscataway, NJ: Rutgers University Press.

Viruru, R. 2005. The impact of postcolonial theory on early childhood education. *Journal of Education, 35*, 7-29.

Walkerdine, V. (1990). *Schoolgirl Fictions*. London: Verso.

Walkerdine, V. (2004). Developmental psychology and the study of childhood. In M.J. Kehily (Ed.), *An introduction to childhood studies* (pp. 96-107). New York: Open University Press.

8

Taking Attendance and Other Rules of Kindergarten:
A Child's Perception of School Literacy[1]
Maureen E. Kendrick

"Let's play teacher," Leticia suggested.[2]

"Okay."

"Okay, put the books away . . . .We're going to read a story and then – I'm Miss Lee, okay – we're going to read a story before we have centres."

"Do we have any work?" I asked.

"No. We don't have any work," she said in her teacher voice then whispered, "Pretend you're talking to your friend while I read the story." Taking her two home reading books out of a plastic bag, she set the Chinese book to one side and held up the English book so that I could see the cover.

"I'm just going to read the English book, not the Chinese one," she explained. "Okay, the story is by McArr," she said in a sweet, sing-song voice, "I'm going to read the story and you have to be quiet, Joelle."

Pretending to talk to the person beside me, I said, "That looks like a good story. I wonder what it's about."

"No, not like that. You have to whisper," Leticia redirected with hand gestures. She continued to pretend to read the story while I whispered to the person beside me.

In a loud, stern authoritarian voice she reprimanded me, "Joelle! Will you stop talking? One more time and it will be time out . . . .Okay, I'm going to start again." Then she directed me, "and you talk for a long, long time." She began to read the book again as I whispered to the person beside me.

"Joelle!" she snapped in her sternest teacher voice, "Time out!" She could not refrain from giggling with pleasure as she said this. "You cry," she instructed.

I began sobbing out loud, "I'm sorry, Miss Lee. I won't talk anymore. Please don't put me in time out."

In her meanest voice she decreed, "No! You're time out! Go!" She pointed to the bedroom door.

"I'm sorry. I'm sorry," I pleaded.

"Say you want your mommy," she dictated.

"I want my mommy," I cried.

"No! No more school for you. Go out." She pushed me out her bedroom door and into the hallway.

"Please let me stay in."

"No, you go out in the hallway. Go! Go out! You stay out there for ten minutes. I'm going to tie you up." She pretended to tie my hands above my head and forced me to stand against the wall.

"You're a very mean teacher," I said, which she responded to with laughter. I sat down in the hallway and waited for her to decide that my time out was over. (Transcript from session 18)

This play narrative serves as a mode of inquiry for this young girl to express and explore her experiences with, and ideas about, the practices associated with school literacy. Her words and actions make evident her unique perspective on classroom rules and routines for literacy. Until recently, there has been little interest in investigating the perspectives of children about aspects of their own lives (Dyer, 2002; Filippini & Vecchi, 2000). Arguably, children's perspectives on their own experiences and learning have the potential to inform educational policy and the evolution of practices that are designed to involve them (Harste, Woodward,

& Burke, 1984; Nutbrown & Hannon, 2003). From a research perspective, however, accessing and understanding young children's views can be methodologically challenging. Drawing on an extensive, year-long case study in which I actively engaged in the play-literacy activities of Leticia, a five-year-old Chinese-Canadian girl (see Kendrick, 2003), I examine how a make-believe play narrative centred on the theme of playing school can reveal a child's hidden perceptions of classroom literacy practices.

Children As Curricular And Research Informants

Educational research is perhaps "one of the last arenas of society where it is still the case that children – especially *young* children – are seen but not heard" (Nutbrown & Hannon, 2003, p. 117). When researchers have endeavored to understand children's perspectives, research methods have largely relied on observational techniques. Far less attention has been given to listening to children and actively soliciting their views. In examining how individuals construct narratives of their own lives and experiences, Welty (1983) makes the distinction between listening *for* a story and listening *to* a story, noting that the former requires a much more engaged and dynamic form of listening (for an in depth discussion on *listening* in early childhood contexts see Rinaldi, 2006). In this research study, I adopted the unique dual-role of play-mate/researcher, which enabled me to more actively listen *for* Leticia's story by entering her play world in a way that would not have been possible had I remained a more passive outside observer. By moving into her play world as a participant, I was better able to understand the meanings she attached to her play narratives, and her perception of the literacy activities embedded within these. Specifically, this dual-role also provided access to Leticia's *funds of knowledge* about a broad range of activities and experiences in her life. Here, I extend Moll, Amanti, Neff, and Gonzalez' (1992) conceptualization of funds of knowledge beyond household contexts to include the strategic knowledge and related activities associated with the functioning and development of school contexts.

I begin from the perspective that children's make-believe play is "a story the players tell themselves about themselves" (Geertz, 1973, p. 237). The story is always comprised of multiple and simultaneous modes of representation including symbolic action, language, gesture, and image (see Kress, 1997). What needs to be emphasized here is that language is only a part of the meaning-making process involved in play. As Kress and Jewitt (2003) argue, any communicative event – including play – involves simultaneous modes whereby meaning is communicated in different ways by images, gestures, and speech. In other words, "meanings are made, distributed, received, interpreted and remade in interpretation through many representational and communicative modes – not just through language" (Kress & Jewitt, 2003, p. 1). This multimodal social semiotic perspective views children as sign-makers who make use of the resources available to them in their specific socio-cultural environment. When children create stories in make-believe play, they use signs – language, images, gestures, actions, objects – to simultaneously communicate the here and now of a social context while enlisting the resources they have 'at hand' from the world around them (Kress, 1997). The sign's intrinsic meanings are not arbitrary but rather, represent what is central to the sign-maker at that particular moment (Kress & Jewitt, 2003). The meanings also reflect reality as imagined by the sign-maker and influenced by his or her beliefs, values, and biases. In this way, the play text has the potential to offer insights into children's stories of self, including individual agency, as well as cultural, societal and environmental conditions surrounding the creation of stories.

When children make up worlds through play, they engage in a serious process of identity making (Holland, Lachicotte, Skinner, & Cain, 1998). From Vygotsky's (1978, 1986) perspective, the free expression of social play provides an opportunity for children to develop new social competencies in newly imagined communities. These imagined communities are narrativized worlds, what Holland and her colleagues (1998) refer to as *figured worlds*. The (re)production of figured worlds involves abstracting significant patterns from everyday life into a set of expectations – or theories – about how such events unfold. Figured worlds are "formed and re-formed in relation to the everyday activities and events that ordain happenings within it" (p. 53). Play, then, becomes a "space of authoring" (p.272) where authorship is a matter of orchestration, of arranging the identifiable social discourses and practices that constitute one's social and cultural resources. These played stories are bricolages (Lévi-Strauss, 1969), a cobbling together of seemingly disparate elements that illustrate a child's perception of how everyday life events take place through a set of enacted behaviors and identities.

Bakhtin's (1984) notion of carnivalization extends my understanding of play as a communicative practice and a means of authoring self. In many ways, I view carnivalization (the carnivalesque) and play as parallel processes. Bakhtin described the carnivalesque as something that is created when the themes of the carnival blend, mutate, and invert social order. With its masks, monsters, games, dramas, and processions, carnival juxtaposes, mixes, and confronts the spiritual and material, young and old, male and female, daily identity and festive mask, serious convention and parody, in a "temporary suspension of all hierarchic distinctions and barriers... and of the prohibitions of usual life" (Bakhtin, 1984, p. 15). During carnival – and play – all are considered equal: "a special form of free and familiar contact reigned among people who were usually divided by the barriers of caste, property, profession, and age" (Bakhtin, 1984, p. 10). The unique sense of time and space afforded by both carnival and play causes the individual to feel he or she is a part of the collectivity, from which arises a heightened awareness of one's sensual, material, bodily unity, and community (Clark & Holquist, 1986). Dialogism is a fundamental aspect of this process whereby multiple voices – each bringing forth a different point of view, a different way of seeing the world – come together in the free and frank communication that both carnival and play permit; although "each [voice] retains its own unity and open totality, they are mutually enriched" (Bakhtin, 1984, p. 56). The aspiration of carnival – and in the case of the present study, play – is to uncover and undermine the hegemony of any ideology that seeks to have the final word about the world. Hence, carnival and play make it possible to renew and illuminate hidden meanings and potentials, while simultaneously projecting an alternate conceptualization of reality.

Context

Leticia, a young Chinese-Canadian girl, is the focus of this chapter. For well over a year, my life interspersed with this young girl's. To understand how she used play to make sense of aspects her life, I focused on the family, community, and classroom activities within which she situated literacy events. I utilized a variety of qualitative research procedures, including conversation records, artefact collection, and combinations of observations and interactions within the context of the home, local neighborhood, and school. Observations always took place within Leticia's everyday routine activities and were never staged. Her play interactions at home were audio taped using a small, handheld tape recorder. Observations of her interactions with family members and friends at home and in the community were recorded as hand-written field notes. Classroom observations were also recorded in writing. Interviews with family members were very much conversational in nature, often taking place at the kitchen table during tea or dinner, and never adhering to any formalized structure. These open-ended conversations were valuable in interpreting and analyzing the literacy activities that occurred within the context of Leticia's play activities. Detailed accounts were also made of the forms and functions of print in the home and at school. The content and purpose of these literacy practices were an important resource for understanding Leticia's use of literacy in her play activities.

In my dual role as researcher-playmate, Leticia saw me almost exclusively as a playmate – her playmate – and paid little attention to my role as researcher. The tools I used as a researcher were of little consequence to her. The tape recorder, for example, was only a novelty on the first day when she was intrigued to hear her own voice on tape, something she had never heard before. My field notebook was also accepted as part of our play relationship. As playmates, we co-created a series of narrative texts, although Leticia initiated the themes and topics of these texts. Perhaps one of the most striking aspects of our relationship was that Leticia recognized that I knew how to play. At the time of the study, I had five nieces and nephews with whom I spent considerable time interacting and playing. I also knew children. I had taught in both primary and secondary school settings, predominantly working with children who spoke languages other than English. As a teacher, I had been involved in teaching drama and was a member of a community theatre group. I was comfortable moving in and out of different roles and understood Leticia's strategies for expressing a range of characters in her play activities. Our relationship, nonetheless, was asymmetrical and not that of peers because it did not involve the same kinds of negotiations of rules, roles, and scripts. Rather, I allowed Leticia to take almost exclusive ownership of the direction of our play narratives.

Leticia's Home and School Context

Leticia is from a multilingual, multiliterate family. Her parents, Howard and Linda, came to Canada at separate points in the early 1980s as refugees from Vietnam. Both of Leticia's parents are ethnic Chinese; they speak several languages including their family language, Chao Chiu, Mandarin, Cantonese, Vietnamese, and English. Howard and Linda have three children: Wilson, seven years old, Leticia, five years old, and Richmond, six months.[3] Their home context was rich in print including newspapers and news magazines written in Chinese, Vietnamese, and English; assorted cookbooks, mostly in English; Chinese horoscope books; English dictionaries; Chinese and English calendars; English encyclopedias; Chinese and English videotapes; computer manuals; and business documents and forms; among other texts. Leticia's family, along with her extended family, lived in an inner city community that bordered on an area known as Chinatown. Linda was reluctant to allow her children to play outside in the local neighborhood because she was concerned about safety in the inner city. Instead, the children primarily played indoors with their cousins. It was a rare occasion for Leticia or her brother to have classmates or neighborhood children over to play at their house.

Leticia attended a Mandarin-English bilingual kindergarten programme. At school, she chose how she would participate in literacy activities. Coloring worksheets, for example, almost always elicited the same half-hearted response. At home, coloring was also something that she did not appear to enjoy, even though she had an interesting assortment of crayons, felts, and coloring books. She was interested in storybooks, though, and listened intently when stories were read aloud in kindergarten. She also enjoyed looking at books during the scheduled times in the kindergarten, and often shared pictures with whomever was sitting next to her. Both her parents and teacher thought she should put more effort into her written work at school, especially her Chinese. Her parents were particularly disappointed that she was unable to write her Chinese name for the duration of her kindergarten year. English printing and speaking came much more easily to her. In fact, Miss Lee, Leticia's kindergarten teacher, described her as one of the stronger English speakers in the class. Her Mandarin, however, was assessed as average.

Leticia's Play Narrative

The play narrative in this chapter transpired over a sustained two-hour play episode. It is drawn from a larger study examining the interconnections among play, literacy, and culture (see Kendrick, 2003). The narrative is exemplary of Leticia's perception of the forms and functions of school literacy, including the role of the teacher as purveyor of literacy. My interpretation of her use of multiple modes of communication in play is represented initially as a multilayered narrative account. The multiple layers of analysis that I undertook involved a close reading of the narrative as a literary text (see DiYanni, 1990; Iser, 1989). I began my analysis by carefully watching the story unfold as Leticia and I co-constructed it. As the story unfolded, I would notice the time and place of the story's action, the characters' dialogue, manner of speaking, and other modes of communicating meaning including how objects, props, and garments were used to create character identities, how written texts were incorporated into the play, and how gesture, image, and action were used to express ideas. As I observed, I also made connections among these details and raised questions that guided my understanding of her meaning-making process. These connections helped me develop inferences (that is, interpretive hypotheses) about the broader significance of the narrative in Leticia's life. Finally, through interpreting the data with her family and her kindergarten teacher, I attempted to come to some conclusion about how the story's meaning might be a reflection of Leticia's own perceptions and experiences.

Taking Attendance and
Other Rules Of Kindergarten

When I arrived at the house that afternoon, Leticia was very anxious for us to play and, not wanting her mother and I to talk for too long, she consistently interrupted us. During her morning kindergarten class, she had been involved in a special school wide cross-age activity. This event became the subject of a make-believe play narrative.

"You need to make a newsletter," Leticia directed me after deciding that I would be Mrs. Hai, the kindergarten aide, and she would play Miss Lee, her kindergarten teacher.

"Oh, I need to make the newsletter, okay."

"I'm going to do morning message," she announced before writing "Goob ne A W" on the board. She read the message back to her students, "Good morning Miss Lee and Mrs. Hai," and then told me that I needed to go to the office "to get something." I asked her if I should finish writing the newsletter when I come back, to which she responded yes. I handed her the newsletter before I left because I wanted to make sure that I was doing it right. I pretended to write Chinese characters the way that I have seen Mrs. Hai write them.

She looked at my newsletter with disappointment. "No, you need to make the newsletter."

"In English or Chinese?"

"English!" she said somewhat exasperated.

"But Mrs. Hai always writes it in Chinese," I explained, thinking that she would want me to do things exactly as they are done in her classroom.

"You don't know how!" she reminded me sharply. "You have to finish. Today, you have lots and lots of time."

"I have lots of time today? Why do I have more time today?"

"'Cause tomorrow we don't have any time to teach other kids. Because tomorrow we have fun."

"What are we going to do?"

"Make crafts and painting. The kindergarten will go with their buddy and they'll go to make craft or painting . . . ."

"Oh, fun. Okay."

" . . . . And we can have some soup."

"Should I put that in the newsletter."

"Yep, and tomorrow will be really, really long centre."

"Oh."

"And they can play in the house after they make craft."

"Where are they going to go to make their craft?" I asked.

"And we are going to watch dragon dancing, okay. And we're going to eat lunch and have fun, and we come home at three. We got a looong day tomorrow. So we don't need to do work."

"Okay."

"All the kids are going to come to our class with their buddy and then we're going to make crafts and eat lunch and watch movies and have a story. But we're going to do centres first. We don't need to work," she emphasized again.

"Okay, we'll do centres first," I repeated her instructions

"Yep. Today we are having a new centre. A pay centre. You buy something and then you need to pay. I need to make a phone call, you teach the kids." She went into the computer room and picked up the disconnected phone that was on the floor under the desk. "Hello," she said into the telephone, "we're getting ready. I need to check which children are going to which classroom. Okay? We're almost ready." She came back to the table in the "classroom" where I was sitting. "The grade one is after so we should be getting ready now. I need a pencil and a paper so that I can take attendance. Today is Linda and [. . .]." She pretended to read a list of names on her blank piece of paper. "We need to write the names here [she pointed to the right side of the page]. Okay, write Edward," she instructed me. I started writing his name, but she quickly stopped me. "Not here! Here." She was very particular about wanting the names written on the very far right side of the page.

"Where do you want me to write?" I asked again.

Her tone was directive. "Down at the bottom where the line is." She pointed to the first line on the right side of the page below the wide top margin.

"What do you want me to write?"

"Edward!" she said impatiently.

She continued to name her classmates one-by-one, as I wrote their names down . . . When I put check marks beside the names, Leticia became annoyed. "You're all wrong. Today is not their turn and then we don't write a check mark."

"Don't put a check mark beside their names?" I asked, somewhat confused.

"If today is their turn to take attendance to the office, then you check it."

"So should I cross off the check marks?"

"Yes!"

I began scribbling over all of the check marks, but she stopped me before I had crossed off all of them. "Wait, stop, stop! Today is Linda and Zhou," she said, wanting me to leave the check marks beside their names.

"Did you take attendance today?" I asked.

"Yes."

"Is everyone here?"

"Iris is away. Tomorrow will be Denise and Gary. If people is not here then they need to take it, then if people here – all the people here – then they don't need to take it."

"If all the people are here, then they don't need to take the attendance to the office?"

"Yeah," she confirmed.

"Okay. Should I bring the attendance sheet?"

"Miss Lee take it, not Mrs. Hai!" she scolded.

"Oh. Should I leave it here for Miss Lee then?"

"Yeah, Miss Lee only need to come [to the office]."

"So is Mrs. Hai in the classroom already?"

"No, Mrs. Hai doesn't go in first [before Miss Lee]," she corrected me. "We quickly got to take attendance."

She looked down her list of names, making a steady tapping sound with her pen on the tabletop as she check-marked the names.

"Okay, all these kids are here." She read each name on the list and instructed me to say, "I am here" for each of the students. She continued to call the names and then paused, "Iris is not here." She continued to take attendance, occasionally commenting "Good," just as her kindergarten teacher does in response to students following the instructions of saying, "I am here."

"Today, it's Denise and Gary," Leticia explained.

"Denise and Gary now take the attendance down to the office?" I asked.

"Yep. Pretend you are taking Denise and Gary."

She returned to the computer room to make a telephone call. "Okay . . . ." she said into the receiver.

"Who was on the phone?"

"Um, Mrs. Bertrand [her school principal]."

"What did she want?"

"She said we need to start now 'cause all the kids already went. The kindergarten is all so slow. Um, William and Leticia need to go to the English kindergarten. All of them, the classmates, need to line up first then go. Okay, wait." She continued to look down her list of names. "We need to go to other class."

"We need to go to the English kindergarten?"

"Mrs. Hai can you take them down."

"To the English kindergarten?"

"Yeah, and come back and take the other kids."

"Leticia and Wilson, come on," I said, pretending to escort the two children to the English kindergarten (the bathroom). "Okay, who's next?" I asked upon returning to where Leticia was standing.

"Okay, Stephen and Lana go to grade six. Jason and Linda go to the grade four. Felix goes, too. And Keena and Ryan need to go, too."

"Where do they go?"

"They need to go to our classroom and get ready. And then they will be able to paint whatever they need, or crafts, or anything else. And all the kids will be going in there and people could go to the other class. Can you take them, Mrs. Hai?"

"Okay." I left and returned for more instructions.

"Mrs. Hai, Zhou needs to go to the grade two."

"To the grade two, okay. There he goes."

"Okay, Leticia and Wilson is done so they could just go to the . . . Wilson go and help his sister . . . We need to sign their name out so that they can play with their brother. Then when they're done, they can go play. Leticia can go with her brother, then if Leticia don't know what to do then her brother will show her."

"Okay."

"Tomorrow afternoon, after school, after kindergarten, Leticia will go to her brother's room. 'Cause Mrs. Hai said she needs to be there in the afternoon. She needs to stay until two o'clock."

"For the craft or for Chinese New Year."

"No, anyone who has any brother and sister in their class. Only those kids can go with Leticia."

"Oh, only if you have a brother or a sister?"

"Yeah. It's almost time to go home."

"What about centres? What about the new centre?"

"That's after. We need to go home now. Um, Leticia could go first, after Wilson. Leanne goes to her sister's class. Jason needs to go home 'cause he doesn't got any brother or sister."

She continued to name each child in her class who has an older brother or sister in the school. These children were to stay at school for the afternoon. She also named the children who didn't have brothers and sisters at school, and indicated that they 'need to go' home.

"So the kids who are staying in their brother's or sister's class, what are they going to do there?"

"Oh, all kinds of stuff. They're going to do all kinds of work. And if the kindergarten don't know, their brother or sister will teach them. And Miss Lee will be there and Mrs. Hai. Come on, let's go!" (Transcript from session 14)

Leticia's Perception of School Literacy

This story is a detailed portrayal of the literacy-related rules and routines of a kindergarten classroom. Leticia casts me in the role of Mrs. Hai (the teacher's assistant in her kindergarten) and herself in the role of Miss Lee (her kindergarten teacher). The assignment of roles establishes a clear relationship of power whereby Leticia has authority over me. She directs my every action, commanding that I 'go to the office to get something' and 'make the newsletter.' She reinforces the power relationship between the teacher and the teacher's assistant on two occasions, the first when she reminds me that 'Miss Lee take [the attendance sheet], not Mrs. Hai,' and the second when she admonishes me with 'No, Mrs. Hai doesn't go in [to the classroom] first.' The ways in which literacy routines are carried out in classroom contexts often have a clear division of labor based on who has authority and power in the situation. At the age of five, Leticia already has her own ideas and perceptions about the nature of the relationship between a classroom teacher and a teaching assistant. In the vignette at the outset of this article, Leticia also explores the idea that teachers have power over students when she reprimands me, rather severely, for talking during storytime. The context of play provides an opportunity for her to experiment with power relationships in relation to literacy. Norton (2000) uses the word *power* to "reference the socially constructed relations among individuals, institutions, and communities through which symbolic and material resources in a society are produced, distributed, and validated" (p. 7). Leticia clearly understands that teachers represent symbolic resources such as language, education, and friendship (Norton, 2000), which place them in a hierarchical relationship to their students and teaching assistants. She uses the status of a teacher to control student behavior and maintain order in her classroom.

In the roles and identities that Leticia constructs in this play narrative (as well as other play narratives), she consistently situates herself in a position of power and authority. Corsaro (1985) suggests that rather than simply reflecting social status, play becomes a context where social status, social power, and shared values are created. From this perspective, it is interesting to consider how Leticia's relative status allows her to explore literacy in ways that she was unwilling to consider within the everyday context of her life in the more subordinate roles of daughter, kindergarten student, and five-year-old Chinese-Canadian girl. In another episode of playing school (see Kendrick, 2003), for example, in her role as teacher, she willingly reads and writes Chinese characters when making a book for her students. The spontaneity with which she writes the morning message is also reflective of her willingness to take risks when she is in a position of authority. Outside of the context of play, she would generally refuse to read or write anything – in Chinese or English – unless she was confident that she could do so with accuracy and fluency. In her role as teacher, she writes the message using her own invented spellings. She reads the message to her students, pointing to each *word*. This example represents one of the few occasions I had to observe Leticia writing without the support of copying a text from a printed source or from oral dictation. How she sees herself as authority (i.e., as the teacher) or subordinate, (i.e., daughter, kindergarten student, five-year-old girl) may very well have a powerful influence on her decision to participate or not participate in particular kinds of literacy practices at school and at home.

Playing school provided an important space for Leticia to construct an imagined identity as a literate member of an imagined school community. Such imagined communities have considerable potential to influence learners' current actions and investment in wanting to learn how to read and write (Kanno & Norton, 2003). Imagined communities present new possibilities for self; moreover, an imagined identity envisioned within an imagined community can significantly influence the kinds of choices learners make about educational practices (Kanno & Norton, 2003). Indeed, they may very well provide a reason and motivation for what learners do in the present. As Kanno and Norton explain, "Our identities . . . must be understood not only in terms of our investment in the 'real' world but also in terms of our investment in *possible* worlds" (2003, p. 248). For many young children possible worlds are represented by make-believe play worlds and the multiple selves they construct within these. For Leticia, her investment in reading and writing appeared to be inextricably linked to an identity of authority. Because learners' visions of the future can be linked to their current actions and sense of self (Kanno & Norton, 2003), perhaps one of the most important benefits of make-believe play for young learners is that it provides an opportunity to imagine themselves as readers and writers long before they are able to read and write print, and a space where multiple identities can coexist. Moreover, play is one of the only spaces in the realm of childhood that allows children the freedom to transpose and invert – to carnivalize – social order for the purposes of trying on – tasting – the language and experience of others (Bakhtin, 1981, 1984).

Following the routine procedures of taking attendance, Leticia sets the scene for the remainder of the plot, which focuses on preparing to have fun. Ironically, it is the preparation for fun – the literacy-related rules and routines of organizing school activities – that becomes the dominant focus of the remainder of the narrative. Her preoccupation with order here is reminiscent of Tasmika in Taylor and Dorsey-Gaines (1988) classic study of family literacy where it was observed that when Tasmika played school, "she did not write 'I love you' messages. Instead she made lists of words and wrote the alphabet" (p. 95). Although Leticia mentions a number of fun activities such as "making crafts and painting," "really, really long centre [time]," and "dragon dancing," and emphasizes that "we don't need to do work," none of these activities actually take place in the play episode. Instead, the day is consumed with tasks such as taking attendance and 'checking the names that go to the rooms.' She executes these routines with painstaking detail, systematically checking off the names of the students in her class, never confusing where they are to go and with whom. For Leticia, school literacy serves the purpose of maintaining order rather than making meaning.

The perceptions Leticia reveals in this narrative also reflect two important ways in which she sees new possibilities for classroom literacy practices. First, her idea of pairing younger and older siblings so that 'if the kindergarten don't know what to do, their brother or sister will teach them,' was not a part of the school activity that had taken place earlier that day. Instead, the idea most likely represents Leticia's desire to have the familiar security of her brother's presence and assistance with tasks she lacks the confidence to complete on her own.[4] Gregory (2001) refers to this interaction between siblings as synergy, a "unique reciprocity whereby siblings act as adjuvants in each other's learning" (p. 309). Leticia's recognition of the value of siblings learning together is indicative of a strategy she relies on as a young literacy learner. She frequently enlisted her brother's help with homework and other literacy tasks assigned by her parents such as book reading. Second, her idea for the new centre, the "pay centre," is an adaptation of shopping scenarios that were integral to her episodes of playing house.

Both the idea of pairing younger children with their older siblings and having a pay centre, complete with cash register and money, are meaningful examples of the how children's perceptions can inform school curriculum. Unlike the writing centre in Leticia's kindergarten classroom, which attracted very few students, her ideas involve reading and writing in much more meaningful ways. As Harste, Woodward, and Burke (1984) emphasize, "experience reveals that when research and curriculum development are conducted in functional language situations [such as play], the use of the child as informant can become a self-correcting strategy for the profession" (p. 51).

Conclusion

Leticia is intimately acquainted with the literacy tasks that help teachers organize and maintain order in their classrooms. For her, school literacy is a conglomerate of rules and routines, which she accurately represents in the play narrative she constructs. Her perception of school literacy is so powerfully shaped by school rules and routines that the vast majority of her school-related play activities are consumed by tasks such as taking attendance, organizing students, and enforcing rules for classroom behavior. When playing school, Leticia also reveals a sense of herself in relation to literacy, which incorporates her perception of school culture, her parents' expectations around literacy learning, and her position within her family and classroom. In her anthropological study of children's make-believe play, Schwartzman (1976) adopts the metaphor of taking a *sideways glance* at play. The metaphor captures the idea that the furtive sideways glance is far more likely to reveal the hidden and obscure than a more direct frontward glance. My role as playmate/researcher enabled me to take a sideways glance at this young girl's perception of school literacy by engaging with her in her play activities. My role as playmate fostered a deeper and more intimate connection between researcher and participant – a relationship that I believe enhanced productive inquiry in this study. As Lawrence-Lightfoot (1997) emphasizes, "Relationships that are complex, fluid, symmetric, and reciprocal – that are shaped by both researcher and actors – reflect a more responsible ethical stance and are likely to yield deeper data *and* better social science" (p. 137-138).

Notes

1 This is a revised and extended version of Kendrick (2005).
2 Pseudonyms are used throughout for the young girl, her family members, and school staff.
3 Children's ages at the beginning of the study.
4 Leticia would often go in search of her brother at recess time, particularly when she didn't have classmates to play with.

References

Bakhtin, M. (1981). Discourse in the novel. In M. Holquist (Ed.), C. Emerson and M. Holquist (Trans.), *The dialogic imagination: Four essays by M. M. Bakhtin* (pp. 259-422). Austin, TX: University of Texas Press. (Original work published 1934-1935).

Bakhtin, M. (1984). *Rabelais and his world* (Trans. H. Iswolsky). Bloomington, IN: Indiana University Press.

Clark, K., & Holquist, M. (1986). *Mikhail Bakhtin.* Cambridge, MA: Belknap Press of Harvard University Press (Reprint edition).

Corsaro, W. (1985). *Friendship and peer culture in the early years.* Norwood, NJ: Ablex.

DiYanni, R. (1990). *Literature: Reading fiction, poetry, drama, and the essay.* New York: McGraw-Hill.

Dyer, P. (2002). A box full of feelings: Emotional literacy in a nursery class. In C. Nutbrown (Ed.), *Research studies in early childhood education* (pp. 67-76). Stoke-on-Trent, UK: Trentham.

Filippini, T., & Vecchi, V. (Eds.) (2000). *The hundred languages of children: Exhibition catalogue.* Reggio Emilia, IT: Reggio Children.

Geertz. C. (1973). *The interpretation of cultures.* New York: Basic Books.

Gregory, E. (2001). Sisters and brothers as language and literacy teachers: Synergy between siblings playing and working together. *Journal of Early Childhood Literacy, 1*(3), 301-322.

Harste, J. C., Woodward, V. A., & Burke, C. L. (1984). *Language stories and literacy lessons.* Portsmouth, NH: Heinemann.

Holland, D., Lachicotte, W., Skinner, D., & Cain, C. (1998). *Identity and agency in cultural worlds.* Cambridge, MA: Harvard University Press.

Iser, W. (1989). *Prospecting: From reader response to literary anthropology.* Baltimore, MD: Johns Hopkins University Press.

Kanno, Y., & Norton, B. (2003). Imagined communities and educational possibilities: Introduction. *Journal of Language, Identity, and Education 2*(4), 241-249.

Kendrick, M. (2003). *Converging worlds: Play, literacy, and culture in early childhood.* Bern, CH: Peter Lang.

Kendrick, M. (2005). "Let's play teacher": A child's perceptions of school literacy. *Scientia Paedagogica Experimentalis, XLI.2,* 175–190.

Kress, G. (1997). *Before writing: Rethinking the paths to literacy.* London: Routledge.

Kress, G., & Jewitt, C. (2003). Introduction. In C. Jewitt & G. Kress (Eds.), *Multimodal literacy* (pp. 1-18). New York: Peter Lang.

Lawrence-Lightfoot, S. (1997). Illumination: Navigating intimacy. In S. Lawrence-Lightfoot & J. H. Davis (Eds.), *The art and science of portraiture* (pp. 135-182). San Francisco, CA: Jossey-Bass.

Lévi-Strauss, C. (1969). *The elementary structures of kinship.* Boston, MA: Beacon Press.

Moll, L., Amanti, C., Neff, D., & Gonzalez, N. (1992). Funds of knowledge for teaching: Using a qualitative approach to connect homes and classrooms. *Theory Into Practice, 31*(2), 132-138.

Norton, B. (2000). *Identity and language learning: Gender, ethnicity, and educational change.* London: Pearson Education.

Nutbrown, C., & Hannon, P. (2003). Children's perspectives on family literacy: Methodological issues, findings and implications for practice. Journal of *Early Childhood Literacy, 3*(2), 115-145.

Rinaldi, C. (2006). *In dialogue with Reggio Emilia: Listening, researching and learning.* London: Routledge.

Schwartzman, H. (1976). Children's play: A sideways glance at make-believe. In D. F. Lancy & B. A. Tindall (Eds.), *The study of play: Problems and prospects* (pp. 208-215). New York: Leisure Press.

Taylor, D., & Dorsey-Gaines, C. (1988). *Growing up literate: Learning from inner-city families.* Portsmouth, NH: Heinemann.

Vygotsky, L. (1978). *Mind in society: The development of higher psychological processes.* Cambridge, MA: Harvard University Press.

Vygotsky, L. S. (1986). *Thought and Language.* Cambridge, MA: MIT Press.

Welty, E. (1983). *One writer's beginnings.* Cambridge, MA: Harvard University Press.

9

We are Here for just a Brief Time:
Death, Dying, and Constructions of Children in Intergenerational Learning Programs
Rachel Heydon

The intergenerational art class is now over. The supplies are packed away and all the children and adult participants have left, yet Julia remains.[1] Well into her eighth decade, Julia sits in her shorts with snow falling behind her outside the window. Always an active person, Julia prefers shorts even in cold weather as they allow her, as she's explained to me, to be unencumbered. One of her daily rituals involves moving, these days with more difficulty than she'd like, around the grounds of the retirement home where she can access a playground belonging to the child care centre that is located in the basement of the home. On these walks Julia's able to observe and talk with the children who share art class with her every Thursday. I've witnessed the children on the playground spot Julia in the cold weather in her shorts, and children like Ethan (four years old) and Amber (five years old) have triumphantly cried her name as they smiled big, excited grins then giggled at her bare legs while comparing them to their own covered ones.

On this particular Thursday, in the wake of art class, Julia looks at a line drawing she's just finished, and she begins to explain it. Pointing to the small smiling faces that she's tucked into corners throughout her drawing, Julia names them her "voices" and says,

> These are the voices from my past and those of the children who call to me from the play area. I am very aware of how limited our time is and how we are connected to the past and to the future. These are the voices that surround me and remind me that we are here for just a brief time.

Shortly after the above exchange, Julia did not arrive with the others for art class, and the children repeatedly asked where she was. As Julia had been ill, some of the adults wondered if today was the day that Julia would finally not make it to class. Then, relief: Greeted with smiles all around, Julia entered the room, took her seat, and joined in the art making.

Whenever I have been a witness to young and old coming together for learning – formally, as in the case of intergenerational art class or informally, such as when I learned at my grandmother's knee – I have been reminded of the Japanese aesthetic of *mono no aware*. Introduced by eighteenth century Japanese scholar Motoori Norinaga, *mono no aware* has been translated as "the sorrow of human existence" and as "a sensitivity to things" (Keene, 1988, p. 86), meaning an apprehension of "the simultaneous existence of beauty and sadness in life" (Dodson, 1993, p. 2). This sensitivity "usually takes the form of realizing the transience of something beautiful" or responding to "the beauty of forms" that are "poised on the brink of dissolution" (Berry as cited in Dodson, 1993, p. 3). The cherry blossom is the quintessential motif of mono no aware.

While *mono no aware* is indeed a very Japanese aesthetic, it is not "uniquely a Japanese sensibility" (Hirakawa, 2005, p. 496) as many cultures have ways of describing the poignancy of the transient or the impermanent. Perhaps this is why I am so struck by the aesthetic of intergenerational learning programs and why I am now turning to wonder of the place of death and dying – as elements of life – within their curricula.

This chapter is based on one element of an ongoing study of intergenerational (IG) shared site learning programs (where child- and elder-care share facilities and programming), hereafter referred to as the study. The objectives of the study, which began in 2004, were to understand critically how forms of curricula, as value-laden entities, are constructed and implemented in such programs. Moreover, the study sought to address the programs relationship to participants' learning opportunities, to the participants' interactions with each other, and to the structure of the social categories they occupy (e.g., childhood and old age). As I have reported elsewhere (Heydon, 2005, 2007, 2008a), I have found that IG art programs in particular have been a vehicle to helping de-pathologize old-age, disability, and childhood and have created opportunities for participants to expand their communication options and identities as capable communicators. I have argued that such opportunities are particularly needed for young children in contemporary times as education has become so closely equated with preparation for the workforce and early childhood education has been specifically targeted as a time to *inoculate* (Stooke, 2004) children against disability through instrumental curriculum that is focused on readiness (Heydon & Wang, 2006). Now I would like to draw on the study's data to explore one area of said programming that is perhaps of import but is rarely represented in the literature: death and dying.

Context of Intergenerational Learning and the Theoretical Framework of the Study

Current Canadian demographic and social trends express the need for innovative ways of educating people who are young and old. In Canada, the proportion of elders will likely greatly increase over the "next four decades" (Spiezia, 2002, p. 109) raising demand for retirement and nursing homes where isolation and depression are common (Kastner, 2004). Simultaneously, a growing number of children require out-of-home care during a very important point in their development (McCain & Mustard, 1999). These trends for elders and children are accompanied by social adjustments such as geographical dispersal that have weakened IG contact (Conyers,

1996). IG shared site learning programs address these needs by building on elders and children as resources. Elders, for instance, can be considered as resources as, overall, they are said to be more educated (LaPorte, 2000) and healthier (Thompson & Wilson, 2001) than ever before. Thus, while improving their own learning, elders may be nurturers of children (Henkin & Kingson, 1999). This notion of older adults educating the young and improving society "through the next generation" (McAdams & de St. Aubin, 1998, p. xx) is at the heart of much IG research and programming. IG learning also recognizes that children have much to offer each other and adults. In the study, for example, children were observed to draw out, motivate, help with idea formation, and give a sense of purpose to the elders with whom they were learning (Heydon, 2005, 2007).

IG learning is studied by a number of fields including gerontology, psychology, education, and other human development specialties (Larkin & Newman, 1997). The many benefits of IG learning programs have been identified in these literatures: Participants, for example, have been reported as experiencing an "increase in self-esteem and usefulness", feeling a "sense of continuity" in their lives, and having opportunities to recognize "lifelong learning at every stage of development" (Brummel, 1989, p. 124). These programs also create possibilities for "understanding" between the generations (p. 124), while fostering acceptance that "aging is a normal and natural part of the life cycle" (Kaplan et al., 2003, p. 5).

Regarding trends in IG research, in recent years research has turned to considering best practices, including ensuring that programming "build[s] on respective strengths" (Kaplan, et al., 2003, p. 7), allows participants consistent contact to foster "meaningful relationships" (Griff, Lambert, Fruit, & Dellman-Jenkins, 1996, p. 5), and is "evaluated cyclically" (Cox, Croxford, & Edmonds, 2006, p. 19). Most of this research draws on developmental theories (most notably that of Erik Erikson) (VanderVen, 1999) and supports evaluation of programming based on instrumentalist theories (Hayes, 2003; Kuehne & Kaplan, 2001) whose goals are to achieve a degree of prediction and control (Habermas, 1972). Undoubtedly this research has been a vehicle to significant IG learning programming, yet its trends can also lead to the danger of naïve pragmatism (Skrtic, 1995), which involves a focus on identifying de-contextualized and generalizable best methods in an attempt to control and predict the outcomes of programming. This can result in too little attention being given to the theoretical or ideological underpinnings of programming or to the effects of programming that are not easily measured or controlled. A gentle corrective to this situation could be for fields that have not traditionally been part of IG learning programs to enter the IG learning conversation and for them to question IG learning phenomena in new ways.

The study is located at the interstices between the fields of IG learning, curriculum studies, and childhood studies and employs a critical theoretical framework with its goal of emancipation (Habermas, 1972). Curriculum studies, in part, considers the answers to the following teaching and learning questions: *What* should be taught? *To whom* should it be taught? *When* should it be taught? *By whom* should it be taught? *How* should it be taught? And *why* should it be taught? (Egan, 1978). Critically investigating these questions is important, and my work with Wang (Heydon & Wang, 2006) and Iannacci (Heydon & Iannacci, 2005) has shown that forms of curriculum can affect people's identity options, quality of life, learning opportunities, and interactions. Significantly, curriculum must be considered at the levels of what is planned to be taught (the *intended curriculum*) and how the curriculum is actually "played out" (the *operational curriculum*) (Eisner, 2005, p. 147). One need also consider the *null curriculum* (Eisner, 2002) where the very absence of teaching something has an effect.

Childhood studies is another interdisciplinary field that "can contribute to an emergent paradigm wherein new ways of looking at children can be researched and theorized" (Kehily, 2004, p. 1). The critical theorizing from childhood studies that undergirds the study is helpful to understanding how children become positioned by curriculum and the adults who create it. The study has already shown, for example, how the curriculum of one IG art program positioned children in "asset-oriented" terms so that their strengths, knowledge, values, and skills were highlighted (Heydon, 2008a).

Why a Focus on Death & Dying?

One of the cornerstones of IG learning curricula is the need to teach children about aging (Basman, et al., n.d.; Lyons, Newman, & Vasudev, 1984; Newman, 1985). There is very little mention, however, of *how* or even *if* such curricula should approach the topic of death and dying. In a literature review of death and dying and IG learning curricula, research assistant, Wendy Crocker and I were only able to find cursory mention of the topic. Hawkins & McGuire (1999) referred to the need to educate adolescent participants on "dealing with loss and grief" (p. 24), though Seefelt (1989) found "lessons on death and dying designed to change adolescents' attitudes toward older adults did not appear to be effective" (p. 190). Nothing was mentioned in these publications about the topic and young children. As for young children, McDuffie (1989) in a one page entry in an IG handbook entitled "What if Someone Dies?" recommended that when talking to children about death and dying one should not use theology, religion, or euphemisms. She then suggested some children's literature on the topic. Nothing was mentioned beyond this, including how to frame the literature. In the same handbook, Cook (1989) addressed the question of whether young children should be shielded from knowledge about death. Again, in just a one page entry, she surmised that children should be given some facts about death within their developmental level "since death is a part of life . . . [and] it may actually be easier for a child to first learn about [death] during an IG visit than to suddenly be faced with the loss of a close loved one" (p. 25). What these facts were, however, was not included. Baring any sustained or in-depth discussion of children and death and dying in IG curricula, there was some scant discussion in an IG guidebook by one of the leaders in the field. This was perhaps the most substantive statement on the topic we could find:

> Don't worry about sparking children's questions on the topic of illness or death, because at the preschool age, their interest is typically matter-of-fact and not fraught with emotional distress. They are curious and the images that surround them on a daily basis should reflect the outside world as realistically as possible so that they can ask questions and become comfortable with individuals who are physically different than themselves. (Kaplan et al., 2003, p. 20)

In another literature review focusing on curriculum on death and dying for young children in general, Wendy and I noticed that sparse attention was given to the subject from the field of education with most authors and publications being from health-related disciplines (for example, nursing and medicine) (see Cole, 2001; MacGregor, 2007; Zolten & Long, 2006). Additionally, the bulk of attention to the topic happened at least twenty years ago (see Childs & Wimmer, 1971; Hare & Cunningham, 1988; Hare, Sugawara, & Pratt, 1986; Moseley, 1976; Ryerson, 1977). Given the gap in the literature and that IG programming happens with elders who are often at the ends of their lives, revisiting the study's data to consider death and dying in IG curricula seemed necessary.

Methodology

Research Questions

The questions that inform the current analysis of the study data are: 1) In what ways (if any) did the intended curriculum of the IG programs represent or deal with death and dying? 2) In what ways (if any) did issues related to death and dying enter the operational curriculum? 3) How do the findings relate to the children's learning opportunities, opportunities for interaction with the elders, and in the ways in which they were positioned?

Method

Using a critical ethnographic methodology (see Carspecken, 1995, 2001), the study was carried out in three IG shared site programs. Sites were chosen for their demographic, curricular, and programmatic diversity. Site Blessed Mother, located in the Pacific Northwest of the United States, offered retirement and assisted living to elders as well as child care to children from six weeks to five years of age. This Catholic IG shared site was over twelve years old and featured numerous opportunities for IG learning and informal IG interaction as the entire building was created with IG programming in mind. As such the child care areas were integrated throughout the building, even in the adults' living areas. Both the child and elder care were run by the same organization. The study focused on the art class in this program, and data were collected from 2004 to 2006. An adults-only art class was also studied at Blessed Mother to act as a comparison. Site Watersberg, located in southwestern Ontario, was a nondenominational, privately run, for-profit assisted living facility for elders that rented space to a private, nonprofit child care organization. The shared site was less than five years old and the building was created with IG programming in mind. Adults and children participated in preplanned IG learning activities, and there was some opportunity for adults to visit the child care centre unannounced. Data were collected here in 2005. Site Picasso, located in a different southwestern Ontario city, was also a nondenominational, privately run, for-profit assisted living facility for elders that rented space to a private, nonprofit child care organization. This site as well offered retirement apartments. Prior to the research, very little IG contact occurred at Picasso, and there was no IG learning programming. In 2006, Picasso consented to having the researchers help them create an IG art program. Data collection here has been ongoing since 2006. All three sites employed early childhood educators (ECEs) who were responsible for the children and recreation therapists (RTs) or the equivalent who were responsible for the adults. There were also administrators responsible for each of these branches of programming. In addition, Blessed Mother employed an art teacher, and for the first year of the study at Picasso, a research assistant taught the art class with an ECE and RT. Table 1 shows the breakdown of participants in the three sites.

Data include videotapes and/or audiotapes of participants during the normal course of their programs; audiotapes of interviews with participants directly before, during, and after programs and interviews of select adult participants and staff; photographs of artifacts from programs; field notes of observa-

Table 1

# of Participants	Blessed Mother	Watersberg	Picasso
Children (ages 3-5 years)	25	37	24
Elders	16 + 10 adults only class	32	40
ECEs	2	7	2
RTs	4	5	3
Administrators	2	2	2
Other	1 IG art teacher, 2 volunteers	n/a	1 family member of adult participant

tions; and any print material including curriculum documents pertaining to the programs. The study focused on the IG curriculum and any related curriculum that pertained specifically to the children. Data were analyzed according to a modified constant comparative method (Handsfield, 2006) that sought to answer the research questions and promote the study's trustworthiness. Data were coded according to predictive themes and pattern-matched. To retain the complexity of the data, data that fit between themes did not automatically discredit themes but rather were included and the discontinuities were presented.

Results

The Intended and Operational Curricula

The intended IG learning curricula in the three sites were developed by various parties. Generally, at Blessed Mother, the ECEs were responsible for the curriculum with the exception of art class which was taught by the art teacher. RTs and ECEs were expected to assist during class. At Watersberg and Picasso, ECEs and RTs shared the development and implementation of IG curricula. The intended curricula of the programs in all three sites did not deal in any way with death and dying. These topics, however, did enter the operational curricula through adult participants dying, the ways the institutions dealt with the deaths, and by faculty and elders' own thoughts, feelings, and sense of preparedness for the topic.

There were elders in all three sites who did die. The greatest number of deaths occurred at Blessed Mother with 8 participating elders deceased by the second year of the study. Only this site told the children when an elder died, though there was no consistent protocol. Gary, an ECE, explained what happened when two residents died and the deaths were included in the building's general morning announcements over the loudspeaker.

> This week, eight o'clock [a.m.], we're starting breakfast . . . and they start the prayers, which is fine, you know, but they get into this we need to pray for two residents who just died. And that's great. Kids need to know about death, but now on the breakfast conversation table one kid says, "They died. Did you hear

that? They died. Oh, no!" when they heard the persons' names. Now, what if it was like Frieda [a favorite adult participant] or someone really dear to us. And that was the first thing they heard? Not through us or a parent or someone telling them through compassion. What if we are sitting and all of a sudden, "We are going to pray for Frieda who just died"? So I went to Jane [the ECE Director] and Sister Mary and Sister is touchy because she's a nun and was in that broadcasting. And I'm sitting with Sister and telling Jane the story. And Sister hadn't heard the story yet, and I'm telling Jane. The first thing, Jane is like laughing, thinking, "Oh, that's funny", and Sister's like, "Oh, that's OK. Kids need to know about death." You're right, Sister they do need to know. Now, Jane help me here. Stop your laughing, 'cause you think you put me in a funny situation for the moment. Kids need to learn things, but in the proper way and time. And I was trying to ask Jane, could you please talk to that person who does the announcements, and please ask them to use a word like deceased, passed, something to where if I choose to explain a situation it'll be my choice at that time in the morning. And I can't tell the [institution] you have to do this, but it'll sure help me as an educator if they could use a different word. If the kids are smart enough to figure it out – great. But just that they [on the loudspeaker] scream "DIED"!

The inclusion of the children in this announcement did not appear to have forethought, and it did not spark any change in the intended curriculum. The data from Blessed Mother do not include any further announcements of this kind, and in fact, volunteers, ECEs, and the art teacher all complained later that they frequently did not hear of elders' deaths until well after the fact.

The lack of a plan for how to proceed with the children following a death was echoed in Jane's telling of the announcement story which she raised when I asked her about the professional development she felt the ECEs needed in order to do a good job in IG programming. Note that in Jane's response, she signals to there being great emotion around the topic.

I honestly don't have a real good view of what [PD for teaching IG] might look like, 'cause I have some ideas of some things, but I don't know if that's really the stuff that people want. Can I just do a little [illustration] of that? . . . I have a new PA speaker right outside the office, and . . . we've been complaining about not having it for about a year and a half, and by golly, they've fixed it. Now, at 8 'o'clock in the morning and at 5 o'clock in the afternoon there's a prayer, which is fine, but Gary, who's in the classroom right next to me was so upset last night with me and the new speaker, because, he says, 'Now, while I'm sitting here having breakfast,' he said, 'I don't mind the prayer. What I mind is when the Sister who's giving the prayer says, "It's time for us to pray for the two residents who died last night." And he doesn't want to have to talk about that over breakfast. That was upsetting to him. And I was kind of laughing at him a little bit about it, 'cause [of] the intensity. But I understand that he wasn't prepared for that to happen, and that maybe he could be prepared better, I guess is why I thought of that story in relationship to your question. That's the sort of topic that, now that we have a speaker, is going to come up much more often as kids hear the word, and they know [what] the word *died* means in preschool, and then they want a teacher who can just have a conversation with them about that.

Despite Jane's observation that the ECEs could benefit from professional development on the topic of death and dying, none of the sites in the study offered any. Staff, faculty, and administrators at all three sites remarked that because IG programming was relatively new in North America, they were the ones who were usually asked to in-service other educators: A job a number of them expressed they did not feel prepared for.

Further to the theme of preparedness was Gary's response to my question, "Have you as a staff talked about how to talk with kids about [death and dying] or when to do it?

Actually we haven't had that sit down conversation as a group [of ECEs] or anything. I've had it with Tammy, a teacher in my room, because she's had a couple of residents on her floor that she visits die, and the kids were close [to the residents], and they talked about it. So we do, but I don't think it's ever been as a group thing. I can't remember ever a group talk about it. But when we do [talk to the children about death and dying], we keep it simple as everything we try to do.

Jane and Gary, over the course of the study, also spoke about some reluctance on the part of many ECEs to fully engage with IG programming, an observation that I had also made at Picasso. Following one of our conversations where death and dying emerged, I tentatively forwarded a hypothesis about this reluctance to Jane which suggested that the null curriculum affected the operational curriculum:

> The more interaction you have, the more questions will emerge, and the more minimal that conversation, the more sanitized everything can be. So that may explain some of the reluctance, even, to enter into those stronger relationships with the other parts of the building [i.e., where young and old meet]. . . . today during class, one of the residents was, she's been ill, and she really had a strong coughing spell . . . And again, I can see how those kinds of issues are things that people, need to be prepared for. But in terms of . . . facilitating [IG] interaction, I have noticed also that there are some [ECEs and recreation therapists] who may be not quite as comfortable moving between the two populations and focused on just the one that they feel responsible for. And sometimes when that happened, we ended up with . . . what looks like what I might call parallel play.

In response, Jane smiled sadly, shook her head and said, "And never the two shall meet. Yes."

RTs at all three sites did talk about not being trained to work specifically with children which could, at least in part, account for the "parallel play" (that is, the sense that people were working *beside* each other but not *together*). Some data, however, point to ECEs fear also potentially being a factor in the ways they operationalized curricula. At Picasso, ECEs Pam and Sandra, in a year and a year and a half of observation respectively, were never seen to initiate conversation or touch an elder during IG art class, and the study documented at length Gary's struggles to become comfortable around elders given his own fears of death and dying in his personal battle with cancer (Heydon, 2005). Despite talking of himself as finally finding a level of comfort with elders, when I asked, "You had spoken in these interviews of being a little apprehensive at first of working with the residents, and then you became more comfortable. And I wondered what you thought made you more comfortable and did your illness affect your perception of your job?" Gary raised a recent incident during an IG activity where he clearly equated elders with death. He explained that his group of children was giving a performance in chapel, and he was crouching behind some pews directing the children:

> I wanted the kids to see me . . . so I could go, "Louder! Louder!" and I'm lying there and all of a sudden this pressure is hitting my spot where I got my radiation [a cancer treatment] . . . I don't want to move around to sit up, because I'm blocking up the aisle. I'm going wow, what's that? I'm torturing myself just lying [there]. I feel my brain start pulsing. I'm like, no, I don't want to be caught dead here with the kids like a resident. I better get up.

The suggestion that one's comfort with a population affected the IG operational curriculum is also something that was hinted at in the example of art class volunteer, Marianne. While Marianne was observed to frequently facilitate IG interaction, she was also recorded as paying particular attention to the elders. She explained this behavior in an interview saying that she often focused on the adults as they were not ECEs first choice of people to work with given that they were often sick and not "cute." Yet Marianne's support of the elders seemed also to support the children. During one art class, Frieda, an elder the children knew well, who had been having breathing problems, had a coughing spell while she was completing an artpiece with two children. Already carting around an oxygen tank with a tube in her nose, this coughing could have been scary for the children (as well as for Frieda); yet during the attack Marianne calmly stroked Frieda's back and spoke to her softly about the artwork. In the presence of Marianne's calm demeanor, the children stood by Frieda's side and when the attack subsided, the team went back to their collective work.

The faculty's perceptions also seemed to affect the intended and operational curricula in other ways. For instance, despite Jane's reference to the need for professional development related to death and dying, there were many inconsistencies in the data about whether faculty, staff, and administration thought there was a need for the topic to enter the intended curriculum. Jane, for instance, talked about how there was perhaps no need to educate children about death and dying, because they did not "really" bond with the residents anyway. Talking about her IG program and the difference between expectations and "reality", she said,

> It seems like a really warm, fuzzy environment, and [ECEs] might feel disappointed sometimes . . . people think every child that comes through this program is going to meet somebody they connect with and love and you'll want to adopt for life, and it isn't going to happen that way, but sometimes it does. And when it does, it's really wonderful. But I'll say in the thirteen years, I can count on one hand the number of individuals that just moved in with us, adopted the kids, kids have loved to see, when that person passed on many people came to their service because they were so much a part of us. So it's not even one a year . . . But on the other hand, on a day-to-day basis, you see many lovely little things happen between residents and kids, and you see a kids' development . . . when they can spontaneously say, "I'll get this for you," or "Let me pick that up and hand it to you," or "I hear somebody's sad. Let's go see what's wrong." Those kinds of things are just a joy.

Wondering if the perceived lack of a number of strong connections between children and elders was reason to negate death and dying in the curriculum, I asked, "You were saying before about that those incredible attachments only happen every now and again, but what do you have to build in, in terms of the death and dying aspects?" Jane replied,

> That . . . is maybe less than you think it might be. . . . Kids will change groups, maybe every year or every

other year. Residents turn over fairly fast. The average age here is about 87, if you can believe it. So only occasionally have we really had that sort of discussion where we talked about a resident [dying] with a group of kids. And a lot of [the children's] families came to say goodbye to that person when they passed away.... More often than that, a person declines and withdraws from us and our kids grow older and they leave before that person passes away. Does that make any sense? It just doesn't happen that often as even I thought it would when I first started here.

Also at Blessed Mother, RT Anna seemed to support Jane's view. When I asked her, "What happens when a resident dies?" she answered, "I haven't really had the chance or observed anything happening with that. I mean a lot of my residents die but none of them have ... I don't think the children were that bonded to certain people who have died." "So they don't notice when residents are gone?" I wondered to Anna, to which she replied,

I've never observed it, but I have heard someone else say that it was hard 'cause there was one particular lady who just loved kids. So when she was gone there's been people who experienced that, but no, no one has passed away that's been really close to the kids that I've noticed. . . . I do think one thing to work on is maybe to find out how to bond more, . . . But it's really amazing how fast the time goes and how short a school year is. I mean they just start coming and it really is hard to find, to get that bond going. Like even our weekly group, it just seems like at the end of the year, it's just when your kids start to make headway and getting to know that particular group [then it's over] . . . . [We do have] babies up to preschool, but the groups all move around. . . . I think for most of the residents they don't remember. They can't remember well enough to know . . . it's great for them [the kids and adults], and they enjoy it, but they can't exactly remember a certain person and know that that's the same person every week.

Anna then said something somewhat incongruous. When I asked if the children knew the elders' names, she emphatically announced, "They do. They do. They have good memories. They don't remember everyone, but most of the people that come a lot they know. They know that that's Jennifer and that's Barbara."

The idea that children did know the elders was substantiated by the study's documentation of some very rich interaction, particularly during art classes (Heydon, 2005; Heydon, 2007; Heydon, 2008b). Consequently, there are data that support the notion that children and adult participants formed relationships that appeared to hold meaning for them, rendering the death of the elders potentially significant or at least noticeable to the children. For instance, staff and faculty, in particular, talked about key adults with whom classes of children formed a bond. In Watersberg, Maureen, a recreation therapist, replied as follows when I asked if she had seen the children get to know the adults well: "I do 'cause I work on the second floor and a lot of them get to know grandma Jaqui.[2] And [the children] ask about her if she's not there . . . so they really do get connected." Grandma Jaqui attended as many IG programs as possible, and the children were seen to hug, kiss, and greet her at her every arrival and departure. Additionally, the observational data are replete with examples of relationships being built between participants at Blessed Mother and Picasso. Participants showed pleasure in seeing each other by giving each other big smiles, saving seats for each other, being disappointed when someone was absent, and chiming out each others' names during the prelude to classes. In the art classes at Picasso, we also observed children and adult participants influencing the images that each made. One such instance involved elder Beatrice and a child participant, and this was a catalyst for death to enter the operational curriculum. Unprompted by anyone other than each other, the participants together chose to depict rabbits during a lesson on texture. Sadly, Beatrice died later that spring before she could see her artwork displayed in the annual art show alongside her friend's. After we packed up Beatrice's piece and sent it to her daughter in another province, her daughter contacted us to say,

> It is . . . very sweet to know about the companion rabbit piece that was made in response to my mom's

image ... it seems comforting, now that she has passed away, to think of the idea of a companion for her! ... My mom used to call the six of us ... her "little bunnies" right up until her passing so it is rather ironic to hear that her last piece was called the Rabbit! ... I was also born on the first day of spring and always felt it was a special time. The day of my mom's funeral, I walked by myself from the funeral home to the reception to just enjoy the sunshine. I realized that all the blossoms were in full bloom ... not a petal had yet fallen .... I felt it was significant that my mom would choose this to be the time to depart.

The staff and faculty did not explicitly refer to Beatrice's death in front of the children. Her rabbit hung beside its companion at the artshow, yet Beatrice's real life child companion stood in front of the artwork by herself with no explanation.

Thus in all circumstances the intended curriculum omitted death and dying, and there was discomfort on the parts of ECEs when the topic entered the operational curriculum. The only exception to the above was one instance in the data that occurred at Watersberg. In an interview, ECE Amelia, talked about her contact with elders and how this affected her personally and professionally. She talked about this in relation to the elders being close to the ends of their lives:

[IG programs have] enhanced my own philosophy about [early childhood education], about bridging that gap between the seniors and the children, 'cause as an adult, we forget that oh yeah, we will get to be that age one time and what we are going to have to look forward to ... seeing how they light up with the kids ... when I get to be eighty or ninety and I can't stay at home anymore, I would love to be at a place like this where I can see children and youth ... see them growing up again, and going okay, there is our future after I'm gone ... for me, it's sort of sentimental too, just to see my uncle ... having him pass, and then going oh well, I can see the benefit from having these children with the seniors – they make them happy. Like, we'll go and deliver papers in the morning and we'll see a few of the grandparents and the kids will be like, "Hi grandpa." They'll sing a song in the dining room in the morning or they'll go in and they'll say, "Hi, have a good day," "How are you?" and you can just see the smiles light up in the seniors' faces first thing in the morning.

I later learned the following about Amelia's group of children from RT Maureen:

A couple of months ago, we had a resident that passed away, and the daycare actually went into the room, the resident's room while she was in bed. She was palliative; they went in to visit her. She only, I think she only lived two days after that. So they [did] build a relationship with her. . . . They went in knowing she was sick.

Watersberg officially followed an emergent curriculum design where any intended curriculum stemmed from what ECEs perceived as emerging from the children's lives and interests. The data do not suggest that the visit to the dying woman was a planned lesson in death and dying, but more of a chance situation as the children daily walked through where the adults lived delivering newspapers and greeting everyone they met. The woman was dying, and the ECEs did not see this as a reason to stop delivering a paper to her. There was no formal lesson or debriefing, however, on death or dying after the woman's death.

Finally, it bears mentioning that the data suggest at least some of the elders thought about death and dying and this may have had an influence on the operational curriculum. Specifically, only one participant at Blessed Mother in the adults-only art class also attended the IG art class. When I asked the adults-only class participants why they did not attend the IG class, elders who the data said liked children, stated things like, "It doesn't fit my schedule." When elder Irene said this, I thought it seemed like an excuse as it was not necessarily true. She then began to speak of her cancer and how it would finally "get her," and she initiated a whole class discussion on death. In this discussion, she said, "They [Blessed Mother] never want you to know who's died. When I die I want them to send out the trumpets so everyone knows. I want to go out with the trumpets!" After this, in reference to the IG class, Irene looked sad and said, "Some children think we're monsters." The data are very complicated in this area. It appeared that Irene, who made me pause every day when I would wheel her back to her room so that she could watch the children play, counted herself out of IG programming. She did not want to scare the children, and she herself was scared and uncomfortable being so close to death. The environment that kept death a secret did not seem to help. Sadly, when Irene died, I learned that her death had not been announced, and there had been no service at Blessed Mother. I was told this was because Irene was a "private person" and she would not have wanted anything broadcast.

Discussion and Recommendations

One cannot help but be touched by the moments in the data: Beatrice's child companion standing alone beside their rabbits at the spring artshow, and Irene who loved children but stayed away from them for fear they would find her a monster. The sadness of these events is countered in intensity only by the extreme beauty and hopefulness of the juxtaposition of youth and old age, life and death in the day-to-day encounters of the children and elders in the IG learning programs. This is the aesthetic of *mono no aware* (sensitivity to the transience of life and youth) that punctuates ECE Amelia's description of her IG learning program. And in the face of all of this, questions resound about the place of death and dying in IG learning curricula. In this chapter, I have asked about death and dying and the intended and operational curricula and how the findings to these questions relate to the children's learning opportunities, opportunities for interaction with elders and the ways in which the children were positioned.

The data are clear that the intended curricula did not deal with death and dying, though it entered the operational curricula. Children were sometimes positioned by adults and the curricula as not bonding with elders and not noticing when elders were absent. If one were to use the same scenarios and replace the children and elders with middle-aged adults, would the reading be the same? The data that demonstrate the links between the children and elders in the programs suggest that the children in the study were not given sufficient credit for being able to build relationships and recognize elders as individuals. The children were also generally constructed as being unable to understand or in need of protecting against troubling information such as death and dying. Elders themselves were even sometimes treated like this as in the case of there being inconsistent or no protocols for informing even them of the death of a peer. While it is outside the scope of the study to say how children deal with knowledge of death and precisely how they should be educated on the topic, it seems that the null curriculum did little to enhance learning opportunities or opportunities for interaction between the generations. Note, for instance, the hesitancy that arose for some ECEs in facilitating IG interaction or even participating in IG learning programs, because they were uncomfortable or afraid, the subsequent lost teachable moments such as when the announcement of the deaths of the elders went out over the loudspeaker, and the case of elders who had much to teach and give to children but stayed away because they did not feel comfortable with their own stage of life. It is thus safe to say that given the presence of death and dying in the operational curriculum, and the negative relationship its omission had to learning and interactional opportunities, death and dying must be part of the intended IG learning curricula.

Data suggest that the topic of death and dying and the reasons for its current treatment in IG curricula are very complex. Indeed the nature of the topic is difficult, particularly given that it is tied tightly to personal fears and belief systems and is perhaps one of the most intimate and important topics that exists yet also one that is somewhat "taboo" (Northcott & Wilson, 2008, p. 20). Consequently, any response to how death and dying should be treated in IG learning programs must itself account for this complexity. The study implies that for any treatment of death and dying in IG curriculum to be helpful vis-à-vis learning and interactional opportunities, the following must at least be addressed: 1) ECEs must recognize how they and the curriculum position children including how they reckon with children's ability to deal with troubling information, and the relationship children have with elders; 2) ECEs must also recognize their own feelings toward death and dying and elders; 3) there must be a comprehensive curricular plan in place for educating children on the topic before elders die, during their dying, and after they have died; 4) all parties involved in IG learning programs must be part of this education and the culture of the institution must support open dialogue on the topic; and 5) there is a need for current and interdisciplinary studies into educating children about death and dying, including studies that consider the socio-cultural contexts of learning about death and dying. Knowledge and subsequent curricular programming will be richer if the socio-cultural contexts of learning about death and dying are complemented by the literature in the area from health professions. Finally, the aesthetic of *mono no aware* might be a way for people working within IG programming to frame the experience, thus allowing all involved to be sensitive to the beauty of the juxtaposition of young and old rather than allowing fears of death to adversely interfere with learning and interaction.

Significance of the Study

While this chapter has obvious significance to the field of IG learning, its focus on the relationship between intended and operational curricula and their corresponding effect on the learning opportunities and positioning of children has implications for all curriculum developed for young children. The study builds on and contributes to research literature in the fields of IG learning, curriculum studies, and childhood studies and is amongst the first studies to employ a critical analytic framework to promote understanding of the theoretical and ideological underpinnings of IG curricula. It is also among the first to consider the place of death and dying in IG learning curriculum and, even more general, early childhood curriculum. The study offers the IG research and early childhood education communities a theoretical alternative for understanding curriculum and programming than that which is currently dominant. It also complements studies that track conceptions of childhood and the ways in which people in this social category are constructed and deconstructed. My hope is that these understandings can be used to ameliorate IG and general early childhood education programming to benefit its participants.

References

Basman, S., Blackman, B., Botticella, M., Coelho, E., Daly, L. A., Liss, J., et al. (n.d.). *Young and old together: A resource manual for developing intergenerational programs.* Toronto: The Ministry of Community and social Services of Ontario.

Brummel, S. W. (1989). Developing an intergenerational program. *Journal of Children in Contemporary Society, 20*(3-4), 119-133.

Carspecken, P. F. (1995). Critical ethnography in educational research: A theoretical and practical guide. New York: Routledge.

Carspecken, P. F. (2001). Critical ethnographies from Houston: Distinctive features and directions. In P. F. Carspecken & G. Walford (Eds.), *Critical ethnography and education* (pp. 1-26). Kidlington, UK: Elsevier Science.

Childs, P. & Wimmer, M. (1971). The concept of death in early childhood. *Child Development, 42*(14), 1293-1301.

Cole, B. V. (2001). Helping children understand death. *Journal of Child and Adolescent Psychiatric Nursing, 14*(1), 5-7.

Conyers, J. G. (1996). Building bridges between generations. *Educational Leadership, 53*(7), 14-16.

Cook, J. (1989). Should young children be shielded from knowledge of death? In W. McDuffie & J. Whiteman (Eds.), *The intergenerational activities program handbook* (3rd ed.) (p. 25). Binghamton, NY: Broome County Development Council.

Cox, R., Croxford, A., & Edmonds, D. (2006). *Connecting generations tool kit: Best practices in intergenerational programming.* Toronto: United Generations Ontario.

Dodson, C. B. (1993, April). *Genji, Keats, and "mono no aware".* Paper presented at the annual meeting of the College English Association, Overland Park, KS.

Egan, K. (2003). Retrospective on "what is curriculum?" *Journal of the Canadian Association for Curriculum Studies, 1*(1), 17-24.

Eisner, E. W. (2002). *The educational imagination: On the design and evaluation of school programs* (3rd ed.). Upper Saddle River, NJ: Prentice Hall.

Eisner, E. W. (2005). *Reimagining schools: The selected works of Elliot Eisner.* London: RoutledgeFalmer.

Griff, M. D., Lambert, D., Fruit, D., & Dellman-Jenkins, M. (1996). *LinkAges: Planning an intergenerational program for preschool.* Menlo Park, CA: Addison-Wesley.

Habermas, J. (1972). *Knowledge and human interests.* (J. J. Shapiro, Trans.). Boston, MA: Beacon Press.

Handsfield, L. (2006). Being and becoming American: Triangulating habitus, field, and literacy instruction in a multilingual classroom. *Language & Literacy, 8*(2). Retrieved January 22, 2009 from http://www.langandlit.ualberta.ca/current.html

Hare, J. & Cunningham, B. (1988). Effects of a child bereavement training program for teachers. *Death Studies, 12*(4), 345-353.

Hare, J., Sugawara, A., & Pratt, C. (1986). The child in grief: Implications for teaching. *Early Childhood Development and Care, 25*(1), 43-56.

Hawkins, M. & McGuire, F. (1999). Exemplary intergenerational programs. In M. Hawkins, F. McGuire, & K. Backman (Eds.), *Preparing participants for intergenerational interaction: Training for success* (p. 11- 27). New York: The Haworth Press.

Hayes, C. L. (2003). An observational study in developing an intergenerational shared site program: Challenges and insights. *Journal of Intergenerational Relationships, 1*(1), 113-131.

Henkin, N., & Kingson, E. (1999). Advancing an intergenerational agenda for the twenty-first century. *Generations, 22*(4), 99-105.

Heydon, R. (2008a). *Communicating with a little help from friends: Intergenerational art class as radical, asset-oriented curriculum.* In R. Heydon & L. Iannacci, Early childhood curricula and the de-pathologizing of childhood (pp. 100- 129). Toronto: University of Toronto Press.

Heydon, R. (2008b). What should I draw? I'll draw you! Intergenerational art for intergenerational learning opportunities and interaction. *Young Children, 63*(3), 80-85.

Heydon, R. (2007). Making meaning together: Multimodal literacy learning opportunities in an intergenerational art program. *Journal of Curriculum Studies, 39*(1), 35-62.

Heydon, R. (2005). The de-pathologization of childhood, disability and aging in an intergenerational art class: Implications for educators. *Journal of Early Childhood Research, 3*(3), 243-268.

Heydon, R., & Iannacci, L. (2005). Biomedical literacy: Two curriculum teachers challenge the treatment of dis/ability in contemporary literacy educa-tion. *Language & Literacy, 7*(2). Retrieved January 7, 2009 from http://www.langandlit.ualberta.ca/archivesDate.html

Heydon, R., & Wang, P. (2006). Curricular ethics in early childhood education programming: A challenge to the Ontario kindergarten program. *McGill Journal of Education, 41*(1), 29-46.

Hirakawa, S. (2005). *Japan's love-hate relationship with the West.* Kent, UK: Global Oriental.

Kaplan, M., Duerr, L., Whitesell, W., Merchant, L., Davis, D., & Larkin, E. (2003). *Developing an intergenerational program in your early childhood care and edu-cation center: A guidebook for early childhood practitioners.* University Park, PA: Pennsylvania State University.

Kastner, J. (Director, Producer, Writer). (2004, September 15, 16 & 19). *Rage against the darkness: Aging: a Canadian snapshot* [Television broadcast]. Toronto: CBC.

Keene, D. (1988). *The pleasures of Japanese literature.* New York: Columbia University Press.

Kehily, M. J. (Ed.). (2004). *An introduction to childhood studies.* Maidenhead, UK: Open University Press.

Kuehne, V. A. & Kaplan, M. S. (2001). *Evaluation and research on intergenerational shared site facilities and programs: What we know and what we need to learn.* Generations United Background Paper: Project SHARE. Retrieved January 23, 2009 from http://intergenerational.cas.psu.edu/Docs/ResearchSharedSites.pdf

La Porte, A. M. (2000). Oral history as intergenerational dialogue in art education. *Art Education, 53*(4), 39-44.

Larkin, E., & Newman, S. (1997). Intergenerational studies: A multi-disciplinary field. In K. Brabazon & R. Disch (Eds.), *Intergenerational approaches in aging: Implications for education, policy and practice* (5-16). Binghamton, NY: Haworth Press.

Lyons, C., Newman, S., and Vasudev, J. (1984). The impact of a curriculum on aging on the elementary school students. *Gerontology and Geriatrics Education, 4*(4), 51-63.

MacGregor, C. (2007). Explaining death to your child. *Pediatrics for Parents, 23*(9), 17-20.

McAdams, D. P., & de St. Aubin, E. (1998). Introduction. In D. P. McAdams & E. De St. Aubin (Eds.), *Generativity and adult development: How and why we care for the next generation* (pp. xix-xxiv). Washington, DC: American Psychological Association.

McCain, M., & Mustard, F. (1999). *Reversing the real brain drain: The early years study.* Toronto: Ontario Children's Secretariat.

McDuffie, W. (1989). But what if someone dies? In W. McDuffie & J. Whiteman (Eds.), *The intergenerational activities program handbook* (3ʳᵈ ed., p. 24). Binghamton, NY: Broome County Development Council.

Moseley, P. A. (1976, April). *Developing a curriculum for death education: How do children learn about death?* Paper presented at the Annual Meeting of the American Education Research Association, San Francisco, CA.

Newman, S. (1985). *A curriculum on aging in our schools: Its time has come.* Paper presented at Generations Together, University of Pittsburgh, Pittsburgh, PA.

Northcott, H. C., & Wilson, D. M. (2008). *Dying and death in Canada* (2ⁿᵈ ed.). Peterborough, ON: Broadview Press.

Ryerson, M. S. (1977). Death education and counseling for children. *Elementary School Guidance and Counseling, 11*(3), 147-173.

Skrtic, T. M. (1995). The functionalist view of special education and disability: Deconstructing the conventional knowledge tradition. In T.M. Skrtic (Ed.), *Disability and democracy: Reconstructing (special) education for post-modernity* (pp. 65-103). New York: Teachers College Press.

Seefelt, C. (1989). Part III: Impacts. Intergenerational programs – Impact on attitudes. In S. Newman & S. Brummel (Eds.), *Intergenerational programs: Imperatives, strategies, impacts, trends* (pp. 185-194). New York: The Howarth Press.

Spiezia, V. (2002). The greying population: A wasted human capital or just a social liability? *International Labour Review, 141*(1&2), 71-113.

Stooke, R. (2004). *Healthy, wealthy and ready for school: supporting young children's education and development in the era of the national children's agenda.* Unpublished doctoral dissertation, The University of Western Ontario, London, ON.

Thompson, E., & Wilson, L. (2001). The potential of older volunteers in long-term care. *Generations, 25*(1), 58-63.

VanderVen, K. (1999). Intergenerational theory: The missing element in today's intergenerational programs. In V. S. Kuehne (Ed.), *Intergenerational programs: Understanding what we have created* (pp. 33-47). Binghamton, NY: Haworth Press.

Zolten, K., & Long, N. (2006), *How to talk to children about death.* Fayetteville, AK: Center for Effective Parenting, Department of Paediatrics, University of Arkansas.

Reconceptualizing Literacies in ECE

10

Taking Turtle Out of the Box:
Multimodal Storytelling in an Urban Kindergarten
Roz Stooke

The children take turns greeting Turtle. They pat his nose or his paw; they whisper into his ear. One of them turns away, but sneaks a peek once Turtle moves on to the next child. Then I set him down beside me. He is a model of appropriate behavior, mostly listening, but occasionally conveying my messages to the children. "Could they please say that rhyme about me. I really like it."

I know a little turtle and he lives in a box
And he swims in the water and he climbs on the rocks.
Well, he snaps at a minnow (that's a little fish)
And he snaps at a flea.
And he snaps at a mosquito.
And he snaps at me.

"Today Turtle's going to be in the story," I tell the children. I begin to walk the battered old puppet up my left arm. "Creepy, creepy, ever so slowly. All the way to the top – and stop," I tell them. Then I flap my left elbow out to one side like a duck. "This is a hill," I explain, "Can you make a hill like mine?" I wait and watch as most of the children mimic me. Then I continue the rhyme and the children join in the actions.

Turtle has climbed the hill to meet his friends for a picnic, but a huge rock is in the way. He can't move the rock by himself.

"He pushed and he pushed and he pushed and he pushed, but that rock wouldn't move. Not one centimeter! Who will help Turtle?" One child suggests Rabbit and demonstrates how Rabbit should go up the hill. "Boing, boing, boing, boing," hops Rabbit. "She'll soon budge that rock in no time with her strong hind legs." But like Turtle, Rabbit "pushed and pushed and pushed" to no avail. The children push too.

"Did that rock move?" I ask them. "No!" they chorus, "Not one centimeter."

"Then who else will help Turtle?"

The children suggest several other animal friends. Each climbs up the hill in its own way and pushes hard, but none of them is able to budge the rock.

"So now what can they do?" I ask.

"They could push together."

So Turtle and Rabbit and all the animals (and all the children) push and push until the enormous rock topples over the edge of the hill and rolls down , arm over arm, faster and faster, accompanied by giggling and squealing, all the way to the bottom.

"And so the friends had their picnic," I say redundantly, "Shall we stretch now?"

Educators who work with young children witness numerous events such as those described in *Turtle's Story*. Greeting a puppet "friend" is a ritual opener for circle time; it invites children to suspend disbelief and enter a storied space where anything might happen, albeit for a brief period of time. Young children, of course, suspend disbelief more often and more easily than do most adults. When one of the children who participated in *Turtle's Story* called out, "Hey, that's a puppet!" the rest of the group paid little attention, even after I conceded that he was right. Adults, on the other hand, are more likely to ask for evidence, and may have intractable views about the nature of evidence and the forms it should take. In recent years, the Early Childhood Education and Care (ECEC) community in North America has been increasingly preoccupied with notions of evidence especially in relation to children's print literacy development and, as Sally Lubeck (2000) pointed out, "professional commitment to play is being eroded" in a "political climate dominated by the language of standards and outcomes" (p. 3).

Given the attention paid to accountability in ECEC over twenty years or more, it is not surprising that storytelling activities are sometimes viewed as peripheral to the "real" business of literacy learning. It has been difficult to make a direct link between storytelling activities and the learning outcomes listed in many standardized curricula and this lack of measurability makes storytelling vulnerable to the panoptic gaze of efficiency-oriented and evidence-based curriculum design (see Petrina, 2004). This chapter nevertheless argues that storytelling activities can be fertile contexts for literacy, and in particular for multimodal meaning making (Jewitt & Kress, 2003; Pahl & Rowsell, 2005). Drawing on field notes and video data collected for a case study of interactive, multimodal storytelling in a culturally and linguistically diverse urban kindergarten classroom, I seek to reposition storytelling as a pedagogical resource for twenty-first-century early primary classrooms.

The chapter is organized into two parts. The first part presents descriptions of interactive, multimodal storytelling activities and cites research pertaining to the "play-literacy interface" (Roskos & Christie, 2001). This research lends support to the idea that such activities playfully "nudge" (Teale, 1999, p. 11) young children toward reading and writing in the conventional sense. I then introduce some recent ideas from New Literacy Studies (Pahl & Rowsell, 2005; Rowsell, 2006) to support my claim that interactive multimodal storytelling activities can be resources for young children's literacy in a broader, multimodal sense. The second part of the chapter focuses on a case study in which I explored the multimodal affordances of interactive storytelling with seventeen children in a culturally and linguistically diverse kindergarten.

Specifically, I discuss three literacy events described in my field notes and draw implications for professional practice.

Interactive Multimodal Storytelling with Young Children

Professional literature for language arts teachers recommends sequencing new learning in the form of a gradual release of responsibility from the teacher to the students (Bainbridge, Heydon, & Malicky, 2008). In Writers' Workshop, for example, teachers often "think aloud" as they demonstrate the writing of specific texts and genres. They also engage in interactive writing, what some teachers call *sharing the pen. Interactive storytelling* is a multimodal equivalent of "sharing the pen." It includes oral storytelling in which children participate by chanting a refrain or retelling parts of the story, acting out a story using gestures, telling a story with the aid of a puppet, draw-and-tell storytelling in which the teller creates a "surprise" drawing during the telling, and flannel board (sometimes called felt board) storytelling (e.g. Sierra, 1987, 1996; Warren, 1990) in which felt shapes are placed on a story board to represent elements of the story, song or rhyme. I focus in this chapter on flannel board storytelling. As in draw-and-tell storytelling, flannel board storytelling produces a visual text. The storyteller tells the story, or rhyme while placing felt shapes onto a large story board often following the left-to-right, top-to-bottom organization used in printed texts, or creating an image that echoes the structure of the story. The finished text is a visual representation of the story, song, or rhyme. In telling the folk song, *Hush Little Baby* (Pinkney, 2006), for example, the storyteller might place the felt shapes on the board in clockwise fashion to form a circle. In telling *Freight Train* (Crews, 1978), the teller might arrange the train cars in a left-to-right, back-to-front sequence to match the image of the train created in Crews' text. The photograph on the next page shows a cumulative representation of foods eaten by the caterpillar in Eric Carle's (1969) classic picture book, *The Hungry Caterpillar.*

An interactive approach to flannel board storytelling emphasizes the co-creation of a text and sometimes produces a visually untidy board as in the photograph of figures from *Brown Bear, Brown Bear* (Martin, 1983) that appears on the following page.

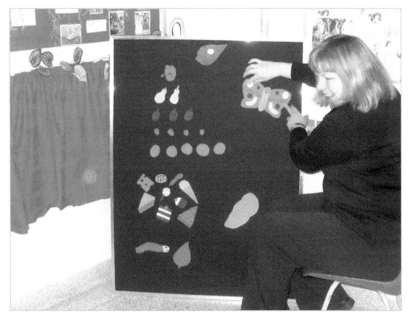

Food *The Hungry Caterpillar's* meal is displayed on the flannel board.

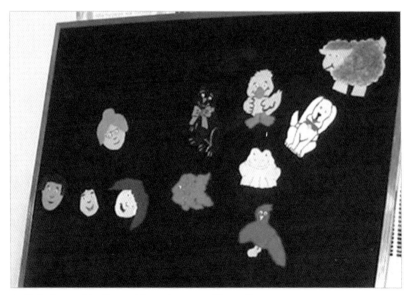

A slightly untidy flannel board storytelling of *Brown Bear, Brown Bear.*

An interactive approach to flannel board storytelling can produce texts analogous to the postmodern picturebooks described by Pantaleo (2008). In one session with the kindergarten children, the children decided to appropriate the mouse and the goat from the rhyme, *A Hunting We Will Go*, which had been told earlier in the session. Such intertextual appropriation is reminiscent of the intertextuality found in Jon Scieszcka and Lane Smith's (1992) *The Stinky Cheese Man and Other Fairly Stupid Tales* where characters from one story regularly turn up in another. Notice too that in the field note below, the familiar "teacher" from Bill Martin's original *Brown Bear, Brown Bear* book is called "grandmother" by the children.

> Field Note (Group Session): The children are bringing in characters from another game. Mouse and Goat belong to A Hunting We Will Go which we played earlier. I'm starting to think of each story session as a story in its own right and I go along with the requests. We hunt through the pieces for A Hunting We Will Go and find the ones the children have asked for.
>
> Roz: So who did the cat see?
>
> Child 1: The cat's going to chase away a mouse.
>
> Child 2: And he's going to scare away the goat.
>
> Roz: Okay, last of all are 1, 2, 3. . .
>
> Several Children: Kids
>
> Roz: Right. The blue horse says "I see 1, 2, 3 children looking at me." And what do they say?
>
> Child 2: I see a grandma looking at me.

The activities explored in my case study were first developed for a series of professional workshops. As a children's librarian working in public libraries, I had invented and improvised several games to extend the possibilities for flannel board activities in story programs. I invited toddlers to help build a snowman from white circles or to help the kittens find their mittens; I asked preschoolers to help decide which of the story character would "go home" first; I often played memory games, sorting games, and matching games with the children after telling a flannel board story in the straightforward way. Encouraged by the children's enthusiasm, I developed workshops for pre-service teachers and later for children's librarians and early childhood practitioners in which a brief presentation and demonstration were followed by a longer period of exploration. The following list of suggestions is summarized from a workshop handout.

Playing With Story Pieces

- Tell a simple story or rhyme using felt shapes.
- Have the children help you to retell a story using felt shapes.
- Start with a bag full of shapes and have the children tell a story together or individually.
- Have children bring objects from home and add them to the bag.
- Play predicting games. (What happens next?)
- Play imagining games. (What if . . .?)
- Play sequencing games. (What happened first? Then what . . and so on.)
- Change the endings, beginnings and other parts of the story
- Play memory games. (Who has gone home?)
- Play sorting games. (Which foods gave the hungry caterpillar a stomachache? Which food do you like to eat?)

If flannel board shapes are to be used by young children:

- Make the pieces large enough for small hands to grasp.
- Avoid layers or attachments as the pieces come apart easily and figures may become too heavy to stay on the board.
- Choose durable materials.
- Be aware of textures – the feel of the pieces.

In their review of research on the play-literacy interface, Roskos and Christie (2001) identified three central theoretical ideas. First was the Piagetian idea that "conscious recollections of facts or past events – is at the root not only of pretend play schemes, but also of the manipulation of a second order symbol system, such as print" (p. 73). Second was the idea that play creates "socio-cognitive conflicts (different points of view)" (p. 73) that necessitate adaptations and promote oral language development. Third was the conceptualization of play as an activity system, one that "affords an opportunity to exercise individual literacy ideas and skills even as it presses for certain kinds of literacy knowledge and interactions" (p. 74).

Although, my exploration into the affordances of multimodal, interactive storytelling draws on each of these theoretical ideas, the third idea only influenced my research recently. Most salient to the early professional workshops were ideas linking symbolic transformations to the promotion of oral language and emergent writing: for example, the claim made by Carol Fox (2003, p. 193) that all storytelling is a form of symbolic transformation and the empirical evidence presented by Pellegrini, Galda, Dresden, and Cox (1991) that children's symbolic transformations in play at age three and a half predict emergent writing skills at age five. Symbolic transformation took place in Turtle's Story when my arm was transformed to become a hill and when the children physically pushed an imaginary rock over the edge of an imaginary cliff. In flannel board storytelling the same principle applies. A white circle can be transformed into a snowball and a rectangle into a box; later, the circle can be transformed again into a wheel and the rectangle into a train car.

Pellegrini and Galda (2000) also reviewed research linking social symbolic play to children's literacy and concluded that symbolic play activities support the development of three kinds of language relevant to emergent literacy: narrative language, expository language, and metacognitive language. Narrative language is supported by functionally explicit play materials such as action figures, a pretend kitchen, or the envelopes and stamps used to stock a post office dramatic play centre. Functionally explicit materials provide children with many cues (p. 61) about how the materials should be used, obviating the need for children to negotiate what the materials will *be* in the activity or story. Paradoxically, expository language is better supported by functionally ambiguous play props. Wooden blocks, for example, or felt circles are relatively open ended props and their meanings must be negotiated and agreed upon before the story can be told. Expository language is foundational to content-area literacy.

> **Field Note (Group Session):** I pick up a bag of felt shapes labeled *A Hunting We Will Go*. I hold up a rectangle of purple felt and ask, "So what's this one, do you think?" I hear several voices say it's a rectangle. "Right, it's a rectangle. Do you remember in the Cat Story we had a piece like this and it was a. . . . " The children remember. "Box," they call out, "It's a box." So we catch the fox and put him in the box and then we let him go.

> **Field Note (Choices Period):** Manchi is standing beside the giant felt board in the storytelling centre, She picks up a plastic straw and tries to make it stick to the felt surface. The straw is bent out of shape. She tries to stick it to the figure of a little girl, but it keeps falling off. Manchi turns to Hannah. Hannah is playing beside Manchi, but she pays little attention to her.

> Manchi: Pretend you were my sister. No – Just pretend you gave me a jumping rope.

> Manchi: Pretend this was my skipping rope.

> Silence.

> Manchi: Pretend it was my birthday again and I turned two years old."

> Silence.

> Manchi: Pretend a dinosaur came along and we tied him with the skipping rope.

> Hannah's interest has finally been piqued. She turns around and moves towards Manchi, all smiles.

As the above excerpt from the case study illustrates, until a rectangle is named as a box or a straw is named as a skipping rope, the rectangle and straw can stand for a variety of things or ideas.

There are limits of course. A rectangle can be a box or a bus or a truck, but once the storyteller adds a series of squares and calls them windows, anyone who insists that the rectangle is still a box must argue the case. By participating in such negotiations, children clarify their wishes and ideas in language. Moreover, once the identity of a prop has been named, any member of the group can keep other playmates on track with comments such as, "You can't move that. It's a stop light." Pellegrini and Galda (2000) note that articulating the rules of their games helps children develop metacognitive language, that is talk about their thinking processes. Metacognitive language is centrally important to the development of strategic reading and writing in school.

In planning activities to explore with the culturally and linguistically diverse kindergarten class, I drew on three axiomatic principles from the field of second language acquisition. First and most important was the well-supported claim that language learners may take upwards of five years of schooling to acquire the language proficiency needed to reach their academic potential (Cummins, 1979). I reasoned that activities in which oral language input is contextualized using gestures, visual images, and real objects support the academic learning of students whose home languages differ from the language of instruction (Cox, 2008) and can, in fact, benefit any child whose academic progress is jeopardized by the dominance of verbal modalities in the classroom. Second was the finding that awareness of generic text structures and story elements scaffolds the composition process for language learners (Bates, 1995). I reasoned that storytelling sessions with the children should therefore aim to visually amplify text structures and explicitly identify story elements such as setting and characters.

The idea that storytelling with traditional materials such as puppets and flannel boards can be a resource for multiliteracies pedagogy has not received much attention in New Literacy Studies literature, perhaps because so much writing in the area of multiliteracies highlights the multimodal affordances of digital texts and environments. Rowsell (2006) explains:

> Multimodality is not a new phenomenon; it has been around for the longest time. The key difference today, however, is that multimodality has become more

sophisticated and more complex in the face of increasing media, technology, texts of all kinds, and popular culture. (pp. 19-20)

What is multimodality? Jewitt and Kress (2003) define a *mode* as a "regularised organized set of resources for meaning-making" (p. 1) and point out that in any meaning-making event the meaning conveyed through any one mode is partial in relation to the meaning of the whole event. The term *multimodal* is most often used to describe new media and popular culture texts such as videogames, but action rhymes, dance, story drama, drawing, painting, Lego building, puppetry, and interactive storytelling are all resources for and products of multimodal meaning making. All communicative activity is, in fact, multimodal, although one mode may be dominant in a specific text.

The recognition that all communication is multimodal has led to a broader definition for the term *text*. Rowsell (2006) writes that a text is "any object from which we make meaning" (p. 149). New Literacy Studies scholars such as Rowsell point out that in school, verbal modes, what Heath (1983) called "ways with words," dominate the communicative space and the majority of texts are print-based whereas outside of school texts are more often visual. In early primary classrooms too, gesture, movement, music, sound effects, and gaze are all important modes of text production. Given the opportunity, children choose the modes that best suit their communicative intentions. However, children in primary classrooms are expected to engage with print in increasingly sophisticated ways and teachers are expected to steer them toward print literacy competence.

New Literacy Studies has much to say to teachers of young children. "Multiliteracies may be more difficult to define and identify in a kindergarten classroom than in one with older learners" (Hawkins, 2004, p. 20), but teachers of young children are very much aware that the communicative spaces inhabited by their students are now deeply influenced by digital culture: "Today's children are growing up in a world where print operates as one among many media" (Mackey, 2006, p. 19) and they are growing up in a world where the distinction between print and digital culture is by no means clear. Many print texts are now read on screen rather than on paper and a growing number of children's picture books can be read as if navigating a website or playing a videogame (Pantaleo, 2008). Such books embed what Eliza Dresang (1999) calls *radical change* characteristics. They may contain split-screen images, multiple conclusions, flashbacks and even hyper-links and they are often self-consciously metafictive (Unsworth, Thomas, Simpson, & Asha, 2005, p. 7). In *The Stinky Cheese Man and Other Fairly Stupid Tales*, for example, the Table of Contents falls on Chicken Licken and The Little Red Hen competes with Jack the Narrator for the right to tell her story. Radical change books may also contain several interrelated storylines as in David Macaulay's (1990) *Black and White* or several perspectives communicated primarily through visual design as in Anthony Browne's (1998) *Voices in the Park*. The fact that many radical change picture books were published before digital culture became so pervasive in the lives of children suggests that the books are not simply poor substitutes for interactive videogames. By the same token, traditional textual forms such as puppet plays and flannel board games are not just substitutes for interactive websites. Flannel board texts, like web-sites, can be updated and redesigned quite easily; they allow children to experiment concretely with intertextuality, multiple conclusions, flashbacks, and graphic devices such as split-screens, thereby avoiding what Mackey (2006) calls "the unchanging stolidity of the book" (p. 18). But flannel board storytelling does not aim to replicate the experience of online media. All storytelling practices embed unique affordances for meaning making, and what gets made depends on what the meaning makers do with the resources available.

To further illustrate this idea, I will discuss a case study in which I explored interactive storytelling with young children in a culturally and linguistically diverse kindergarten. Three child-initiated storytelling events are presented and considered in light of recent writing in New Literacy Studies (see Jewitt & Kress, 2003; Pahl & Rowsell, 2005; Rowsell, 2006) and children's literature (Dresang, 1999; Pantaleo, 2008). Finally, I reflect on personal learning gleaned from my visits with the children and draw implications for educators whose longstanding commitment to playful curricula is vulnerable to further erosion in this "political climate dominated by the language of standards and outcomes" (Lubeck, 2000, p. 3).

The Study

The case study was conducted in one culturally and linguistically diverse urban kindergarten classroom in British Columbia's Lower Mainland. Once a week during a rainy May and June, I packed a bag with puppets and other props for storytelling and headed down the mountain from my university office to spend the morning with seventeen students and one or both of their teachers. The elementary school was located in one of the poorest neighborhoods of the region. Many of the students had arrived there after long and arduous journeys as refugees; their families' lives had been disrupted by violence, transience, and extreme poverty. It was the playful nature of my proposed activities that appealed to the principal since he wanted, above all, for the school to be a safe and nurturing space for students to grow and learn.

The purpose of the study was to explore with the children some of the activities developed in the professional workshops and, specifically, to learn what the children did with the stories and games when left to their own devices. I visited the classroom six times to share stories, each time conducting a half-hour session with the whole class. Following each large-group session the teachers scheduled a thirty-minute Choices period during which children were permitted to visit any activity centre in the classroom and to move from one centre to another as long as they did not disturb or hurt another child. I created a storytelling centre in the classroom and provided the children with access to materials similar to those employed in the group sessions: felt shapes, flannel boards, puppets, a white board and wipe-off markers. I remained in the classroom during Choices periods as a participant observer along with Carol, a graduate research assistant and Linda, an experienced video-ethnographer. Carol and I observed children in the storytelling centre and made field notes while Linda filmed children engaged in multimodal activities.

One methodological challenge arose when Linda, Carol, and I noticed that children's multimodal storytelling events were not restricted to the storytelling centre. Accepting that it would not be possible to document all multimodal meaning-making events, we decided to focus primarily, although not exclusively, on events in which children made use of the materials from the storytelling centre.

The video data were reviewed and discussed with Carol, Linda and the two teacher-researchers who had hosted the study. The teachers were especially interested in the group sessions. They were genuinely impressed by the children's level of engagement in the multimodal activities and pointed out that my efforts to engage children in print-based activities were notably less successful. I was most interested in what the children were doing (or not doing) with the resources – by which I meant the communicative resources provided in the group sessions and the material resources we had placed in the storytelling centre. The question I address here is: What are some characteristics of the texts that children created as they engaged with the storytelling materials during Choices periods? I begin with Connor and Jake's story in which a triceratops pushed down a tree.

Video Data (Choices Period): Connor and Jake always seem to sit together in the group sessions. Now they are playing together on a small flannel board mounted on an easel. Jake is on his knees, rummaging in the plastic materials tubs for felt shapes. (Across the room, children are rummaging in Lego tubs in much the same way.) Connor appears to be building a tower of shapes – triangles, rectangles, circles. He starts at the bottom of the board and places triangles and rectangles one above the other. The image of a tower or skyscraper comes to mind. I wonder if the draw-and-tell Cat Story we made in last week's storytime has inspired his creation. I too had used simple shapes and started at the bottom of the board. "Triangle, triangle, circle, square. Can that be a face I see in there? And so on.

Connor is singing quietly to himself as he works. "Over in the meadow," he sings.

We learned that one the first week and I had left copies of the words with the teacher.

"Na na na na na na na," sings Connor to the tune of Twinkle, Twinkle, Little Star.

Jake's head comes into view. He presses a fish shaped felt piece flat onto the board and turns to Connor.

Jake: This is a shark.

Connor: (dismissively) That's a fish. (He goes back to building and humming "Over in the Meadow.")

The boys work side by side, covering the board with a variety of shapes, but not in any pattern discernable to me.

Connor: (singing) Over in the meadow . . .

Jake: No. Let's not do that. (pause) I said let's do something else.

Connor: Okay, let's get rid of all these except the doggie, right?

Jake: And the tree.

They run their hands down the board and scoop all but the dog piece into the trough on the easel. Then Jake places a tree onto the board close to the lower right hand corner.

Connor: (singing to a new tune) The doggie climbs up the tree and then he got stuck. (now talking) Okay, let's get the bats on. (Sings) There were two bats.

Jake takes a pink and a yellow butterfly and places them above the tree. They must be the bats.

Jake: (singing the same tune as Connor) A mama bat and a baby bat and they got stuck.

Connor: (Singing) The bat came along. The whale came along/

Now Connor disappears from view. Jake is adding felt shapes to an already overburdened tree. He uses the flat of his hand in an effort to make them stick. The easel shudders and the cumulative weight of the pieces in the tree makes the felt tree trunk begin to buckle. The whole sculpture looks very unstable.

Jake: Whoa!!!

Jake presses the felt sculpture back onto the board more carefully this time.

Then Connor's head pops into view on the far side of the board. He's holding a dinosaur shape and looking around to see where it should go.

Connor: Okay (Singing again as he walks the triceratops shape across the board toward the tree.) The triceratops came along and he pushed down the tree.

Without missing a beat, Jake joins in the singing.

Jake and Connor: (to the same tune) Then there was nobody in the tree.

The tree and all its pieces fall to the ground. Connor and Jake are doubled over, laughing with delight. The story appears to be over.

What Linda recorded with her ethnographer's eye was a snapshot of two boys transforming familiar material and linguistic resources into new forms. The *Triceratops* story resembles structurally the story in which *Turtle* and his friends pushed the rock down the hill. The parallel sentences "The bat came along. The whale came along" echo the structure of lines from several stories told during group sessions as well as stories commonly found in books for young children. A certain amount of mixing up had taken place, but mixing up can be very creative and productive as Anne Haas Dyson (2001) explains:

Children situate, or recontextualize, aspects of new activities (new concepts, new symbolic tools, and new social practices) within the meaningful frames of old, familiar activities . . . This recontextualization allows children a sense of competence and agency – indeed, this allows them sense. (2001, p. 411)

An important quality of the *Triceratops* story sequence was the interactive, multimodal nature of its production. Visual, linguistic, aural and tactile modes of expression were all evident in the video data and a great deal of switching and changing of materials and text-making strategies took place before the boys settled into the more conventional *Triceratops* narrative. There were, in fact, several texts created before the *Triceratops* was introduced, but the earlier texts were effectively deleted, by wiping the board clean.

Another noteworthy characteristic of the *Triceratops* story sequence was the collaborative nature of its production. Connor took the lead in the telling, Jake contributed the bats, supplying appropriate narrative lines as he placed them on the tree. Moreover, Jake needed no prompt to sing "Then there was nobody in the tree." I inferred that Jake shared in the joke at the end of the story and realized that the story needed to be brought to a close before it physically fell apart. Two related characteristics commonly associated with digital text production were evident in the final moments of the *Triceratops* story. Connor's improvisational move to have the Triceratops knock down the tree and thereby to save the story from a disaster precipitated by Jake's over enthusiastic layering of shapes demonstrates both interactivity and immediacy. The material affordances of the felt entered into Connor's design decisions which were very much *in the moment*.

Lesley Lancaster (2003, 2007) claims that even very young children distinguish between drawing and writing although the marks they make may be indistinguishable to adults. Following Lancaster's advice to observe closely the actual processes of text production and listen to what children are saying, I reviewed the video data many times and concluded that Connor's tower of shapes was pictorial in nature. I noticed, for example, that neither of the songs Connor sang as he created the tower appeared to be semantically related to the resulting image. Neither was there a discernable verbal narrative. By contrast, in creating the Triceratops story, the boys incorporated singing into the design process. They used sing-song voices for the actual narrative and reserved talk for directions and negotiations. The flannel board too was incorporated into the design process. It functioned as a kind of screen so that the text was reminiscent of an animated short film.

It is not easy to speculate on children's intentions when they are playing by themselves. My field notes contain an account of text making in which a child I call Mirella was placing shapes onto the board in what I took to be "pretend writing." While I was speculating on whether Mirella's actions demonstrated an understanding of print concepts, her teacher read the text as an example of patterning, a topic she had been teaching to the class. The most salient characteristic of this event, however, was that Mirella was prepared to "mess up" her work to preserve the privacy of her intentions.

> **Field Note: (Choices Period):** Mirella is placing a variety of shapes onto the board. Beginning at the top left corner of the board, she proceeds to make a row. Halfway across she stops, then returns to the left hand edge and begins another row directly below the first. She creates several "lines of text" this way so that the board resembles the left-hand page of an open book.
>
> Then her teacher approaches and asks her if she is making a pattern. Mirella remains silent. The teacher then invites her to play a guessing game. She places several shapes onto the board and asks, "Can you guess my pattern?"
>
> Mirella pauses to look, but still says nothing. Then she looks away and randomly places shapes all over the board, any which way, covering up her earlier lines of text.

While little was learned about Mirella's intentions, her actions can tell teachers something about the limits of our well-meant interventions. The teacher's attempt to "nudge" Mirella toward a mandated activity was not successful, perhaps because, as Kress (1997) reminds us, children choose the "stuff" that is most apt for their purposes. They do not appropriate practices unless an authentic purpose presents itself. It is worth noting here that neither my field notes nor the video data contain evidence of children initiating any of the sorting and matching games they were happy to play in group sessions. I concluded that the games, while engaging for the children when a teacher was present, were also seen as work. In group sessions they expected to work. Now they expected to play.

Perhaps the most easily overlooked characteristic of classroom text making is that it is infused with identity. Connor and Jake's story was an action adventure communicated in a distinctly physical manner, Moreover, it lacked the moral message of its parent text, *Turtle's Story*, and in spite of the negotiations that took place between the boys about what they would do next, it proceeded with little discussion about the nature of the symbolic transformations. When Jake said, "That's a shark," Connor dismissed the idea with "That's a fish." When Jake picked up a butterfly and declared it to be a bat, there was no discussion and no argument. Connor and Jake's matter-of-fact approach to negotiation brings into view a link between children's identity construction and unequal relations of power. Their text-making can be compared to the less successful negotiations between Manchi and Hannah that follows. Earlier in the chapter, I cited a conversation between Manchi and Hannah to illustrate the kinds of conversational work children do to establish the identity of a functionally ambiguous play prop such as a drinking straw. In the following excerpt from the video data, Hannah consistently refuses to enter into Manchi's story even though the props, a set of felt numerals, are relatively explicit.

Video Data (Choices Period):

Manchi: Pretend this was the best party ever. And then I changed back to myself. And then I cut my hair again. And then I was this many old. (She looks at the collection of felt numbers on the board.)

Hannah: Let's do 100 years old. (She starts to rearrange the numbers.)

Manchi: Don't! You ruined the best party. (She calms down and resumes telling.) Pretend it was the best party ever. Pretend I always grow my hair and cut my hair. Pretend I don't like you because you got long hair. (She picks up a large zero.) Pretend I was not born yet, so I was zero.

Hannah: I don't want you to grow your hair.

Manchi: Pretend it was the best party ever and then we sang Happy Birthday (sings the song). Pretend I was just singing and singing and you didn't know my name. And you were 36 (She places a backwards 3

next to a 6. And we were so old. And then you were 60.
And then I changed my clothes and cut my hair.

Hannah: No more cutting hair! And that's not the best
birthday ever. You can't always say that.

Manchi's preoccupation with short and long hair was part of
her identity resource kit. So was her tendency to fit the felt
numerals into her birthday party theme. But the fact that her narrative failed to meet Hannah's rather stringent expectations was
also contributing to her identity as a learner and member of the
classroom community. I wondered if the girls held differing
understandings of what counts as a story, a suspicion supported
by Hannah's earlier interactions with Manchi in which she
remained aloof until Manchi produced a recognizable story beginning. In the second exchange, Hannah critiques Manchi's repeti-
tion of the phrase "best party ever." Their conversation harks
back to Pellegrini and Galda's (2000) comments about the value of
metacognitive language for children's later content learning, but
the value of the interaction in this case seems to be overshadowed
by its exclusionary consequences. The conversational exchanges
between Manchi and Hannah trouble romantic notions of play.
Socio-dramatic play events, like all aspects of social life, can be
organized by unequal relations of power (Roskos & Christie, 2001),
and in this situation, the unequal power relations between the two
girls may have been exacerbated by Manchi's status as an English
language learner and by the institutional context. Storytelling in
school makes demands over and above those of casual conversation and although Manchi's refusal to abandon the phrase "best
party ever" suggests that she wanted her story to stand out from
everyday talk, her story does not exhibit the conventional story
grammar present in the *Triceratops* story. From Hannah's perspective, Manchi was not saying "it" right:

From [a] Bakhtinian vantage point, a key theoretical
distinction is made . . . between primary interactional
encounters (e.g. casual conversation) and more
complex institutionally embedded ones. These more
complex, or secondary, genres build on, and in varied
ways incorporate primary ones. . . . Whether a quick
greeting, a performance rap, an analytic commentary,

or a postmodern novel, all texts are responses to others' voiced turns and sound against the landscape of communicative possibilities. Young children's repertoire of kinds of voiced turns – of communicative practices – informs their judgments about saying "it" right. (Dyson, 2006, p. 11)

Manchi was not the only one who failed to meet Hannah's expectations of storytellers. In this final excerpt from my field notes, Hannah reminds me of the rules for my own game.

> **Field Note (Choices Period):** Our group stories are over. I am kneeling on the rug in the middle of the room sorting through all the felt pieces, making sure they go back into the right bags. Hannah flops down beside me and slips her right hand inside the Turtle puppet. She taps me on the shoulder then on my left arm.
>
> I am not so easily distracted. I assume Hannah just wants to visit. But after a few more seconds, her head suddenly appears under my left elbow so that I have to stop what I'm doing.
>
> She eyes me with wonder and exasperation.
>
> "Come on, Roz!" she insists in a decidedly bossy tone. "Make a hill."

Closing Remarks

A busy kindergarten classroom is no place for theorizing. Once I realized I was "stuff" for Hannah's story, I entered into her plans with good humour. First *Turtle* climbed my hill. Then Hannah was joined by two friends and I was transformed into a garden wall while *Turtle, Caterpillar,* and *Worm-in-the-Apple* crawled all over me in search of food. It was a carnival in the Bakhtinian tradition. The three puppets collided, batted each other on the nose and happily competed for space until they had worn out the joke and the "chain of signification" (Kress, 1997, p. 47) came to an end. Only later did I question why, once the circle time was over, I had so thoughtlessly consigned *Turtle* to his conceptual box.

An immediate response to the question is that once *Turtle* was back in his box, I ceased to be a storyteller and assumed the role of researcher. The children, of course, recognized no line between the two roles. For a few minutes Hannah saw in me neither storyteller nor researcher, but only a resource for story making and companionship. A more considered response to the question, however, would add that the conceptual box to which I consigned *Turtle* was one in which I live most of the time. In my communicative world, stories unfold against a flat background. Not paper necessarily, but definitely flat. I recall that when my own children were first introduced to television, they cried because we couldn't turn back the pages. Nowadays children (including mine) are more likely to be frustrated by images on paper because they want to see what lies behind the images (Mackey, 2006, p. 18). For Hannah too, stories appeared to take place in the round and there was no such thing as a backstage.

This second response may seem incongruous in the context of an exploration of multimodal storytelling, but it is an honest one. For the most part, I resisted the temptation to nudge children toward print literacy and even when I lapsed in my resolve, I was quick to notice that the children simply nudged back. What I failed to internalize was the idea that, unlike me, students of Hannah's generation may well be thinking primarily in terms of multimodality and not necessarily in terms of words, yet alone printed words (Rowsell, 2006, pp. 19-20). If Rowsell is right, and I believe she is, it is no longer enough to say that young children "weave together symbols of all kinds . . . to orchestrate literacy events long before language alone can serve them" (Siegel, 1995, p. 457). We need to understand that children are orchestrating literacy events in a world where language alone cannot fulfill their communicative intentions.

How, then, should teachers of young children navigate these radically changed communicative spaces? Certainly children will need greater access to new technologies than is currently available in many early primary classrooms, but Pantaleo's (2008) work with students in elementary classrooms demonstrates that learning to appreciate the interactive complexity of printed texts can support 'net-age' children's understanding of "the ways in which the text is producing pleasure and how it is positioning them as interpretive agents" (Unsworth, Thomans, Simpson, & Asha, 2005, p. 9). In any case, abandoning the teaching of print literacy is not an option for primary teachers. Like Mackey, I suggest that we acknowledge "what print can do very well and, equally importantly, what it does not do as well as other media" (p. 19). Finally, and most importantly, I would draw readers' attention to evidence in my case study data that interactive storytelling activities and other multimodal meaning-making events were not only deeply engaging for the children, but also afforded opportunities for them to create texts characterized by interactivity, immediacy, and complexity – nouns more often associated with digital culture (Unsworth, Thomas, Simpson, & Asher, 2005) than with oral storytelling. It is entirely possible, then, that the erosion of a commitment to play in early primary classrooms will not achieve the policy goal of preparing children for twenty-first century adult life and might in fact undermine policy makers' intentions.

Acknowledgments

The study was funded by a Simon Fraser University President's Research Grant and made possible by the generosity and imagination of the seventeen children who participated in the study, their teachers, and their principal. I would like to acknowledge the valuable practical support provided by my research assistant, Carol Doyle Jones and the incisive eye of video ethnographer, Linda Hoff, who saw the possibilities for the research before I did. Finally I would like to thank Jon Callow for his very helpful feedback on an earlier draft of the paper.

References

Bainbridge, J., Heydon, R., & Malicky, G. (2008). *Constructing meaning. Balancing elementary\language arts* (4th ed.). Toronto: Thomson Nelson.

Bates, L. (1995). Promoting young ESL children's written language development. In M. Venna, V. Corrigan, & S. Firth (Eds.), *Working with bilingual children.* Clevedon, UK: Multilingual Matters.

Browne, A. (1998). *Voices in the park.* New York: DK Books.

Carle, E. (1969). *The very hungry caterpillar.* New York: World Publishing Co.

Crews, D. (1978). *Freight train.* New York: William Morrow & Co.

Cox, C. (2008). *Teaching language arts: A student-centered classroom* (6th ed.). Boston, MA: Pearson

Cummins, J. (1979). Cognitive/academic language proficiency, linguistic

interdependence, the optimum age question and some other matters. *Working Papers on Bilingualism,19,* 121-129.

Dresang, E. (1999). *Radical change: Books for youth in a digital age.* New York: Wilson.

Dyson, A. H. (2001). Donkey Kong in little bear country: A first grader's composing development in the media spotlight. *The Elementary School Journal, 101*(4), 417-435

Dyson, A. H. (2006). On saying it right (write): "Fix-its" in the foundations of learning to write. *Research in the Teaching of English, 47*(1), 8-42.

Fox, C. (2003). Playing the storyteller: Some principles for learning literacy in the early years of schooling. In N. Hall, J. Larson, & J. Marsh (Eds.), *Handbook of early childhood literacy* (pp. 189-198). London: Sage.

Hawkins, M. R. (2004). Researching English language and literacy development in schools. *Educational Researcher, 33*(3), 14-25.

Heath, S. B. (1983). *Ways with words: Language, life and work in communities and classrooms.* New York: Cambridge University Press.

Jewitt, C., & Kress, G. (2003). Introduction. In C. Jewitt & G. Kress (Eds.), *Multimodal literacy* (pp. 1-18). London: Peter Lang.

Kress, G. (1997). *Before writing: Rethinking the paths to literacy.* London: Routledge.

Lancaster, L. (2003). Moving into literacy: How it all begins. In N. Hall, J. Larson, & J. Marsh (Eds.), *Handbook of early childhood literacy* (pp. 145-153). London: Sage.

Lancaster, L. (2007). Representing the ways of the world: How children under three start to use syntax in graphic signs. *Journal of Early Childhood Literacy, 7*(2), 123-154.

Lubeck, S. (2000, April). *On reassessing the relevance of the child development knowledge base to education: A response.* Paper presented at the Early Education/Child Development SIG , AERA, New Orleans, LA.

Mackey, M. (2006). Implicit understandings in the reading classroom. In J. Rowsell (Ed.), *Family literacy experiences: Creating reading and writing opportunities that support classroom learning* (pp. 18-19). Markham, ON: Pembroke.

Martin, B. (1983). *Brown bear, Brown bear, what do you see?* New York: Holt, Rinehart, and Winston.

Macaulay, D. (1990). *Black and white.* Boston, MA: Houghton Mifflin.

Pahl, K., & Rowsell, J. (2005). *Literacy and education: Understanding the New Literacy Studies in the classroom.* London: Paul Chapman.

Pantaleo, S. (2008). *Exploring student response to contemporary picturebooks.* Toronto: University of Toronto Press.

Pellegrini, A., Galda, L., Dresden, J., and Cox, S. (1991) A longitudinal study of the predictive relations among symbolic play, linguistic verbs, and early literacy. *Research in the Teaching of English, 25,* 215–35.

Pellegrini, A., & Galda, L. (2000). Children's pretend play and literacy. In D. Strickland & L. Mandel Morrow (Eds.), *Beginning reading and writing* (pp. 58-65). New York: Teachers College Press.

Petrina, S. (2004). The politics of curriculum and instructional design theory/form: Critical problems, projects, units, and modules. *Interchange, 35*(1), 81-126.

Pinkney, B. (2006). *Hush little baby.* New York: Greenwillow.

Roskos, K., & Christie, J. (2001). Examining the play – literacy interface: A critical review and future directions. *Journal of Early Childhood Literacy, 1*(1), 59-89.

Rowsell, J. (2006). *Family literacy experiences: Creating reading and writing opportunities that support classroom learning.* Markham, ON: Pembroke.

Scieszka, J. (1992). The stinky cheese man and other fairly stupid tales (L Smith, Illustator). New York: Viking.

Siegel, M. (1995). More than words: The generative power of transmediation for learning. *Canadian Journal of Education, 20*(4), 455-475.

Sierra, J. (1987). *The flannel board storytelling book.* New York: H. W. Wilson.

Sierra, J. (1996). *Multicultural folktales for the feltboard and readers' theater.* Phoenix, AZ: Oryx.

Teale, W. H. (1999). Libraries promote early literacy learning: Ideas from current research and early childhood programs. *Journal of Youth Services in Libraries, 12*(3), 9-16.

Unsworth, L., Thomas, A., Simpson, A. M., & Asha, J. L. (2005). *Children's literature and computer-based teaching.* Maidenhead, UK: Open University Press.

Warren, J. (1990). *Animal patterns: Multi-sized patterns for making cut-outs, puppets and learning games.* Washington, DC: Warren Publishing House.

11

Toys as Text:
Critically Reading Children's Playthings
Kimberly Bezaire & Linda Cameron

. . . to imagine is to begin the process that transforms reality.
  bell hooks, 1990, p. 9

I n our research observing children socialize together and in our examination of toys and play practices with our graduate students, we have noticed some disconcerting changes wrought by consumeristic toy producers upon contemporary children. These concerns are not solely our own. If you know young children or work with them, you likely have noticed little girls playing at being teenage sisters, rather than mothers and babies – pretending to be dating, shopping, and clubbing in Kindergarten dress-up corners. You may wonder about the sheer volume of children's products found on so many store shelves and in so many homes. Of course, these practices raise other questions. Grandparents, socialized to purchase the hearts' desires of their grandchildren, how do they understand children's consumer markets? What has the microchip done to children's imagination? Throughout our research, questions like these continually trouble us. An examination of the children's consumer toy market, in particular, offers a revealing look into the texts of many children's everyday lives, and prompts critical questions regarding the conditions of learning and living for today's children.

In fields of philosophy and education, play and make believe have long been positively associated with life and learning in childhood (Elkind, 2003; Jenkinson, 2001, Kavanaugh, 2006). However, current research challenges us to view and value play from holistic perspectives that give heed to the complexities of twenty-first-century childhood (Alliance for Childhood, 2004; Cameron, 2006; Elkind, 2003). Children at play are considered to be optimally engaged in opportunities for physical exertion, practice of social skills, and chances to develop resources through and confidence in activities that are personally meaningful to them (Anderson, Moffatt, & Shapiro, 2006; Kavanaugh, 2006). Further, play and make believe are associated with developing complex, abstract cognitive and socio-emotional processes including receptive and expressive language, symbolic representation, and complex social dialogue and negotiation (Bergen, 2001). While colloquially child's play might be equated with simplicity and ease, educational research offers informed and textured accounts of children actually involved in complex literate behavior – imagining, constructing, and narrating their experience of the world, *as it is* and *as it could be* (Engel, 2005a; Kavanaugh, 2006; Podlozny, 2000; Roskos & Christie, 2001). In peak/authentic play activity, children are involved in creative, imaginative processes which connect with the full range of their senses and draw upon their multiple intelligences (Gardner, 1993, 1999). Play is a whole body activity.

Theorists and philosophers suggest that these creative engagements, experiences, and connections are key to critical thinking, inquiry, and agency (Samson, 2005). At its most powerful and fully realized, make believe offers opportunities to construct one's own identity, imagination, and ways of being.

> Play opens a temporary ontological space, where one can be imaginatively detached from present reality to allow outside-the-box thinking; distance and so offer-

ing a new objectivity; imaginative possibilities; re-alignment of roles, priorities, restraints; and, a re-weighting of what matters. (Lee Bartel, email correspondence, September 15, 2007)

Creative, imaginative, critical ways of thinking provide means through which to unlearn, to challenge, to problem solve, to work life out vicariously, and to imitate others as well as to find ourselves – to make meaning. Through play, children are fully engaged using many sign systems – linguistic, visual, auditory, gestural, spatial – and in combining these modalities, move beyond traditional conceptualizations of language and literacy teaching and learning. Play and make believe *are* multiliteracies, offering multiple ways of experiencing, representing, responding to, working through and inquiring about ideas and the world. Pretending, building, collecting, singing, rhyming, gesturing, dancing – arguably, the most powerful aspects of play occur within the hearts and minds of the children engaged in this most personal and meaningful activity (Cameron, Bezaire, & Murphy, 2007; Edwards, Gandini, & Forman, 1998).

Despite these claims, experts are concerned that in the context of hurried twenty-first-century childhood, the time, space, and materials required for meaningful play are being pushed to the margins of children's lives (Alliance for Childhood, 2004; American Academy of Pediatrics, 2006; Cameron, 2006; Elkind, 2006a, 2006b). Increasingly intrusive consumer advertising and children's participation in broad, lucrative global markets are central to our concerns that today's children are growing up too fast, too soon. How are today's aggressive media marketing affecting children's ideas, values and beliefs – the memes – surrounding consumerism, gender, race, class? How is the hidden curriculum impacting the present and future health and happiness of children? How does the culmination of these forces shape their hearts, minds, and imaginations?

Toytexts: Connections and Considerations

Contemporary childhood – characterized by intensifying consumer culture and electronic media – requires children to engage in ever more subtle and complex ways of making meaning, which involve literacies that are multimodal and intertextual

(Carrington, 2003; Center for Media and Child Health, 2005; Rideout, Vandewater, & Wartella, 2004). Popular children's toys offer an illustrative example, crossing a range of modes, messages, markets, and meanings. Because marketing pursues profits with a singular focus, marketers amplify their ads through the use of complex behavioral manipulation that promotes desire for new technologies and corporate brand familiarity. The seductive nature of marketing has a serious effect on some Western childhood experiences at the turn of the millennium, presenting families and educators with serious dilemmas. Whereas pandemics, poverty, and armed conflict threaten childhood in many global contexts, in Western industrialized nations commercialization is considered a contributing factor to the erosion of childhood as a human right – children's entitlement to childhood as a "separate space from adulthood" (UNICEF, 2004, p. 3; Linn, 2008).[1]

Exploiting changes in family life and social patterns, children represent three lucrative opportunities to corporations: primary, future, and influence markets. With many children having significant disposable income, as well as a lifetime of purchases ahead of them, marketers in the 1990s recognized them as lucrative targets in both primary and future markets; hence, they expanded their efforts well beyond the traditional limits of marketed candy and breakfast cereals (McNeal, 1998). Further, in an age of *responsive parenting* and *time crunched* households where adults are more likely to run errands in the company of children and consider children's input in family decision-making, marketers have exploited the influence that children can exert on the purchases of parents and grandparents. The award-winning documentary, *The Corporation* (Achbar & Abbott, 2003) describes how marketers employ "the nag factor" to prompt children's influence on parental spending on a wide array of products, from fast food to holiday vacations. Recently, new marketing techniques, as revealed in *Consuming Kids: The Commercialization of Childhood* (Barbaro & Earp, 2008), employ children's abilities to understand and effectively communicate marketing messages in more persuasive ways to adults at home – a more palatable, and even more effective device, as compared to "pester power." These developments raise a host of important questions. What are the possible impacts on family relationships and on children's developing identities? What are the ethical and political implications of these marketing practices? What are the implications for our conceptualization of text and literacy learning?

Connections Down the Pink and Purple Aisle[2]

Emily, six years old, walks down the pink and purple aisle, scanning a multitude of dolls stacked high upon the toy store shelves. At her eye-level and within reach, she finds a Hannah Montana Holiday Christmas doll. Recognizing this character, Emily proudly relates her knowledge and "connection" to this media character and her "real-life" personae, teenage multimedia personality Miley Cyrus. Emily regularly watches the "family-friendly" Hannah Montana cable television show, and saw the G-rated "Best of Both Worlds" concert movie at a friend's birthday party. Emily knows the lyrics to songs such as "Pumpin' Up the Party" and "If We Were a Movie," mimicking Miley's vocal style and choreographed dance moves. Classmates are adorned with Hannah/Miley clothing, lunchboxes, backpacks, school supplies, jewelry, and children's cosmetics. Many wore long blonde wigs and mini-skirts for Halloween. While surfing the Internet at a friend's house, Emily has viewed Miley's music videos, tabloid video clips, as well as Miley's "homemade" youtube personal page. On the playground, Emily heard some grade four girls talk about Internet photos of Miley in the shower, and that these were "for her boyfriend," but Emily isn't quite sure, yet, what this may mean. While in line at the grocery store, and in a medical waiting room, Emily has viewed Miley's controversial Vanity Fair cover, as well as recent fashion photos featuring Miley alongside adult celebrities on "best dressed" lists. Hannah Montana products – CDs, books, DVDs, CD-ROMs – are popular items, featured prominently in children's toy catalogues, as well as Emily's school book fair and monthly book order program. Many of her classmates portrayed Hannah/Miley at the school's annual lip-synch talent show. Emily picks up the Hannah Montana doll and proceeds down the toy aisle, looking at row upon row of fashion dolls – Bratz, "My Scene" Barbie. . . .

What connections is Emily making between these multiple texts? What play scripts do these toys, television shows and movies, and Internet clips suggest? How might these texts influence Emily's understanding of gender, identity, success, and sexuality? Multimedia texts, such as these, risk going critically unexamined by child consumers and adults alike. In comparison to the hurried and sophisticated child consumer, teachers, and parents are often not as knowledgeable or informed in respect to the modes and messages embedded in children's consumer products (Carrington, 2004). However, our understanding of how children construct their knowledge and understanding – from experience and engagement with the world around them (Dewey, 1938) – indicates the importance of adults' thoughtful and informed engagement into this aspect of children's worlds. We need to read critically children's playthings, viewing this media as not "merely a neutral giver of pleasure to small children," but also as "distinct cultural and material artifact(s), representing current themes in mass culture," including "prevailing views about gender and childhood" (Carrington, 2003, p. 92; see also Sutton-Smith, 1986).

Because children's abstract thinking and understanding evolve out of their material actions (Wood, 1998), the lived curriculum of toys has the potential to be central within the everyday lives of children, especially since many children privilege these experiences as their most personally meaningful.

In our many conversations with young children regarding their favorite toys and media characters, we are provoked by children's explicit understanding of social capital associated with ownership – whether physical and symbolic – of toys and various multimedia, including their associated play scripts. If we are seen to critique the toys, children will sometimes defend their favorite media – that it's worthwhile, enjoyable, important. Yet, we have also heard children express concern for younger age groups, with respect to a toy being too scary or precocious. "Kids in Kindergarten shouldn't be playing with that doll. That looks more like for grade eights", observes seven-year-old Michael,[3] commenting on a Bratz doll. Or seven year old Sasha, "That toy is too violent for little kids."

These conversations are important for teachers and parents to tap into and perhaps provoke some thoughtful dialogue and reflections about the overheard conversation at a time when it does not interrupt the children's play. For example, we asked a group of children what they think makes a toy scary and then to compare a selection of toys according to the collaboratively developed criteria. In co-creating these criteria, the children took greater ownership in critically applying them to marketed products and in discerning what they thought was appropriate for them. It also opened up an interesting conversation about fears and how to manage them. It pointed out to us that what we assumed would be scary to kids was not necessarily right and that it differed across culture, gender, and age. As Vivian Vasquez (2001) suggests, engagement in a *critical curriculum* allows various social justice and issues of equity to emerge that can then be used to "interrogate, obstruct, contest, and/or change inequitable situations" (p. 66). Moreover, it empowers kids by giving them critical literacy tools.

Children do read their playthings, but they also have varied experiences that affect their comprehension and their ability to play. Listening and watching Sam and Ahmed, we noticed that the boys' knowledge and skill with Lego has a prominent place in their everyday classroom play. As well as building with the classroom's ample supply of mixed up Lego bits and pieces, each boy brings choice pieces and figures from home, along with the visually detailed instruction booklets that accompany today's elaborate Lego designs. They go online to look at what is possible and comment on what is too complicated. The boys value the complex and intricate nature of these Lego kits as well as the toys' cross-marketed connections with Star Wars and Indiana Jones, yet their classroom teacher laments the lack of open-ended creative play she associates with her childhood memories of Lego. The boys play exclusively together, as they own of the choice figures and are experts on the movie storylines and the aligned play scripts: "No Matthew, you can't play that way. The Clones don't fight each other. You don't even know who Commander Cody is?" Occasionally, Sam seems overwhelmed by the specificity of the toy's directions, his eyes welling up with tears of frustration when he can't find a particular piece or his model doesn't match exactly the one in the booklet. Despite his frustrations, he remains a loyal consumer and promoter of the toy. Yet, when discussing a classmates' choice of toy, children seem to move easily towards skepticism, sometimes bordering on cynicism, and openly express negative critical judgements. "She looks like a criminal. She's scary," observes six-year-old Ethan matter-of-factly, critiquing a classmate's Goth fashion doll. Likewise, Holly responds with criticism of Ethan's Star Wars action figures: "That's violent," she admonishes, "No guns at school!" As adults, we may agree with both children's assessments, but simply agreeing with them does not help children look past their own consumer loyalty to examine critically the messages being conveyed to them through their toys. How do we go *deeper* with our inquiry and understanding?

We reconceptualize understandings of curriculum from an holistic perspective, one that takes into account children's many ways of knowing (Elkind, 2003; Engel, 2005b) and their many languages (Edwards, Gandini, & Forman, 1998). Not limited to cognitive skills or knowledge, this reconceptualization includes social, cultural, emotional, embodied, and enacted understanding. Observing children at play, we recognize multiple ways of experiencing, representing, responding to, working through, and inquiring about ideas and the world. Play (the curriculum of children) makes visible children's cognitive, linguistic, socio-cultural, and socio-political processes. Considering literacy from a socio-cultural perspective, children are viewed as active meaning makers, developing foundational knowledge and understanding through everyday social interaction (Anderson, Moffatt, & Shapiro, 2006; Wells, 1986). Consequently, we would argue, in this era of consumer media and digital technologies, children's toys and multimedia have increasing potential to influence children's foundational understanding. Recognizing the increasing importance of critical and media literacies within our early childhood classrooms, we have come to view toys *as* text, defining *toytexts* as "objects which involve children in social meaning-making processes through their acquisition, interaction, and play – Toytexts are symbolic objects, material artifacts which convey meaning and references to the social world, as children 'decode' and invest meaning in these objects and in play contexts" (Cameron & Bezaire, 2009). Defined as such, our inquiry has been driven by an action research project (Creswell, 2005), conducted with teachers as agentive research partners.

The Toytext Project

Have you toured a toy store lately? With over 200 pre-service and graduate student participants, each with specialized interest and backgrounds in early learning and play, we critically examined many toy stores, and found the results to be disheartening. Noting store layout and design, categories and types of toys, price ranges, quality and durability, as well as packaging, promotion, and cross-marketing, the participants considered issues surrounding gender, race, class, and language. We visited big-box department stores and independent–educational toy stores with the intent of exploring issues of accessibility and affordability and questioning the effects of commercialization and mass merchandising. We examined the play and learning potential of the most popular toys, returning to the research literature to consider children's play and learning processes and critically examining manufacturers' and advertising claims. Some of the guiding questions for the inquiry have included:

- Are there toys that are unstructured that might facilitate imaginative play and maybe even socio-dramatic play?

- Are there toys that might elicit storying? Problem solving? Working through ideas? Acting? Developing worlds? Working through issues? Trying on roles? Experimentation? Exploration? Fantasy?

- What toys would invite being active rather than just being a spectator?

- What kinds (categories) of play might result in the use of particular toys? For example, nurturing or caregiving play with dolls, violent play with guns, adult mimicking play, sexual play, construction, etc.

- What kind of gendered or racial messages are being transmitted in a region of Canada considered perhaps the world's most linguistically and racially diverse?

- What economic resources are necessary to purchase chosen merchandise?

- What claims about learning are the manufacturers making and does the toy appear that it might deliver the goods?

- What cross marketing is happening?

- What is the best and worst toy you found and why?

Exploring these questions was very provocative as students considered the results from their perspectives as educators (some as parents, also) and as citizens invested in and concerned with the welfare of children. Students one by one presented their data that often mourned the loss of childhood play and of childhood itself. Particularly poignant were their reflexive comparisons of current toy market trends to their most memorable childhood play experiences. Focus group discussion with participants largely related a shocked recognition of how much hasn't changed (i.e., gender and racial stereotyping), while attuning to the extent to which today's childhood experience has morphed, becoming static, sedentary, and spectator-based as compared to previous generations' outdoor wandering, freedom, and freeplay. Participants often felt overwhelmed by the sheer volume, range, and number of toys commenting on how there was so much more stuff than in the past. Throughout their participation in this research, students were encouraged to consider results through the lens of curriculum studies by asking questions such as: What is the curriculum? What are the messages and memes? What are the implications for teaching and learning at home and at school? The teachers reconceptualized their responses and responsibilities as a result.

Pink and Purple, Blue and Black: Gender Stereotyping

Toy stores, particularly more economical department stores, divide and organize toys according to stereotyped gendered layout and design. Participants such as Daniela Bascuñán,[4] a Masters student, parent, and elementary teacher, characterized these divides as "segregation" offering "very gendered or very specific roles, discouraging imaginative play." Toys were further stereotyped and limited in selection and packaging. Girls' toys were generally marketed in pink and purple and are separated from the boys' black, blue, and army camouflage toys and packaging.

As in previous generations, girls' toytexts embody stereotyped messages about household work, nurturing, and beauty, with domestic play props, baby dolls, and fashion dolls still dominating girls' sections of stores. However, twenty-first-century twists in consumer marketing emphasize glittery invitations to be a desperate housewife or pop princess through sexualized play props and marketed media personae. Citing sexualized play scripts, heavy make-up, high heels, and sexy clothing, study participants found the Bratz collection of dolls most alarming. With marketing titles such as "Rock Angelz", "Funk Fashion Makeover" and "Be Prom Perfect," study participants noted dolls with bare midriffs, mini-skirts, and fishnet stockings. Moreover, they were shocked to consider the Kindergarten-Primary school age group to whom these toys are marketed. Neophyte elementary school teacher and new scholar Sarah Roebuck noted, "Pornification of fashion . . . I find this appalling" [Bratz dolls being marketed to ages 4+]. A Pre-service Kindergarten teacher observed, "Punk it up in rockin' rebel style. Do we really want our four-year-olds dressing up like punks and becoming rebels . . . and we wonder why children are growing up so fast these days?" Yet another Kindergarten teacher questioned, "Instead of playing with the dolls, you get to make rock music videos and songs . . . adding tattoos, make-up, gloss and powder to the face . . . Is this really appropriate for a five-year-old to engage in?" A pre-service teacher stridently remarked, "The Rock Angelz Tour Bus features a 'rock star party on wheels,' including a Smoothie Bar, Hot Tub(!) and Primpin Stations . . . might as well be a 'Pimpin' Station! Give me a break." Daniela Bascuñán further added, "Jewelry, money and sex" are overt themes in today's girl aisle, as *bling*, make-up, highly sexualized dress-up clothes, and faux designer bags feature prominently."

Conspicuous toys missing from the girls' section included science and inquiry possibilities, construction materials, outdoor playthings and sports equipment. These toys were most often found only in the boys' section. Are only boys to be scientists, physically fit, or architects?

The boys' toy aisles were described as dark in color and theme. Characterized by blue, black, and camouflage-patterned packaging, boys' toys most often depict themes of aggression, violence, conflict, and horror. Where yesterday's G.I. Joe or soldier figures also featured these themes, today's action figures display stylized, hyper-masculine bodies, with "muscles upon muscles." Toy packaging and marketing advertisements portray boys at play with angry facial expressions, engaged in aggressive play with

"Power Gear," "Ultra Blast Weapons," and "extra Ammo." Cars, trucks, and construction toys were among the toys found in the boys' aisle, along with outdoor toys and sports equipment.

In "educational" toys stores, toys are more often organized according to toy category (i.e., construction, make believe), rather than strictly gendered toy aisles. The more obvious stereotyped toys (i.e., Barbie dolls, Bratz dolls, soldier toys, toy guns) are most often absent from these stores, with store staff/managers explaining that these toys are not viewed as educational (i.e., to more affluent "discerning" customers). However, though more subtle, the gender lines were still clearly drawn in these stores, with pink and purple for girls and camouflage colors for boys still a prominent theme. Princess toys and baby dolls were also targeted at girls while medieval war toys and gadgets reigned for boys. Toys that provided children with props for parenting were for the purpose of mothering with no baby dolls found that little boys may find appealing to parent. Participants in this study were troubled by these observations and noted that in their experience, fathers' are increasingly hands-on participants in their children's lives. Likewise, science toys were gender stereotyped and marketed in brown and green packaging that mirrored the tones used for other boys' toys. No pink or purple was evident in the science section and few girls were featured prominently on science toy packaging.

Toy stores presented a false dichotomy, depicting children's interests and activities as though the genders are separate and limited in their play. Within postmodern scholarship, " . . . gender is positioned as a form of fantasy play, a game in which the behaviors of 'girls' and 'boys' are acted out" (Thornton & Goldstein, 2006, p. 517). While observable gender differences exist, and inform us in interesting ways about possibilities for parenting and teaching, they are complex and inclusive, rather than simple and separate (Thorne, 2002). For example, boys have been observed to engage in rough and tumble play most often, and the physical aspects of boys' play has traditionally been the focus of this area of research (Jarvis, 2007; Pellegrini & Smith, 1998). However, recent ethnographic study of rough and tumble play suggests that mixed-gender rough and tumble play involves narrative and complex social interaction – gender differences being subtle and related, rather than separate and distinct (Jarvis, 2007). Derman-Sparks's (1989) work points out that the learning context for young children needs to be free from both gender-bias and sexism.

Why do toys for three to five year olds present exaggerated depictions of gender and limit play choices and potential for developing minds and bodies, especially in an era when we pride ourselves on the choices and options available to adult men and women? Make believe play offers children space to re-enact and make meaning of their everyday lives and to imagine possible future selves, lives in which gender identities are increasingly complex and textured and where gender equity is a common expectation within today's homes and workplaces.

Out of Reach: Cultural and Racial Misrepresentation

Our study participants catalogued a severe lack of dolls and play props representing racial, linguistic, and cultural diversity. Baby dolls were almost exclusively blond and blue-eyed, with few dolls of "color" simply dyed a generic darker color, rather than depicting diversity in the appearance of eyes, hair, and skin shade. Fashion dolls were mainly Caucasian. When "dolls of color" were in evidence, they were literally marginalized as they were placed out-of-reach on the stores' top shelves. These dolls were often styled in "ethnic" dress and designed as collector items for White consumers.

Although department stores offered multiracial dolls, they were mainly found in the Bratz product line. Overtly sexualized in appearance, Bratz product included suggestive play props and risqué play themes. These dolls with a "passion for fashion" were considered to be the most disturbing by our study participants. "Seeing children depicted in a sexually provocative and racially insensitive manner disgusted me," observed a male elementary teacher and Masters student, "There should be no place for high mini-skirts revealing panties in children's toys." Usha Shanmugathasan surveyed a department store in a neighborhood she considered racially-diverse and asserted, "The only ethnic looking doll was the 'Bratz Genie' which only served to 'exoticize' the 'Other'". Some playhouses offer multicultural family figures, but these toys are few and far between, with dolls more often embodying racialized stereotypes: Ninjas and Cowboys and

Indians. "The most disturbing thing I saw was the lack of racial diversity and the horrible messages this sent . . . the Asian Family set of dolls was "particularly upsetting because the dolls did not have eyes, they just had straight lines where their eyes should be," observed training teacher Sandy Tzogas, while exploring a "very expensive and upscale toy store."

Participants also noted a lack of toys and books representing linguistic diversity, as products were almost exclusively offered in English, with a few products available in French. Yet, nearly 43% of Toronto's population speak a mother tongue other than English or French (Statistics Canada, 2007). For our participants whose work focuses on early years education and emphasizes early language and literacy development, the implications were alarming. As literacy research reveals and educational policies reflect, literacy experience in a child's home language contributes in significant ways to overall language and literacy development (Ontario Ministry of Education, 2007).

In the metropolitan Toronto area, where over 36% of the population identifies as a visible minority (Statistics Canada, 2005), hence the lack of toys portraying diversity cannot simply be traced to a lack of demand. Disturbingly educational toy stores were also observed to be homogenous in terms of their stock. "No Black or Asian firefighters," noted Stephanie Carrasco-Rodriguez, a pre-service teacher and parent. When store managers/staff were questioned about the homogeneity of the products they sold they cited neighborhood demographics to justify a lack of representation, assuring our investigators that toy stores in other areas of the city likely meet the needs of diverse populations. Interestingly, our participants were representative of Toronto's diverse population and they felt these responses were indicative of racism. The participants often felt invisible, as people of color, and felt that they did not belong. These classist and racist assumptions were compounded within toy stores, perhaps no more so than in upscale stores where a white, unilingual (i.e., English-speaking) consumer-base was assumed. Many families, and, indeed, many of our teachers, cannot see themselves nor their children on Canadian toy shelves. Daniela Bascuñán observed:

> My search for a doll that looked more like my daughter took me to all mainstream toy and department

stores, only to be met with, "I'm sorry. We don't get regular shipments of them. We don't usually carry black dolls." (At this point, I had given up on finding a "Latin American" doll, and was hoping to find anything that represented the diversity of my daughter's real world.) At every store, I have spoken to sales staff or to managers about this issue of non-representation of the many communities that make up Toronto, to no avail.

Look, Push, Look, Wait:
"Educational" and Electronic Media

A review of our study data, as well as trends documented in the toy trade media, reveal a proliferation of electronic media such as videogames, computer games, and learning systems (Fonda, 2004; Canadian Press, 2005). These products, first designed for schoolagers, extended to preschoolers during the early years of our data collection, and are now featured prominently in advertising for toddler/infant toys. Traditional toys – board games, stuffed animals, books – now feature electronic add-ons which have increased price points and limited active play opportunities. Our study participants questioned the value of products that require little action or involvement as 'players' but rather as spectators to microchip and battery-operated toys and games. "Educational toys often do all the talking . . . children just listen and press corresponding buttons or touch the screen," observed Masters student and elementary school teacher Anni Wong. Toy packaging often makes educational claims, citing specific developmental skills, reminiscent of a crude developmental checklist – not the fully engaging, interpersonal, active, open-ended learning opportunities we know actually prepare children's developing minds for present and future learning (McCain & Mustard, 1999). We question this limited conceptualization of learning, which misinforms and miseducates families regarding the true play-value of these expensive items and the most effective means of supporting young children's learning. The American Academy of Pediatrics (2006) recently issued a report outlining their serious concerns about the reduced playtime for children and their parents, as hurried lifestyles and academic pressures negatively impact essential family time. Recommendations from their report include: the provision of active and ample, unscheduled, independent, nonscreen time in order that children have time to be creative, to reflect, and to decompress. They also emphasized the benefits of unstructured toys (p. 187).

The Kaiser Foundation (2005) research review on the role of electronic media in the lives of infants, toddlers, and preschoolers revealed that, while the sale and marketing of children's DVDs and computer games has exploded in recent years, there is "no reliable information about very young children's exposure, attention or interaction" with electronic media (p. 2). Reviewing this report, our participants expressed concerns that families may view such purchases as an "investment" in their children's education. The implications were particularly disturbing for those who taught in schools with families who experienced low socio-economic status. Participants were troubled by the high prices of products that made unsubstantiated educational claims. Money and time – all the more precious for the substantial number of our Canadian families who live with poverty – can be easily misplaced on heavily marketed items, when educational research affirms children's success is fostered through enjoyable family time spent sharing books, talking, solving problems in playful ways and engaging in a variety of literacies. Doctoral student, professional author, and experienced elementary school teacher Katherine Luongo-Orlando noted that "most toys with award winning labels or electronic features have expensive price tags." She believed that this was possibly sending contradictory messages to families who struggle to provide their children with quality early learning experiences. We question the real value of expensive electronic items such as small televisions (13" screens in pink, with Cinderella and Bratz motifs marketed at girls, and black/Batman TVs for boys) that were designed with children's bedrooms in mind and found alongside matching DVD players and a full assortment of lengthy DVD movies.

Our study participants are advocates for children and often viewed as experts who are requested for advice on children's toys and family involvement in education. This inquiry provided informed, reconceptualized direction to assist them in advising families and in choosing appropriate materials for their classrooms.

Where is Play?

Regarding the educative value of today's toys, study participants most frequently and strongly related their concern regarding observed market trends that limit the potential for freeplay.
They catalogued an increasing range and number of products
which were structured and had a single-use. These so-called creative kits featured a one-time, one-use activity (e.g., cosmetics and
body tattoos, learning games with prescribed outcomes, assemble
and display collectors items, etc.). These products were designed
with speedy consumption in mind, rather than fostering engaged
and sustained play and learning. Instead, these products forward
an underlying curriculum that teaches consumption and conformity.

Through design, packaging, and advertising, today's toys
increasingly prescribe the gender, age, and possible activities of
the play participants. While such designations may effectively
create consumer markets and protect companies from liability
(e.g. not for children under 3 years), socio-cultural perspectives on
early learning inform us that it is precisely through playing, communicating, and solving problems with diverse others that our
zone of proximal development is expanded, thus creating the conditions for learning to occur (Cameron & Bezaire, 2007).

Memories of childhood experience informed the participants'
analyses and many reflected on how cross-marketing had come to
limit the freeplay potential of yesteryear's most popular, creative
materials. Perennial favorites such as Playdough and Lego, were
now largely cross-marketed (e.g., McDonald's Playdough, Dairy
Queen Playdough, Star Wars Lego, Bionicle Lego), with instructions and potential activity being predetermined and unimaginative. Daniela Bascuñán noted, "It is extremely difficult for parents
to find toys that are not related to TV or movies . . . the stories
themselves are very dry and lack inspiration, fun or creativity."

The results of this study reveal pricing patterns whereby the
most popular toys were also the most expensive. "Toys seem to
have become fashion items," training teacher Jacqueline Brown
suggests, "that identify certain types and classes of individuals." In
focus group discussions, we continued our inquiry, considering
questions of personal subjectivity and notions of idealized or
romanticized childhoods and nostalgia, and after sifting through

these subjectivities, we asked again, "What are the implications for teaching and learning? What are the texts? What is the curriculum?"

Mindful of research about childhood and early childhood education, *Toytext Project* participants identified what they considered to be optimal toytexts, celebrating science/problem-solving toys, wooden blocks, open-ended houseplay items, diverse baby dolls, and open-ended construction toys. This category of toytext was least often displayed in prominent positions in the store. Art educator Julie Bell observed that these toys were "at the back of the store, in the last row . . . I wonder whether a child would even see them?" We advocate that optimal toytexts be assured prominent placement in stires and ample time and space in our early childhood classrooms. Let the "business" of toytexts and multiliteracies, play and learning, be our business as early childhood educators as we consider ways to respond to the provocations presented by this inquiry.

Multiliteracies and Make Believe

Charles Paschal (2008) highlights the importance of educator's creative and critical thinking – emphasizing "emergent learning and reflective practice" on the part of teachers and principals – in ensuring quality early learning and care for young children. He reminds us that we will need to be different in the future than we are today, that the purpose of initial teacher and in-service training for teachers involves developing "truly reflective practitioners." Thus, *The Toytext Project* served as a provocation for participants, with the hope that teachers will be moved toward action, critically reflecting on their own personal choices as consumers, as well as the role they play within their classrooms as a part of a larger social context/system. When teachers allow, acknowledge, and engage in children's popular consumer texts, they open up the possibility of challenging children to be critical, thinking deeply and meaningfully about text. In allowing consumer toytexts into the classroom, the toys do not become the basis of the curriculum – doing so would be tantamount to promotion or collusion. Rather, as teachers who recognize toys as text, we invite critical inquiry and engagement, offering opportunities to make connections between multiple texts and to develop more complex, critical understandings. *Culture Jamming* is a "technique where existing mass media texts are transformed in such a way as to act as public and social commentary on the media itself," with a purpose to "speak against corporate or mass media images" (Albers & Harste, 2007, p. 16). A Wonder Woman doll may be intertextually linked to all sorts of consumer products: Halloween costumes, DVDs, clothing, jewelry. But when a teacher places that doll alongside, perhaps, the class' favorite Jillian Jiggs picture book, a photo of a local female firefighter (a recent classroom visitor), and engages the children in conversations and inquiry around what it is to "be a superhero," we disrupt corporate scripts, and explore the critical potential of popular texts in the classroom. This teaching and learning terrain is, admittedly, tricky. Dyson (2003), in her study of children's play and literacy, considers the means and meanings that popular culture images and personas hold for young children:

> Popular images appeal, in part, for precisely the same reason they disconcert: they feature dominant desires and pleasures about, for example, power, wealth, and beauty, which themselves reflect interrelated societal constructions like age, gender, race and class. Using such texts is a way in which children can imagine themselves older and hipper; that is, those texts are toys for a kind of dress-up play. . . . (pp. 28-29)

In acknowledging and exploring what children find pleasurable or inviting, by providing multiple texts that explore, expand, and extend children's interests and emergent learning, and through thoughtful scaffolding, teachers engage in some gentle culture jamming, supporting children's critical meaning-making processes. As Kress (1997) explains, these processes are foundational to literacy practices in a changing world:

> The communicational landscapes of today, their relation to current forms of work and to current forms of pleasure, demand a recasting of our thinking about representation in the most far-reaching form. The world, now, is no longer a world in which written language is dominant. (p. 5)

Spy Team Investigation

"We're not spies yet," Austin asserts, adjusting the utility belt he has fashioned from a cardboard box and duct tape at the classroom's construction centre. "We're still kids, right?" Kyle replies, patting his cardboard moustache, a key part of his disguise. He glances nervously between Austin and Evan, who stands with his legs widely spaced, arms extended, a grimace on his face – Evan's self-made disguise is in place, as he signals "ready for action."

The boys begin to circle each other, kicking in the air with fists and feet, making gutteral noises and one-word exclamations, spinning in tandem. Austin is "the boss," with Kyle and Evan seemingly teaming up against him. "When we're practicing, we're all against our boss, right?" "The boss is the best, and we're all against him." "Don't really kick me. Just pretend," Austin clarifies. This rough and tumble play admittedly causes some tension for the classroom teacher, as does the spy team play theme. However, rather than shutting down the play, Stephanie watches, questions and engages with the boys in exploring their interest in spy agents. Through observation and dialogue with the children, she discovers that this play scenario is intertextually linked to various popular texts, including Spy Agent Lego toys, the feature film *Spy Kids*, *Spy Academy* television show, and various spy gadgets purchased at both upscale educational toystores and a local discount store.

Small group discussion, and observation of playground play reveal that the appealing aspects of spy agents includes solving puzzles, cracking codes, playing on teams, communicating with walkie talkies, and working with gadgets. Spy agents are described as brave, smart, tough, and sneaky, but further inquiry also reveals them to also be loyal, creative, and sometimes co-operative. Still, fighting persists as a key element, presenting the classroom teacher with a puzzle of her own. Stephanie offers ample time, space and creative arts materials, as well as her interest and assistance, as children design their own toytexts and play props and compose their own play scripts during freeplay times. She incorporates and links spy role-playing to curriculum expectations, as children become word detectives, searching for the little words inside of bigger words or listening for letter blends by reading aloud into walkie talkies fashioned from plastic pipe. Books such as *Harriet the Spy*, *Henry And Mudge and The Sneaky Crackers*, and *Superhero ABC* are provided and become popular books for shared reading. Connections are made, conversations abound, and inquiry continues and varies within the classroom community, as various other interests are explored and expanded (i.e., a project on African animals, families' plans for Spring Break).

Aspects of spy team that continue to cause tension include practice fighting, and stealing things. Small and large group discussions explore the difference between real and pretend fighting, as well as negotiating rules for what is acceptable and unacceptable to the classroom community. "Is killing a bad guy okay?" "Can girls be a spy boss?" "Should there be such thing as a boss?" Interest in consumer toytexts also persists, and Stephanie fields questions from concerned parents and skeptical colleagues – "Is the curriculum adequately being covered?" "Don't these themes encourage violent play?" "It's so noisy in your classroom!" While these questions sometimes cause anxiety, they, too, lead to dialogue; Stephanie makes use of classroom documentation (i.e., anecdotal notes, digital photography, artifacts) to make children's learning visible.

Returning to the questions concerning how to think about what our classrooms could invite, include, and inquire around, we should be cognizant of the possibilities and potential of everything that enters the classroom and becomes the curriculum. As teachers, we are reminded that the toytext becomes the connection to the curriculum, so play centres – play props and settings – need to reflect the population of the classroom. The props that we place provide invitations. When a child brings in something, it's the invitations we offer as we scaffold that influence where the play and meaning making can go, opening the curriculum, not closing it down with a script. For example, what happens if G.I Joe comes to school and we invite him into the sandbox? What sort of stories might emerge?

What are the implications for our early childhood education classrooms? Why does this matter? Should these toys be invited into our classrooms? If so, what might happen? Although we may want to stop these consumer texts at the doors of the classroom, child care, or parenting centre and insist that Bratz dolls, Game Boy games, or Star Wars figures be relegated to backpacks, should we? While our walk down the toy aisle may yield alarming results, we caution against an alarmist reaction. Although we advocate for finer toy options for our children, rather than stylized portrayals of precocious sexuality and simplistic violence, we do not suggest banning these toytexts from classrooms. Stephen Kline (1999), considers the communicative power of toys and cautions that "in adopting this 'hands-off' attitude [adults] are missing an important opportunity to communicate with children" regarding our own values and perspectives (p. 14). Rather, by recognizing the multimodal, multiliteracies potential of engagement with children's familiar toytexts, we would assert that much potential exists for playful, critical, and deep engagement within supportive social environments.

Classroom playthings, rules, and routines also provide everyday texts for children's play and learning. Healthy sexuality and body awareness are important for young children, as are opportunities to safely engage in conflict and asserting one's autonomy and power. Some of these opportunities include:

- mirrors in dress-up corners,

- dress-up clothes of all sorts,

- rich sensory experiences in which children enjoy and engage all five senses,

- creative movement with which to experiment, express, and enjoy their bodies,

- self-portraiture with art materials and photography,

- time out-of-doors in natural environments,

- rough and tumble play, tools and gadgets (real and invented),

- freedom to make loud noises, to test and negotiate limits.

These opportunities offer positive, protective experiences and media through which children can create, (re)play, and (re)imagine their everyday lives and possible future selves.

When ECE educators are "down on the floor," observing and documenting how children play, attempting to discern and make visible their varied meaning making and problem-solving processes, they learn more about the varied ways children connect to everyday texts. By attuning communication skills, by listening and entering children's play in thoughtful, timely ways, ECE educators can sensitively protect children's sense of wonder, foster critical thinking, and lovingly communicate and interrogate their values.

Creative, active play offers children "multimodal ways of representing meaning . . . [and] meaningful, personal ways of understanding and representing knowledge" (Cameron & Bezaire, 2007, p. 10-11). Kress (1997) provides evidence of his young children's journey to literacy and learning through detailed descriptions of their meaning making through make believe play about their stories, their imaginative use of play props and household objects, and their art pieces and developing writing attempts and interest in print – using all sorts of semiotics moving from one to the other.

Classrooms that provide options for varied and multimodal ways of knowing and constructing meaning, tools that inspire, toy-texts that kids connect with, ideas that abound, ample invitations for unstructured play, large blocks of time to expand, elaborate, and extend meaning, modeling of a critical examination of materials and ideas, play partners that engage and collaborate, stories that provide roots and wings, and caring teachers are early childhood delights. As Brian Edmiston (2008) suggests:

> When children play, in imagination they fully enter worlds that may be as engaging and complex as the cultural narratives that they draw upon which include their retold experiences, the stories they have read, and the movies they have watched. When adults play with children they can likewise enter those worlds not to observe but to participate with children, not only to listen but to interact and shape meaning, and not only to enter imagined space-times but to explore possible ways of acting and identifying with other people in the world. (p. 12)

Play is indeed a gift! It is a gift that promises to feature what is significant to the growing and developing child: a chance to think, wonder, question, imagine, pretend, solve problems, inquire, interact, laugh, cry, try! It is not limited to time or place or to anyone. It allows children the freedom to be anything that they choose to be, to do anything they want to do, and to have fun. It is complicated, however, and we do need to assure that we do our best to foster wisdom and sagacity along with pleasure. Is it not the right of the child (and the teacher!) to be able to play? Lego – play well!

Notes

[1] This is not to suggest that there is an absence of poverty in Western nations.

[2] A creative construction based on study of the children's consumer market.

[3] The remaining data in the chapter involving children are based on field note observations. All of the children's real names have been changed.

[4] The teacher/researchers submitted their observations for the purpose of publication and wanted to be identified by their real names.

References

Alber, P., & Harste, J. C. (2007). The arts, new literacies, and multimodality. *English Education, 40*(1), 6-20.

Alliance for Childhood. (2004). Childhood essentials: Fostering the full range of human capacities. In C. Cordes & E. Miller (Eds.), *Fool's gold: A critical look at computers in childhood* (pp. 45-66). Retrieved August 31, 2006 from http://www.allianceforchildhood.net/projects/computers/computers_r eports_fools_gold_download.htm

American Academy of Pediatrics (October 9, 2006). *The importance of play in promoting healthy child development and maintaining strong parent-child bonds.* Retrieved November 16, 2006, from http://www.aap.org/pressroom/ playFINAL.pdf

Achbar, M. [Producer], & Achbar, M., & Abbott, J. (Directors). (2003). *The Corporation* [Motion picture]. Canada: Zeitgeist Films.

Anderson, J., Moffatt, L., & Shapiro, J. (2006) Reconceptualizing language education in early childhood: Socio-cultural perspectives. In B. Spodek & O. N. Saracho (Eds.), *Handbook of research on the education of young children* (2nd ed.). Mahwah, NJ: Lawrence Erlbaum Associates, Publishers.

Barbaro, A. [Producer], & Earp, J. [Director]. (2008). *Consuming Kids: The Commercialization of Childhood* [Motion picture]. USA: Media Education Foundation.

Bergen, D. (2001). *Pretend play and young children's development.* ERIC document ED458045

Canadian Press. (2005, November 14). Traditional toys (plus) best, testers say. *The Toronto Star* [online]. Retrieved from www.thestar.com

Cameron, L. (2006). Play held hostage by the 'bully' excellence. *Touchstone 36th Annual Conference Proceedings: Council of Drama and Dance in Education,* 6-10 Retrieved November 3, 2008, from http://www.oise.utoronto.ca/ newsletters/december_06/CODE%20Touchstone%20Fall%202006%20Issu e%20-%20web%20edition.pdf

Cameron, L., & Bezaire, K. (2009). Toytexts: The power and potential of play in 21st century schooling. In D. Booth & S. Peterson (Eds.), *On screen and in print in children's literature.* Winnipeg, MB: Portage & Main Press.

Cameron, L., & Bezaire, K. (2007). Art-full play: Wonder-full learning. In M. Hachiya (Ed.), *Prospects for new early childhood education through art.* Yamagata, JP: Research Center for Children's Art Education, Tohoku University of Art and Design.

Cameron, L., Bezaire, K., & Murphy, S. (2008, July). *"Ready or not, here I come!": Play as multiliteracies.* Paper presented at the 19th Annual International Whole Language Umbrella Conference, National Council of Teachers of English, Tucson, AZ.

Carrington, V. (2003). 'I'm in a bad mood. Let's go shopping': Interactive dolls, consumer culture and a 'glocalized' model of literacy. *Journal of Early Childhood Literacy, 3*(1), 83-98.

Carrington, V. (2004). Texts and literacies of the Shi Jinrui. *British Journal of Sociology of Education, 25*(2), 215-228.

Center on Media and Child Health. (2005). The effects of electronic media on children ages zero to six: A history of research. Washington, DC: The Henry J. Kaiser Family Foundation.

Creswell, J.W. (2005). *Educational Research: Planning, Conducting, and Evaluating Quantitative and Qualitative Research.* (2nd ed.). Upper Saddle River, NJ: Prentice Hall.

Derman-Sparks, L. (1989). *Anti-bias curriculum: tools for empowering young children.* Washington, DC: National Association for the Education of Young Children.

Dewey, J. (1938/1997). *Experience and education.* New York: Simon and Schuster.

Dyson, A. H. (2003). *The brothers and sisters learn to read: Popular literacies in childhood and school cultures.* New York: Teachers College Press.

Edmiston, B. (2008). *Forming ethical identities in early childhood play.* New York: Routledge.

Edwards. C. P., Gandini, L., & Forman, G. E. (1998). *The hundred languages of children; the Reggio Emilia approach advanced reflections* (2nd ed.). Santa Barbara, CA: Greenwood Press

Elkind, D. (2003). The lasting value of true play. *Young Children, 58*(3), 46-50.

Elkind, D. (2006a). *The hurried child: Growing up too fast too soon* (New Edition). Cambridge, MA: Da Capo Press.

Elkind, D. (2006b). *The power of play: Learning what comes naturally.* Cambridge, MA: Da Capo Press.

Engel, S. (2005a). The narrative worlds of 'what is' and 'what if'. *Cognitive Development, 20*(4), 514-525.

Engel, S. (2005b). *Real kids: Creating meaning in everyday life.* Cambridge, MA: Harvard University Press.

Fonda, D. (2004, December 6). Zapped!: How the toy industry is being outplayed by video games this holiday season. *Time Magazine,* 52-54.

Gardner, H. (1993). *Frames of mind: The theory of multiple intelligences.* New York: Basic Books.

Gardner, H. (1999). *Intelligence reframed: Multiple intelligences for the 21st century.* New York: Basic Books.

hooks, b. (1990). *Yearning: Race, gender and cultural politics.* Boston, MA: South End Press.

Jarvis, P. (2007). Monsters, magic and Mr Psycho: A biocultural approach to rough and tumble play in the early years of primary school. *Early Years: An International Journal of Research and Development, 27*(2), 171-188.

Jenkinson, S. (2001). *The genius of play: Celebrating the spirit of childhood.* Goucestershire, UK: Hawthorn Press.

Kaiser Foundation (2005). *A teacher in the living room?: Educational media for babies, toddlers and preschoolers.* Menlo Park, CA: Henry J. Kaiser Family Foundation.

Kavanaugh, R. D. (2006). Pretend play In B. Spodek & O. N. Saracho (Eds.), *Handbook of research on the education of young children* (2nd ed.). Mahwah, NJ: Lawrence Erlbaum Associates, Publishers

Kline, S. (1999, June). *Toys as media: The role of toy design, promotional TV and mother's reinforcement in the young males (3-6) acquisition of pro-social play scripts for rescue hero action toys.* Paper presented at ITRA Conference, Halmstadt, Sweden. Retrieved June 24, 2008, from http://www2.sfu.ca/media-lab/research/toys/toymedia.pdf

Kress, G. (1997). *Before writing: Rethinking the paths to literacy.* New York: Routledge.

Linn, S. (2008). *The case for make-believe: Saving play in a commercialized world.* New York: New Press.

McCain, M., & Mustard, F. (1999). *Reversing the real brain drain: Early years study.* Toronto: Ontario Children's Secretariat.

McNeal, J. (1998, April). Tapping the three kids' markets. *American Demographics, 20,* 36-41.

Ontario Ministry of Education. (2007). *Supporting English language learners in Kindergarten.* Toronto: Author.

Paschal, C. (2008). *Early years education Ontario network.* Meeting Minutes of December 10, 2008.

Pellegrini, A. D., & Smith, P. K. (1998). Physical activity play: The nature and function of a neglected aspect of play. *Child Development, 69*(3), 577-598.

Podlozny, A. (2000). Strengthening verbal skills through the use of classroom drama: A clear link. *Journal of Aesthetic Education, 34*(3-4), 239-275.

Roskos, K., & Christie, J. (2001). Examining the play-literacy interface: A critical review and future directions. *Journal of Early Childhood Literacy, 1*(1), 59-89.

Rideout, V. J., Vandewater, E. A., & Wartella, E. A. (2003). *Zero to six: Electronic media in the lives of infants, toddlers, and preschoolers.* Menlo Park, CA: Kaiser Family Foundation.

Samson, F. (2005). Drama in aesthetic education: An invitation to imagine the world as if it could be otherwise. *Journal of Aesthetic Education 39*(4), 70-81.

Statistics Canada. (2005, January 25). *Visible minority population, by census metropolitan areas, 2001 Census.* Retrieved January 5, 2009, from http://www40.statcan.gc.ca/l01/cst01/demo53c-eng.htm

Statistics Canada. (2007, December 12). *Population by mother tongue, by census metropolitan area, 2006 Census.* Retrieved January 5, 2009, from http://www40.statcan.gc.ca/l01/cst01/demo12c-eng.htm

Sutton-Smith, B. (1986). *Toys as culture.* New York: Gardner Press.

Thorne, B. (2002). Do girls and boys have different cultures? In *The Jossey-Bass Reader on Gender and Education* (pp. 125-152). San Francisco, CA: Wiley .

Thornton, C. D., & Goldstein, L. S. (2006). Feminist issues in early childhood scholarship. In B. Spodek & O. Saracho (Eds.), *Handbook of research on the education of young children* (pp. 515-531). Mahwah, NJ: Erlbaum.

UNICEF. (2004). *The state of the world's children 2005: Childhood under threat.* New York: author.

Vasquez, V. (2001). Constructing a critical curriculum with young children. In (B. Comber & A. Simpson, Eds.), *Negotiating critical literacies in classrooms.* (pp. 55-66) Mahwah NJ: Lawrence Erlbaum Associates, Publishers

Wells, G. (1986). *The meaning makers: Children learning language and using language to learn.* Portsmouth, NH: Heinemann.

Wood, D. (1998). *How children think and learn.* Malden, MA: Blackwell.

12

Reconceptualizing Early Childhood Literacy Curriculum: An Eco-Justice Approach

Kelly Young

Recent efforts to reform the Ontario curriculum through a revitalization of environmental education have not been successful. Rather than expanding environmental education to encompass the entire curriculum, the Ontario Ministry of Education's 2007 report (re)unites environmental education solely with scientific inquiry to the exclusion of other important discourses. This development falls in line with an established history in Ontario of equating environmental education with scientific study. By tracing the origins of environmental education in North America to its Indigenous roots, and subsequently to a division between science and Indigenous environmental education models, I map out an historical trajectory of the ways in which environmental education has been and continues to be dominated by a science model that reinscribes a mechanistic and commodified approach to environmental education. In response to these failed curriculum reform efforts, I offer an eco-justice education framework as an integrated reconceptualist approach to early childhood literacy curriculum and, then, elaborate on its practical applications in order to help foster critical cultural and ecological literacy in early childhood curricula.

An eco-justice education framework illuminates the ways in which language – specifically, root metaphors – are linked to the development of anti-ecological ways of knowing and being that exclude human relations with the natural world (Bowers, 2001, 2006). I use this framing to reconceptualize early childhood literacy curriculum in order to facilitate a greater understanding of the ways in which sustainable relationships with the earth are important parts of the educational process. Throughout this process I a) delineate the ways in which root metaphors play a major role in informing cultural narratives that mediate human relationships with natural and reconstructed environments, b) address the reality that Indigenous Knowledge (IK) is often overlooked in environmental education curriculum decision-making processes, and c) offer an integrated eco-justice educational framework with practical application for early childhood literacy curriculum.

At a time when environmental education has been absent from Ontario's curriculum for nearly a decade, and when the eco-logical footprint is at a crisis level, the Ontario Ministry of Education (OME) commissioned a working group to review several ways in which to infuse the Ontario curriculum with environmental education (OME, 2007). Participants from across Ontario were asked for input. During a meeting with the working group that I was invited to address, I indicated that the origins of environmental education in North America can be traced to both a scientific model and IK (Sheridan, 1994; Young, 2006). I suggested that an Indigenous model be explored in order to infuse and reform environmental education in keeping with its origins. The working group however, ignored this vital information and produced an approach to environmental education based solely on a scientific model in their report, *Shaping Our Schools, Shaping Our Future* (2007). Unfortunately, the report reproduced the illusion of an ecologically sound method of environmental education as it replicates the very Enlightenment principles that have framed our interactions with the environment over the last several centuries. The report employs Eurocentric language steeped in scientific root metaphors that ultimately reinscribe an anthropocentric and individualistic approach to environmental education curriculum (Bowers, 2001, 2005, 2006, 2007). For example, the reports states that "responsible environmental citizenship incorporates problem solving, hands-on learning, action projects, scientific inquiry, higher order thinking, and cooperative learning" (p. 6). Environmental education is once again aligned with scientific inquiry as its sole model of understanding. A cultural analysis of the environmental crisis was not included in the report.

The report also states that environmental education promotes "environmental literacy that requires a mix of knowledge, vocabulary, key concepts, history, and philosophy" (p. 6). The report however failed to address IK in terms of informing curriculum reform. It is my steadfast belief that early childhood literacy curriculum be infused in a cross-curricular manner with environmental, ecological, and cultural literacy informed by *both* a scientific model and IK through an eco-justice approach.[1] What follows is an historical overview of the origins of environmental education, including outlines of several models of environmental education curricula informed by IK, linked with a reconceptualization of early childhood literacy curriculum theory and practice through an eco-justice educational framework.

The Origins of Environmental Education in North America

The origins of environmental education curricula in North America can be traced to their roots in the natural world through Ernest Thompson Seton's (1912) appropriation of Indigenous Knowledge into his program of *woodcraft*. Seton was the first non-Indigenous environmental educator to openly and consistently ground his educational methodologies in the ways of the Anishinaabe, Pueblo, and the San Ildefonso Apache near his Seton College of Indian Wisdom.[2] Seton enacted a form of Saulteaux environmental education that he learned from his own experiences with cultural authorities and also from the San Ildefonso Apache and the Haudenosaunee (largely from the correspondence with E. Pauline Johnson, the Haudenosaunee poet). Through his ideal model of the Indian, he developed his Woodcraft League in order to teach an approximation of place-based environmental education to youth. By drawing upon an example of how environmental and sustainable educational values were integrated into the cultural life of Indigenous peoples and how these ethics were infused through every dimension of cultural practice, Seton devised a program of study that engaged traditional cultural teachings in what dominant culture came to know as outdoor and environmental education. Engagement with woodcraft lore and nature study were essential experiential components followed by the symbolic domains of craft and storytelling. Although he may not have been able to address all Indigenous protocols of these traditional approaches accurately, he worked to teach youth about organic cyclical cultural practice through ritual and ceremony that resulted in an identity shift toward a naturalized state of being and the assumption of an approximation of Indigenous practices in traditional territories.

Seton's model of environmental education involved practicing traditional ceremony and ritual in spite of not having cultural authority, but also without instilling fear about "turning Indian" among his participants (Deloria, 1973; Shepard, 1982; Turner, 1980). Environmental education then, was initially an Indigenous cultural accomplishment that attempted to provide for settler culture practices of naturalizing personal and cultural identity to North America. Doing so also prevented antagonism towards the enviroment bread from the fear of a foreign and seemingly hostile land. Environmental education was an invitation to learn how to be Indigenous to North America by undertaking the work that cultural authorities assigned. Historian and Seton scholar, Wadland (1978) outlined Seton's environmental education model that involved athletic and woodlore proficiency, craftsmanship and survival techniques, and nature study (see pp. 276-362). All of the protocols involved a socialist model of mythic ritual that emphasized the importance of developing a healthy relationship between humans and the natural environment in a community setting and through cultural practices that involved Indian games of skill (p. 359).

The Scouting movement found its ethos in the environmental education roots aligned through Seton's Woodcraft League and his experience of Plains Ojibway or Saulteux culture that he experienced in Manitoba, Canada.[3] That ethos was initially developed to indigenize youth in/to North America and, hence, worked to establish a version of Indigenous teachings that accorded to settler culture responsibilities and duties to North America. These responsibilities involved, among other things, learning how to live in balance with the Earth and elaborated on the expectation that all peoples have contributions to be make to the harmony and balance envisioned by Indigenous Peoples.

In contrast with Seton's youth-based Indigenous environmental education model, Baden-Powell, captured the fundamental fear of "going Indian" in his paramilitary scouting and guiding movement (Sheridan, 1994; Young, 2006). Baden-Powell's (1909, 1918/1936; Baden-Powell & Baden-Powell, 1912) version of environmental education through the Scouting youth movement misappropriated Native ideas in Seton's woodcraft, and in an historical progression, Seton's model of environmental education (that worked to adhere to a partial Indigenous worldview) was replaced by Baden-Powell's paramilitaristic scouting and guiding movement, which was organized as forces prepared for the English in the Boer War in order to promote citizenship and character-building through skill and craft.

Paradoxically, Baden-Powell's youth movement became the foundation in the development of anti-ecological imperial habits of mind within contemporary environmental education exercises, thus perpetuating conditions as injurious to the originators of environmental education as the traditional territories of North America. Therefore, early in the twentieth century, learning to become native to North America ceased to be a focus of environmental education. For example, Scouting practices created internal dispositions and cognitive processes that came to guide ways of thinking and behaving about the twin fears of "turning Indian" and of the natural world (Young, 2006). The formation of anti-ecological imperial habits of mind in Baden-Powell's youth movement finalized a reaction against the possibility of fulfilling Indigenous environmental educational practices and undertaking their transformative spiritual and cultural potential (see Sheridan, 1994; Turner, 1980; Wadland, 1978; Young, 2006). Seton's model, however, was not the only model developed; Cajete's (1994) and Henley's (1989) contribution to environmental education are also important examples of practices that draw upon IK to produce a more just approach to the environment

Exemplary Models of Environmental Education

In addition to Seton's model of environmental education, Cajete's (1994) model provides an opportunity to help learners develop a deeper understanding of our role in an unbalanced world. He writes:

> Many of these thinkers are exploring alternative cos-
> mologies, paradigms and philosophies. They are
> searching for models that may sustain Nature rather
> than destroy it. Many of these thinkers have found
> that Indian cosmologies offer profound insights for
> cultivating a sustainable relationship to place, and a
> spiritually integrated perception of Nature. These are
> needed to address what has become a global crisis of
> ecological relationship. (p. 81)

Cajete outlines an environmental education model that a) engages the natural world by drawing on traditional systems of Indian education, b) explores "alternative approaches to education that directly and successfully address the requirements of Indian populations during this time of educational and ecological crisis" (p. 21), and c) "integrates, synthesizes, organizes and focuses the accumulated materials from a wide range of disciplines about Indian cultures and Indian education toward the evolution of a contemporary philosophy for American Indian education that is Indigenously inspired and ecologically based" (p. 22). By drawing on an Indigenous nature-centred philosophy, Cajete connects nature, humans, community, and spiritual ecology through education.

For Cajete (1994), Western science can benefit from an integrated model when partnered with IK. In Indigenous epistemology, one can only make meaning of something when it is understood in relation to all aspects of human life that involve the mind, body, and spirit. IK, then, has to do with being spiritually and physically integrated with spatio-temporal landscapes and involves knowledge, practices, and beliefs about the interrelatedness of humans and the physical environment. Within an IK framework, knowledge is inseparable from cultural, spiritual, and environmental contexts. IK is rational but has been marginalized by an existing Western science paradigm (Deloria, 1973). For Longboat (2008), rationality and dialogue are key ingredients in establishing the discourse of sustainability that involves a refusal to disassociate sacred from secular knowledge; moreover, rationality and dialogue are required in the development of cognitive models reflecting both the interrelationship of organisms that comprise Creation, as well as, the vast and ancient rotational patterns of the cosmos. This biocultural concept of rationality possesses, articulates, and embodies the rationality of Creation that Lovelock (1995) describes otherwise as the sentience of GAIA, a theory that the earth is alive (see Lovelock, 1988). An Indigenous view of knowledge draws upon Creation Stories and involves an understanding of the duty to respect all living things, human and nonhuman. Environmental and sustainable education requires principles for naturalizing cultural identities within a biocultural context (Longboat, 2008). For Cajete, (1994) an integrative model forms the basis for an ecologically centred approach to environmental education.

A third model of environmental education can be found in Henley's curriculum. Henley's (1989) account of *Project Rediscovery*, involves a cross-culturally diverse First Nation's based environmental education project enacted through summer camps on traditional territories. For his Earth-based model of experiential environmental education project, Henley outlines twelve principles that infer, at the core, respect and authority: 1) contact with the land that is in keeping with Native traditions, 2) food gathering that follow principles of conservation and stewardship, 3) small group dynamics that promote kinship, 4) teachings by Native Elders, 5) cross-cultural practices through the tradition of passing an eagle feather, 6) two week camping sessions, 7) sharing activities that promote self-expression, 8) solo expeditions for a sense of personal achievement, 9) physical exercise, 10) leadership skills, 11) environmental and cultural learning, and 12) follow-up through annual camping trips. These twelve steps amount to a curriculum where experiential activities and storytelling complement all traditional activities. Henley's curriculum brings together story, myth, and scientific knowledge through Native-based environmental education.

All three models, Seton, Cajete, and Henley have characteristics in common that involve humans in a cultural and ecological development of being through ecologies of stories enacted through storytelling in natural landscapes as *integrated* curricula.

In addition, these programs provoke an ecological development of identity where people begin to identify themselves more closely to their local environment. These models of environmental education are in opposition to Baden-Powell's imperial model that is linked to the social and moral reform movement whereby discipline and morality provide a framework for gendered citizenship practices through narratives of nationhood (Hall, 1996). Scouting employed character building strategies through an environmental education much akin to Outward Bound. In this model, nature is little more than the challenge necessary to survival, and the character development corresponding to this activity focused on domination and control as *alienated* models.

An integrated model is not new. Since first contact between the displaced European, African, and Asian Indigenous Peoples and the Indigenous Peoples of North America, Indigenous North Americans have tried to teach settlers how to live in balance and appropriately experience *being* within North American landscapes. What followed was a systematic apartheid of Indigenous Peoples through a growing tendency toward European spiritual disenfranchisement and domination over landscape through a sentiment of "progress" achieved through fear. For example, captivity narratives sent a panic throughout Europe and so fears grew about the possibility of becoming naturalized (Turner, 1980). These fears, in the form of imperial cultural narratives, were perpetuated for over 400 years manifesting themselves into Scouting, Brownie, and Girl Guide handbooks (among other texts) that formed the basis of environmental education for that same duration of presence in North America. Many of the curricula found in the handbooks that were originally intended to naturalize identities to North America through traditional systems of Indian education were altered in the name of colonial-imperial advancement, thus resulting in a development of anti-ecological imperial habits of mind through cultural practices (Young, 2006).

These cultural practices emphasize the ways in which, as Devereux (1996) suggests, "culture stands between the individual and the natural world" (pp. 24-25). Scouts, Brownies, and Girl Guides exemplify an Imperial cultural system (sacred teaching) made of history and fear in contrast with an IK system made of myth and spirituality because "the new antimythological myth was history" (Devereux, 1996). For Seton (1912), Cajete (1994), and Henley (1989), myth (sacred teaching) continues to be a focus in a natural system while history remains a focus in a cultural system as found in Baden-Powell's model. Ultimately, Baden-Powell's discourse creates unsustainable practices through the development of anti-ecological imperial habits of mind that directly contradict the profound affect, as demonstrated by more recent research, that the natural world has on children's perceptions of their environments in early development (see Cobb, 1959; Coles, 1990; Nabhan, 1997; Nabhan & Rosenberg, 1997; Shepard, 1982). Restricting curricula to a solely human act is inherently anthropocentric; to avoid this approach to our enviroment, a reconceptualization of curriculum is required.

Despite Orr's (1992) plea that "all education is environmental education" (p. 81), only the education models of Indigenous culture have accomplished an ideal objective where curriculum is not a solely human affair. There are many reasons that environmental education became a wholly human affair. For example, landscapes lost their veracity under the regime of print in the agricultural era. As a corollary, learning about the relationship between story and place, which occurs mainly through intergenerational knowledge being passed down culturally, diminished in the evolution of settlement and sedentary habits of mind that have been fully expressed in the development of urban architecture (see Abram, 1996; Bowers, 2003; Bowers & Flinders, 1990; Bringhurst, 2002; Brody, 2000; Sheridan, 2002; Solnit, 2000). With population growth, indoor urban education became the dominant model further promoting human alienation from the natural world despite a growing field of environmental education in North America.

Environmental Education in North America

Carson's (1962) influential work *Silent Spring* invited humans to question their own relationships with the natural world. Her work is often positioned as the dawning of contemporary environmental education. In addition, throughout the middle to latter half of the twentieth century, the Scouting movement, based in imperial cultural narratives, expanded globally. At the same time, contemporary environmental education in North America continued to develop in higher educational settings with a division between environmental studies and environmental science eventually emerging.[4] Environmental studies involved data that primarily focused on human aspects using subjective investigation in relation to environment as data, while environmental sciences used data divided into specializations, such as biology, chemistry, geography, and physics or "natural sciences" using objective investigation of environment (Longboat, Kulnieks, & Young, 2009). With environmental sciences primarily measuring, classifying, and quantifying data, "a predictive model that could then be universalized and generalized" became increasingly tied to an economic consumer-producer model through an "objective" analysis (p. 4). This process of legitimization is increasingly tied to global economics. Eventually by "the early 1970s, courses in environmental education began to be offered and the first program of study in environmental studies in Canada was offered at Trent University in Peterborough, Ontario" (p. 6).

During this period of change, naturalists and biologists developed the earth sciences, IK was increasingly informing the field of ethnobotany, and environmental studies programs were growing across North America. By the 1980s, deep ecologists and Indigenous scholars were influencing "the growing field of eco-justice education that aims to broaden understanding of environment through collaborative processes across disciplines and cultures" (Longboat, Kulnieks, & Young, 2009, p. 8).[5] While science remains the dominant paradigm of environmental education, there is a growing interest in the collaboration of IK with science models as evidenced by the development of an Indigenous Environmental Studies program at Trent University in 2000 that integrates IK and scientific inquiry through a nature-based experiential program (Longboat, 2008).

Eventually, over time and across North America, K-12 education became a solely indoor activity save for a few outdoor environmental education programs that were never fully infused across the curriculum; they continue to diminish across Ontario due to financial cutbacks. A hyper-separation between humans and nonhumans in educational settings predominantly became a taken-for-granted way of knowing and being. In contemporary times, 95% of life takes place under a roof. Former Adbusters, Environmental Editor, Nicholson-Lord (2006) writes:

> No other society in history has lived so cocooned from the routine vagaries of climate and weather – the crop failures, food shortages and environmental reverses that have vexed humanity since prehistory but that have also demonstrated how we rely on nature for our survival. Up to 93 percent of Westerners' lives are now lived indoors. Research suggests that 99 percent of Americans spend less than one day in a lifetime in conscious sensory contact with nature. Out of 1,440 minutes a day, Britons average just one minute in the countryside or seaside.
>
> We live, in short, in a new evolutionary habitat – a roofed-in-terrain composed of a succession of boxes that fit around us like the layers of a Russian doll (house, car, train, office, bar, city). The main avenue of release from this manufactured world is itself a fiction – the virtual (nonspatial) worlds of Internet, television, iPod, mobile. More crucially, we treat bubble concepts – most notoriously, the market economy – as real, allow them to rule our thoughts and lives. (p. 1)

These habits define the lives of those fully assimilated into a sedentary life. These habits are cultural and are reproduced through dominant cultural narratives that have fully adopted a taken-for-granted view that environmental education is a wholly human affair. Is teacher education not still, perhaps more so, the colonial project of complete assimilation for everyone? Is *nature attention disorder* not the single greatest educational development and accomplishment of the colonial-alienated model? And since it was Baden-Powell's curriculum that altered these cultural practices away from natural practices, then is it not education's responsibility to realign what was misaligned by turning to eco-justice, an emerging field of research and pedagogical practice that is increasingly being adopted by faculties of education across North America as an integrated framework from which to base reconceptualist early childhood literacy curriculum.

An Eco-Justice Framework

Eco-justice n., the condition or principle of being just or equitable with respect to ecological sustainability and protection of the environment, as well as social and economic issues. (*OED*, 2008)

Linking *ecology*, (derived from the Greek, *oikos*, meaning "household," as the study of relationships), *justice* and *pedagogy*, eco-justice in its broadest conceptualization involves a cultural analysis of environmental degradation and social oppression informed through an interdisciplinary approach to educational theory and practice.[6] Within the field of *eco-justice education*, many theorists argue that language carries forward root metaphors that reproduce cultural epistemologies and ontologies in terms of identity-formation and human and nonhuman relations (see Bartz, 2007; Bowers, 2001, 2002, 2006, 2007; Bowers & Martusewicz, forthcoming; Gaylie, 2007; Kulnieks, 2006, Longboat, Kulnieks, & Young, 2007; Martusewicz, 2005; Martusewicz & Edmundson, 2004; Young, 2005, 2008). The following essential aspects of an eco-justice education framework were identified by Bowers and further refined by Bowers and Martusewicz (2004):

1. Analyzing the deep cultural assumptions or root metaphors that underlie both social inequalities and ecological degradation and are carried forward inter-generationally.

2. Recognizing the relationship among the domination of nature and the domination of oppressed groups such as women, indigenous peoples, and ethnic groups both locally and across the globe.

3. Ending the practices of exploitation and cultural colonization by Western industrialized nations on the cultures of the "South" (e.g., "Third World" which is now more commonly referred to as "Majority World" cultures).

4. Revitalizing the commons (e.g., water, air, land etc.) in order to achieve a healthier balance between market and nonmarket aspects of community life.

5. Ensuring that the prospects of future generations are not diminished by the hubris and ideology that drives the globalization of the West's industrial culture.

6. Reducing the threat to what Vandana Shiva refers to as "earth democracy" – that is, a decision-making system and a sense of responsibility that recognizes the right of natural systems to reproduce themselves rather than to have their existence contingent upon the demands of humans.

An eco-justice approach involves, among other things, a cultural and ecological analysis of root metaphors (patriarchy, anthropocentrism, ethnocentrism, individualism, progress, mechanism, economism) that frame a Western mindset by reproducing hierarchies that conceptualize humans as superior to nature and animals; conceptualize scientific inquiry as superior to experiential and Indigenous Knowledge; reinforce oppressive relations; conceptualize print as superior to oral tradition; and espouse a privileging of notions of "progress" that perpetuate a consumerist society in lieu of valuing "traditions" that espouse noncommodified relations (see Bowers, 2001, 2002; Bowers & Martusewicz, 2004). Root metaphors are explanatory frameworks derived by the mythopoetic narratives and powerful evocative experience that influenced thinking and behavior across a wide range of cultural experience (Bowers, 2001; Merchant, 1980). Since these root metaphors are embedded in, and are taught as part of the dominant discourse through a privileging of cultural narratives that perpetuate anti-ecological relationships, it is the work of eco-justice educators to name these metaphors and cultural narratives and reveal the ways in which classroom curricula mediate identity-formation, attitudes, and perceptions.

Reconceptualization of Early Childhood Literacy Curriculum

My proposed reconceptualization of early childhood literacy curriculum draws upon the origins of environmental education as outlined earlier through models proposed by Seton (1912), Cajete (1994), and Henley (1989) together with an eco-justice framework. I then seek to integrate these models into the scientific inquiry model as outlined in the Ontario working group's report *Shaping*

Our Schools, Shaping Our Future (2007). I am ultimately proposing a reconceptualized curriculum that involves identifying practices that help humans get over an obsession with development, progress, and consumerism"and consider how dominant cultural narratives perpetuate anti-ecological habits of mind. Dominant cultural narratives include taken-for-granted notions of human domination over the natural world through a commodification of "natural resources" into a celebrated story of "progress" based on a myth that consumption of these resources are endless and have no boundaries. These narratives are featured everyday in the media, conveying a message that bigger and more is better, new and improved products are superior to older ones, and that progress is the inevitable trajectory of civilization while tradition is somehow backward.

By bringing together as many elements of an eco-justice framework as possible with Indigenous models, I propose to integrate four elements into a cross-curricular approach to early childhood literacy. This approach enables children and educators to explore root metaphors that reproduce hierarchies and anti-ecological habits of mind by examining commodified versus non-commodified relationships (intergenerationally, in communities, and in curriculum practices). This curriculum integration includes an analysis of Western and Indigenous cultural narratives through storytelling and situates learning as experiential and nature-based as much as possible in order to make necessary connections between human consumption and its impact on natural ecosystems and future sustainability. This integrated model promotes a mix of cultural and environmental literacy involving IK and Western cultural narratives and focuses on naming and comparing commodified and noncommodified relationships that impact natural ecosystems.

As mentioned early in this chapter, the Ontario working group's (2007) report identified six aspects for "responsible environmental citizenship" and further suggested that environmental education promote "environmental literacy" (p. 6). In so doing, however, it failed to acknowledge that cultural literacy is essential in developing ecological habits of mind. My integrated model extends the report's six identified aspects of environmental education by incorporating IK and eco-justice through 1) problem-solving, involving a consideration of impacts of sustainability for future generations; 2) cooperative learning comprising intergenerational members of the community; 3) hands-on learning entailing experiential and nature-based engagements whenever possible; 4) action projects involving an inclusion of intergenerational knowledge and cultural storytelling; 5) scientific inquiry that engages an inclusion of Indigenous ways of knowing to promote a "mix of knowledge" (p. 6); and 6) an integration of higher-order thinking skills where the ways in which all things are interrelated and interdependent are explored through an analysis of root metaphors. Environmental education can only serve to promote ecological literacy if it is entirely grounded in a critical cultural and ecological literacy that in turn draws upon an integrated approach of scientific inquiry and IK. Within an Early childhood literacy curriculum, this entails fostering the cultural literacy skills necessary to counter the cultural narratives that proclaim that bigger and more is always better. Moreover, by introducing concepts early in order to promote traditional non-commodified relations as important aspects of healthy living, early educators begin an important process to build upon further in the junior-intermediate and senior years. An eco-justice infused curriculum involves a cross-curricular approach that integrates social sciences, geography and history, media and technology, and the arts within the context of early childhood literacy curriculum as it brings together hands-on learning, critical inquiry, problem-solving, cooperative learning, and cultural storytelling.

Eco-justice in Early Childhood Literacy Curriculum: Vocabulary Building

The Ministry of Education's revised 2006 documents, *The Ontario Kindergarten Program* and *The Ontario Curriculum Grades 1-8*, do include suggestions for raising environmental issues as part of the curriculum. However, they do not specifically help students mediate culture's role in perpetuating the environmental and social crisis. Elementary language arts curriculum reconceptualized through an eco-justice framework can enhance the existing curriculum because it involves developing an analysis of cultural narratives through inquiry. Regardless of grade level, it is important to introduce concepts by beginning with metaphor, since all language is metaphorical in nature, and in its simplest form, metaphor is an analogy: this is like that. *Comparisons* will help students to name the analogs that reproduce mechanistic root metaphors instead of ecologically-based ones (Bowers, 2001, 2002; Bowers & Martusewicz, 2004). Examples include: How is the body like a clock or computer? (revealing a mechanistic root metaphor). How is it different? How is the body like a plant (repositioning the body through an ecological root metaphor)? Language is clearly a tool that can at once reveal and hide meanings. Esteva and Prakash (1998) write:

> Tools redefine and reshape the human condition. Modern tools have transformed their users and operators into extensions of or in the image of the machine. And no other tool serves to have had a more profound impact on the human condition than the alphabet. It transformed men and women during a long historical process, into texts . . . (p. 73)

Developing an eco-justice oriented repertoire of *guiding questions* can help to facilitate comparisons and will help in building an *eco-justice vocabulary*. For example: How is a stream like a drain? How is it different? This is an important comparison of two similar things that essentially act in the same manner (both move water toward a larger body of water). How do we treat these same things differently? Which word, *drain* or *stream* is derived from a mechanistic root metaphor? Which one is derived from an ecological root metaphor? Why does it matter? Would you put different things in a stream versus a drain? These are examples of how language mediates relationships (Martusewicz, Lupinacci & Edmundson, in review). For younger children, reformulating these questions might include asking what associations come to mind for the words *drain* and *stream* and eventually exploring these in local communities. Ultimately, developing a comparison guide for naming root metaphors will be useful in integrating an eco-justice action project.

Developing an Eco-justice Action Project: All about Me and My Local Community

Beginning with cultural storytelling about *self* and *community* as foci for an eco-justice action project, students apply eco-justice vocabulary to an active investigation of dominant cultural narratives. However, before young children are able to report on their own relationships, they will benefit from having stories read aloud to them as these can provides models for understanding the foundation of relations. Stories, in the form of fables, fairy-tales, adventures, fantasy, and so on engage and stimulate the imagination. They provide the possibility to broaden understandings, sympathies, and experience. Regularly listening to stories can promote an understanding of causality, as Egan (1989) suggests:

> Children, in coming to make sense of increasingly sophisticated stories, come of necessity to develop an increasingly subtle sense of causality. They learn problem-solving and the forming and reforming of hypotheses in the light of further knowledge. They become familiar with an increasingly wide range of human emotions and ways of responding to them: a good story will stimulate sympathy and actively develop the emotional life. (p. 85).

Understanding causality will ultimately help students to discover cause-and-effect relationship between culture and the environmental and social crisis, which is ultimately one of the hopes for eco-justice education.

Because it helps children recognize causality, story plays an important role in teaching young children about their relationships to others and their environment. As students listen to a variety of stories and learn to tell their own stories, in their own words and with their own storytelling voices, they better understand how they are connected to their culture and enviroment and can begin to discern the differences between commodified and noncommodified relationships. Students research and tell stories about the current and past practices of their parents, grandparents, great-grandparents, aunts, uncles, and community elders that do not dependent on monetary exchanges (games, songs, traditional crafts, gardening, etc.). Students compare these traditional noncommodified relationships with their current relationships that are predominantly commodified and report their findings in various forms (drama, oral presentations, music, poetry, letters, media advertisements, etc.) that integrate reading, writing, listening, speaking, viewing, and representing. Students can then continue to build an eco-justice vocabulary by comparing how they relate to humans and the natural world via consumer and nonconsumer practices.

Ultimately, students compare themselves in terms of two distinct forms of relationships – commodified and noncommodified – with elders and further explore how language and cultural practices perpetuate hierarchies that celebrate notions of progress over traditional practices. (Bowers, 2007). For example, students can compare traditional food preparation with fast food consumption; natural settings with indoor human-made settings; music (playing an instrument) with commercial production of music; arts (making crafts) with purchasing crafts; historical landscape/architecture with contemporary landscape/architecture; face to face relations with computer mediated relations; oral traditions with print-based traditions. As students are introduced to classification schemes, they can begin to classify relationships into commodified/noncommodified associations in the same way that they currently classify items by color, numbers, shapes, animals, plants, sounds, and so on.

As part of an eco-justice action project, students investigate the differences between past traditional ways of knowing and being with contemporary practices through an analysis of various cultural practices. Students also compare traditions of Indigenous peoples with non-Indigenous elders whether through oral storytelling, films, or storybooks. In Western society, each cultural practice (food, arts, etc.) is embedded in a larger dominant cultural narrative that privileges progress and consumerism over traditional experiential practices. In naming these cultural practices, students will learn to recognize cultural patterns (Bowers, 2007). Connections to dominant cultural narratives in media can then be explored and compared.

Analyzing cultural practices as outlined above involves comparing past and present ways of knowing and being. For example, when addressing the difference between approaches to traditional food preparation and today's fast food consumption, consider the following guiding questions: How is food preparation and consumption different? Why is it different today? How do Indigenous peoples approach food preparation? Students can share their food stories. In addition, further integration of eco-justice vocabulary concerning food could address food growth, distribution, and waste (composting, gardening, planting, soil nutrients, fertilizers, harvest, preserving, and preparing food) through an investigation into local versus global approaches to food production.

When focusing on a comparison between natural settings and human-made ones, consider the following guiding questions: How are trees repositioned as an exclusive product and article for trade (commodity) for humans to use and consume? What does it mean when we describe a forest as a woodlot, natural resources, timber or lumber, rather than woodland? Children can explore the differences and similarities between trees described as forest versus trees described as wood for building houses.

When addressing the difference between human relationships in an oral society and a print-based society, consider the following guiding questions: What is the difference between an oral traditional society and a print-centric society? How have relations been changed and mediated via the computer and Internet? What methods of communication did elders use and why? How are these different from contemporary modes of communication? Children can compare and classify these differences as a group with the teacher. These discussions can outline how oral cultures did not use print but, rather, told stories for days and sometimes even weeks. Children of oral traditions learned stories by listening to an Elder. Children can explore how Western children learn stories via oral storytelling, print, film, etc.

Concrete examples of early childhood literacy events can include but are not limited to a reconceptualization of "show and tell" that can be realigned with tradition versus consumer products. Handmade items can be shared and if possible the class could be conducted outdoors. Letters to Santa can be redirected to have students write to Santa about traditional cultural practices or hand-made gifts and why they are important. Dr. Seuss' (1974) *The Lorax* is an excellent resource that brings together themes of progress, capitalism, and the commodification of trees and their devastating effects on the environment and on animal species in a rhyming sequence. Parallels can be draw to real life issues.

Other considerations include comparing historical local architecture and landscape with contemporary geography and mapping out the visual and aerial aspects and physical layout of community (past and present). This will naturally move into a consideration of what forms of enclosure are part of everyday life – water, airways, woodlots and pastures, privatized land, state ownership, patents, works of art, Internet, land, roadways, and so on. Consider the following guiding questions: Where are greenhouses in the community? Where are farms located? How have land, water, airways, pastures, and so on been enclosed and privatized? Again, questions can be modified for younger children through a comparison and classification of pictures as they can identify the difference between natural landscapes and human-made ones, fenced-in areas versus free-range areas, farms versus cities.

Throughout an eco-justice action project, there is an ongoing review of the ways in which cultural practices impact the ecological crises that include the effects of global warming, melting ice-caps and the destruction of polar regions, water shortage and the commodification of water, degrading of ecosystems, greenhouse gases, loss of species, hunger and food shortages, and so on. Connections can be made to a dependency on consumer relationships and a penchant for self-sufficiency and autonomy. As the cultural narratives that align humans with consumer relations are revealed and noncommodified relations are explored, teachers can helps students make cross-curricular connections to the impacts that these taken-for-granted notions have on natural ecosystems through social studies, the arts, and media and technology.

Conclusion

Returning environmental education to its origins by fostering cultural literacy and ecological habits of mind in early childhood literacy involves a study of relationships. By returning to the origins of environmental education – IK and the educational models of Seton (1912), Cajete (1994), and Henley (1989) – in conjunction with the emerging eco-justice field, I have proposed several considerations of these approaches that need to be brought forward as important considerations for (re)conceptualizing early childhood literacy curricula through an eco-justice pedagogical approach to language and experiential learning. One outcome of this approach, and there are more to be discovered, is the construction of an eco-justice vocabulary through guided questions and comparisons. This vocabulary can then applied to a cross-cultural eco-justice action project through a cross-curricular analysis of dominant cultural narratives and their role in mediating relationships.

A deep human analysis of dominant cultural narratives needs to be central for a transformative relationship to develop with the natural world. By addressing the environmental crisis, as a crisis of culture that, then, becomes a crisis of education, it is my radical hope that my promotion of a reconceptualized early childhood literacy curriculum based upon an eco-justice education framework will open up possibilities for educators to think about the ways in which they are implicated in and positioned by dominant discourses that perpetuate anti-ecological identity-formation and habits of mind. Restricting literacy to a social act that humanity engages in diminishes the relationship of language to the nature world until it vanishes and becomes indiscernible. An eco-justice education approach makes explicit the implicit; that is, it magnifies the important differences between a noncommodified cultural approach to knowing and being and a dominant, seductive Western consumer cultural approach. Eco-justice pedagogy helps learners mediate between these with a hope for a sustainable future.

Notes

1 In an effort not to essentialize Indigenous Knowledge (IK), for the purpose of this chapter, IK refers to the form of sustainable environmental knowledge and practices produced by Earth-based peoples that have been sought across the world in order to inform environmental issues and environmental education. My own research is specifically informed by the traditional knowledge of the Anishinaabe and Haudenosaunee. In my research and teaching, I draw upon my own experience of IK in several ways. Specifically, I have learned that while there has been a division between IK and Western science in many academic settings, an integrated model that brings these two areas together into an emerging Indigenous environmental studies discipline is growing across North America. (See Longboat, Kulnieks, & Young, 2009).

2 Seton College of Indian Wisdom moved to Santa Fe, New Mexico. Seton designed and built Seton Castle and founded the "Seton Institute of Indian Lore," a training camp for leaders of recreational organizations based on the North American Indian traditional way of life. His college drew upon IK traditions and continued to employ these teachings through his conclusive work at the Seton College of Indian Wisdom, which saw San Ildefonso Apache Elders teaching their wisdom in the first college credit course ever taught by Indigenous North Americans. See http://www.etsetoninstitute.org

3 Seton's (1912) experiential and nature-based curriculum was primarily intended for boys, but it eventually branched out to include girls through the Scouting movement that included Girl Scouts, Girl Guides, Brownies, Boy Scouts, and Cubs.

4 For a literature review on the relationship between environmental science and IK see Young, 2007.

5 See Berry (1995, 1996), Capra (1996), Lovelock (1988), Maturana and Varela (1998), and Snyder (1990) who were writing about experiential learning and the seminal writings of Bateson (1972), Basso (1996), Bringhurst (2002), Cajete (1994), Cruikshank (1981), Kane (1995), Laduke (1999), Orr (1992), and Sheridan (1994).

6 Eco-justice draws upon such disciplines and fields as ecofeminism (Fawcett, 2000; Griffin, 1995; Merchant, 1980; Plumwood, 1994, 2002; Shiva, 1993; Taylor, 1997; Warren, 2000, 1997), Indigenous Knowledge and Indigenous environmental studies (Apffel-Marglin & PRATEC, 1998; Basso, 1996; Bowers & Apffel-Marglin, 2004; Cajete, 1994, 2000; Chase, 1993; Cruikshank, 1981, 1990; Kane, 1995; Kulnieks, 2006; Laduke, 1999; Longboat, 2008; McGregor, 2004; Norberg-Hodge, 1992; Sheridan, 1994; Sheridan & Longboat, 2006; Wilson, 2002; Young, 2006), and perhaps finds its most profound influence from theorists in the fields of deep ecology, sociology of knowledge and socio-linguistics (Abram, 1996; Bateson, 1972; Berger & Luckmann, 1967; Berry, 1995; Bowers, 2003; Bowers & Flinders, 1990; Bringhurst, 2002; Brown, 1977; Cobb, 1959; Illich, 1970; Lakoff & Johnson, 1980; Leopold, 1948; Mander & Goldsmith, 1996; Mulhausler, 1996; Orr, 1994; Ortony, 1979; Polanyi, 2001; Shills, 1981; Snyder, 1990).

References

Apffel-Marglin, F., & PRATEC. (1998). *The spirit of regeneration: Andean culture confronting western notions of development.* London: Zed Books Ltd.

Abram, D. (1996). *The spell of the sensuous: Perception in a more-than-human world.* New York: Pantheon Books.

Baden-Powell, R. (1909). *Scouting for boys: A handbook for instruction in good citizenship through woodcraft.* Ottawa: National Council of Boy Scouts of Canada.

Baden-Powell, R. (1918/1936). *Girl Guiding: The official handbook.* London: C. Arthur Pearson, Ltd.

Baden-Powell, R., & Baden-Powell, A. (1912). *The handbook for Girl Guides or how girls can help to build the empire.* London: Thomas Nelson and Sons.

Bartz, S. (2007). Using ecojustice principles in an elementary school world cultures curriculum (parts 1&2). *The EcoJustice Review: Educating for the Commons, 1*(1), 1-6.

Basso, K. (1996). *Wisdom sits in places: Landscape and language among the Western Apache.* Alburqurque, NM: University of New Mexico Press.

Bateson, G. (1972). *Steps to an ecology of mind: Collected essays in anthropology, psychiatry, evolution, and epistemology.* San Francisco, CA: Chandler Pub. Co.

Berger, P., & Luckmann, T. (1967). *The social construction of reality: A treatis in the sociology of knowledge.* Garden City, NY: Anchor.

Berry, W. (1995). *Another turn of the crank.* Washington, DC: Counterpoints.

Berry, W. (1996). Farming and the global economy. In W. Berry (Ed.), *Another turn of the crank.* San Francisco, CA: Counterpoints.

Bowers, C. A. (2001). *Educating for eco-justice and community.* Athens, GA: The University of Georgia Press.

Bowers, C. A. (2002). Toward an eco-justice pedagogy. *Environmental Education Research, 8*(1), 21-34.

Bowers, C. A. (2003). *Mindful conservatism: Rethinking the ideological and educational basis of an ecologically sustainable future.* Lanham, MD: Rowman & Littlefield Publishers.

Bowers, C. A. (2005). *The false promises of constructivist theories of learning: A global and ecological critique* (complicated conversation). New York: Peter Lang Publishing.

Bowers, C. A. (2006). *Revitalizing the commons: Cultural and educational sites of resistance and affirmation.* Langham, MA: Lexington Books.

Bowers, C. A. (2007). *Handbook for faculty on how to introduce cultural commons and ecojustice issues into their courses.* Retrieved July 6, 2008, from http://cabowers.net

Bowers, C. A., & Apffel-Marglin, F. (2004). *Re-thinking Freire: Globalization and the environmental crisis.* Mahwah, NJ: Lawrence Erlbaum Associates.

Bowers, C. A., & Flinders, D. J. (1990). *Responsive teaching: An ecological approach to classroom patterns of language, culture and thought.* New York: Teachers College Press.

Bowers, C. A., & Martusewicz, R. (2004). *The ecojustice dictionary.* Retrieved January 25, 2008, from http://www.ecojusticeeducation.org

Bowers, C. A., & Martusewicz, R. (forthcoming). Ecojustice education and the revitalization of the commons. In E. Provenzo (Ed.), *Encyclopedia of the social and cultural foundations of education.* New York: Sage Publishers.

Bringhurst, R. (2002). The tree of meaning and the work of ecological linguistics. *Canadian Journal of Environmental Education, 7*(2), 9-22.

Brody, H. (2000). *The other side of Eden: Hunters, farmers and the shaping of the world.* Vancouver, BC: Douglas & McIntyre.

Cajete, G. (1994). *Look to the mountain: An ecology of indigenous education.* Skyland, NC: Kivaki Press.

Cajete, G. (2000). *Ecology of Native American community.* Athens, GA: University of Georgia Press.

Capra, F. (1996). *Web of life: A new understanding of living systems.* New York: Anchor Books.

Carson, R. (1962). *Silent spring.* Boston, MA: Houghton Mifflin.

Chase, A. (1993). Traditional ecological knowledge: Wisdom for sustainable development. *The Australian Journal of Anthropology, 4*(3), 245-247.

Cobb, E. (1959). The ecology of imagination in childhood. *Daedalus: Journal of the American Academy of Arts and Sciences, 88*(Summer), 537-548.

Coles, R. (1990). *The spiritual life of children.* Boston, MA: Houghton Mifflin.

Cruikshank, J. (1981). Legend and landscape: Convergence of oral and scientific traditions in the Yukon Territory. *Arctic Anthropology, xviii*(2), 67-93.

Cruikshank, J. (1990). Getting words right: Perspectives on naming and places in Athapaskan oral history. *Arctic Anthropology, 27*(1), 52-65.

Deloria, V. J. (1973). *God is red.* New York: Dell Publishing.

Devereux, P. (1996). *Re-envisioning the earth: A guide to opening the healing channels between mind and nature.* New York: Simon & Schuster.

Egan, K. (1989). *Teaching as story telling: An alternative approach to teaching and curriculum in the elementary school.* Chicago: University of Chicago Press.

Esteva, G., & Prakash, M. S. (1998). *Grassroots post-modernism: Remaking the soil of cultures.* New York: Zed Books.

Fawcett, L. (2000). Ethical imagining: Ecofeminist possibilities and environmental learning. *Canadian Journal of Environmental Education, 5*, 134-147.

Gaylie, V. (2007). Teaching teachers in a learning garden: Two metaphors. *The EcoJustice Review: Educating for the Commons, 1*(1), 1-4.

Griffin, S. (1995). *The eros of everyday life.* New York: Doubleday.

Hall, S. (Ed.). (1996). *Questions of culture and identity.* Thousand Oaks, CA: Sage.

Henley, T. (1989). *Project rediscovery: Ancient pathways - new directions.* Vancouver, BC: Western Canada Wilderness Association.

Illich, I. (1970). *Deschooling society.* New York: Harper & Row.

Kane, S. (1995). *Wisdom of the mythtellers.* Peterborough, ON: Broadview Press.

Kulnieks, A. (2006). Rediscovering traditional teaching and language learning: Interpreting a journey of story, song and dance at camp Gazerers. The *Canadian Journal of Environmental Education, 11,* 143-156.

Laduke, W. (1999). *All our relations: Native struggles for land and life-selection.* Cambridge, MA: South End Press.

Lakoff, G., & Johnson, M. (1980). *Metaphors we live by.* Chicago: The University of Chicago Press.

Leopold, A. (1948). *A Sand County almanac, and sketches here and there.* Oxford: Oxford University Press.

Longboat, D., Kulnieks, A., & Young, K. (2009). Beyond dualism: Toward a transdiciplinary indigenous environmental studies model of environmental education curricula. *The EcoJustice Review: Educating for the Commons, 1*(1), 1-18.

Longboat, D. R. (2008). *Owehna'shon: A (the islands) Kawenoke the Haudenosaunee archipelago: The nature and necessity of biocultural restoration and revitalization.* Unpublished doctoral dissertation, York University, Toronto, ON.

Lovelock, J. (1988). *The ages of Gaia: A biography of our living earth.* New York: WW Norton & Co.

Lovelock, J. (1995). *Gaia, a new look at life on earth.* Oxford: Oxford University Press.

Mander, J., & Goldsmith, E. (1996). *The case against the global economy, and for a turn toward the local.* San Francisco, CA: Sierra Club Books.

Martusewicz, R. (2005). Eros in the commons: Educating for eco-ethical consciousness in a poetics of place. *Ethics, Place & Environment, 8*(3), 331-348.

Martusewicz, R., & Edmundson, J. (2004). Social foundations as pedagogies of responsibility and eco-ethical commitment. In D. Butin (Ed.), *Teaching context: A primer for the social foundations of education.* Mahwah, NJ: Lawrence Erlbaum Publishers.

Martusewicz, R., Lupinacci, J., & Edmundson, J. (in review). *Teaching for diversity, democracy and sustainability: An ecojustice approach.* New York: Routledge.

Maturana, H., & Varela, F. (1998). *The tree of knowledge: The biological roots of human understanding.* New York: Random House.

McGregor, D. (2004). Coming full circle: Indigenous knowledge, environment and our future. *American Indian Quarterly, 28*(3-4), 385-410.

Merchant, C. (1980). *The death of nature: Women, ecology, and the scientific revolution.* San Francisco, CA: Harper & Row.

Muhlhausler, P. (1996). *Linguistic ecology: Language change and linguistic imperialism in the pacific region.* London: Routledge.

Nabhan, G. (1997). *Cultures of habitat: On nature, culture, and story.* Washington, DC: Counterpoint Press.

Nabhan, G., & Rosenberg, J. (1997). Where ancient stories guide children home. *Natural History, 106*(9), 54-61.

Nicholson-Lord, D. (2006, January/February). Drink fresh snow. *Adbusters,* p. 1.

Norberg-Hodge, H. (1992). *Ancient futures: Learning from Ladakh.* San Francisco, CA: Sierra Club Books.

OED. (2008). Eco-justice. *The Oxford English dictionary.* Retrieved May 16, 2008, from   http://www.britannica.com/EBchecked/topic/436518/The-Oxford-English-Dictionary

Ontario Ministry of Education. (2006a). *The Ontario curriculum grades 1-8.* Toronto: Queen's Printer for Ontario.

Ontario Ministry of Education. (2006b). *The Ontario kindergarten program.* Toronto: Queen's Printer for Ontario.

Ontario Ministry of Education. (2007, June). *Shaping our schools, shaping out future.* Toronto: Working Group on Environmental Education, Ontario Ministry of Education.

Orr, D. (1992). *Ecological literacy: Education and the transition to a postmodern world.* Albany, NY: State University of New York Press.

Orr, D. (1994). *Earth in mind: On education environment and the human prospect.* Washington, D C: Island Press.

Ortony, A. (Ed.). (1979). *Metaphor and thought.* Cambridge, MA: Cambridge University Press.

Plumwood, V. (1994). *Feminism and the mastery of nature.* London: Routledge.

Plumwood, V. (2002). *Ecological culture: The ecological crisis of reason.* New York: Routledge.

Polanyi, K. (2001). *The great transformation: The political and economic origins of our time.* Boston, MA: Beacon Press.

Seton, E. T. (1912). *The book of woodcraft and Indian lore.* London: Constable & Co.

Seuss, D. (1974). *Dr. Seuss story time.* New York: Random House.

Shepard, P. (1982). *Nature and madness.* San Francisco, CA: Sierra Club Books.

Sheridan, J. (1994). *Alienation and integration: Environmental education in Turtle Island.* Unpublished doctoral dissertation, University of Alberta, Edmonton, AB.

Sheridan, J. (2002). My name is walker. *Canadian Journal of Environmental Education, 7*(2), 193-206.

Sheridan, J., & Longboat, D. (2006). The Haudenosaunee imagination and the ecology of the sacred. *Space and Culture, 9*(4), 365-381.

Shils, E. (1981). *Tradition.* Chicago: University of Chicago Press.

Shiva, V. (1993). *Monocultures of the mind: Perspectives on biodiversity and biotechnology.* Penang, Malaysia: Third World Network.

Snyder, G. (1990). *The practice of the wild.* New York: North Point Press.

Solnit, R. (2000). *Wanderlust: A history of walking.* New York: Penguin Books.

Taylor, D. (1997). Women of color, environmental justice and ecofeminism. In K. J. Warren (Ed.), *Ecofeminism: Women, culture and nature* (pp. 213-226). Bloomington, IN: Indiana University Press.

Turner, F. (1980). *Beyond geography: The western spirit against the wilderness.* New York: Viking Press.

Wadland, J. (1978). *Ernest Thompson Seton: Man in nature and the progressive era 1880-1915.* New York: Arno Press.

Warren, K. J. (Ed.). (1997). *Ecofeminism: Women, culture and nature.* Bloomington, IN: Indiana University Press.

Warren, K. J. (2000). *Ecofeminist philosophy: A western perspective on what it is and why it matters.* New York: Rowman and Littlefield.

Wilson, E. O. (2002). *The future of life.* New York: Knopf.

Young, K. (2005). Developing ecological literacy as a habit of mind in teacher education. *The EcoJustice Review: Educating for the Commons, 1*(1), 1-7.

Young, K. (2006). *Girls of the empire: The origins of environmental education and the contest for brownies and girl guides.* Unpublished doctoral dissertation, York University, Toronto, ON.

Young, K. (2007). Environmental educational leadership and its origins. In W. Smale & K. Young (Eds.), *Approaches to educational leadership* (pp. 220-236). Calgary, AB: Detselig Enterprises Ltd.

Young, K. (2008). Ecological habits of mind and the literary imagination. *Educational Insights, 12*(1), 1-9.

Young, K., Martusewicz, R., & Kulnieks, A. (in review). *The eco-justice education reader.* New York: Routledge/Taylor & Francis.

13

Colonization, Literacy, and the Body:
A Critical Narrative of Culturally and Linguistically Diverse Children in Early Childhood Education
Luigi Iannacci

In previous research (Iannacci, 2007a), I have forwarded a conceptual model and set of criteria for engaging in critical narrative research. Through this work, I have found that the links between a researchers' lived experience and what/how they research must be explored in order to fully understand and assess their inquiries. Like Diane Reay (1998), I suspect that "all research is in one way or another autobiographical or else the avoidance of autobiography" (p. 2). This notion has resonated with me throughout the sometimes painful process of confronting and reflecting on my autobiography while developing research. As these experiences have fostered critical questions that shape and are the impetus for my inquiry, it is necessary for me to begin this chapter by briefly sharing some of them as they provide a background and context to this study and make explicit how the personal becomes manifest in knowledge formation. This process works to dispel the notion of research as objective, rejects the idea of universal truths, and resists making claims in the knowledge it constructs; these aims are imperative to forwarding the validity of critical narrative research (DeLuca, 2000). Traditionally this personal connection to research has been understood as problematic in reductionistic and formalistic lines of inquiry, a "black mark on the slate to be wiped clean" and "something to be ignored" (Clandinin & Connelly, 2000, p. 40). Critical narrative research, however, allows access to these personal experiences in order to fully capitalize on and position the researcher's subjectivity as an asset that enriches rather than compromises their inquiry. To this end, I offer up some of my personal and professional experiences of being a child learning ESL, a teacher of culturally and linguistically diverse (CLD) children, and a researcher exploring CLD children's literacy experiences in Early Childhood Education (ECE) in order to enrich the research presented in this chapter.[1] These experiences have been edited and revised from previous sources (Iannacci, 2005) to contextualize the perspective I bring to this inquiry.

Background/Context:

Almost immediately after the start of my grade one year, my first language proved problematic for the school I attended and I was placed in a special education class where literacy curriculum was comprised of fragmented English language learning through vast numbers of phonics sheets. My parents were called to the school and told to begin speaking to me in English at home. As they had a great deal of trust in and respect for teachers and schools and wanted me to succeed, they were willing to follow the school's request. This began a long and troublesome journey of cultural and linguistic assimilation and loss throughout my childhood and early adolescence. By the time I had left high school, I had begun to reclaim some of my first language and culture as a result of being part of a community who shared similar experiences of growing up Italo-Canadese.

This continued in university and culminated in research I explored during that time that focused on the education of Italian immigrant children and children of Italian immigrants. After completing my undergraduate degree, I taught Kindergarten as a teaching assistant in Malton, Ontario, the same community in which I was raised. My introductory year of teaching altered the trajectory of my personal and professional life as I worked with an inspirational teaching mentor who ignited my passion for teaching young children.

I entered a Bachelor of Education (B.Ed.) program the following year. Many of the issues I had struggled with as a child resurfaced as a result of observing the experiences of young children learning ESL during one of my placements. I subsequently became deeply interested in how to support these students within the classroom.

After my Bachelor of Education, I again taught in Malton. Although I was left uneasy by some of the experiences I had in my B.Ed., I took great comfort in the fact that when I entered the teaching profession, English as a second language educators were staffed in even the smallest of schools to support immigrant children or children of immigrants whose first language was not English. I recognized myself within these children and felt that at the very least, schools were recognizing their needs.

As time went by I began to notice that most of the ESL programming presented language in isolated and fragmented ways and from an assimilationist perspective, which from experience, I knew to be problematic and ineffective. Despite this, I held on to the fact that students learning ESL were to a much lesser extent being inappropriately evaluated using culturally biased tests which would inevitably indicate a learning disability. Although the programming and support being offered was far from ideal, what I saw allowed me to proceed in my chosen vocation in good conscience. It felt good to know that these children had more than I had had and that some progress had been made in ensuring that they were not rendered completely invisible and marginalized within the Ontario school system.

However, as the years passed, I noticed that the number of ESL educators working within schools was decreasing. With the elected conservative government, I witnessed the deterioration of services and support offered to students learning ESL who were now less supported than they had been previously. In addition, the mandatory standardized provincial testing for *all* students that was being put in place was extremely disconcerting.

I began a Masters of Education in 1997 with the intent of being better able to understand how to provide and advocate for students learning ESL. The experience developed my voice in ways that I had not been able to as an elementary school student or teacher, and I was a better teacher for it. Although graduate school was deeply satisfying, it also left many questions. I wondered how much had really changed for children learning ESL in the twenty-two years since my initial experiences and what progress and/or regressions school systems had made providing for them. My return to teaching provoked more questions and confirmed my need to critically examine what was happening to them.

Although no ESL positions were available when I returned to teaching, the voice I had developed and knowledge gained were assets in the position I acquired. I became a special education resource classroom teacher (SERC), which meant teaching and running a comprehensive class. The self-contained class housed students who had been formally identified as having a variety of exceptionalities through the Identification and Placement Review Committee (IPRC) process. I was shocked by the number of students learning ESL who had been identified as learning disabled and placed within the class. Although this very large school was located in a highly diverse area where many new Canadians settled, it did not have an ESL teacher or program. While reviewing Ontario Student Records (OSR's), I discovered that none of the students learning ESL in my class had ever received ESL support. They were inappropriately tested, formally identified as learning disabled, and placed in special education classes or provided with special education support shortly after immigrating to Canada. Considering my personal experiences, my Master's research, and the ensuing questions, I found the situation ironic and disturbing. As personally and professionally satiating as teaching the comprehensive class was, eventually I knew it was time to formally explore questions cultivated as a result of my personal, professional, and academic experiences and piqued during my teaching.

With this in mind, I decided to pursue a Ph.D. in education to explore the questions I had regarding culturally and linguistically diverse children's literacy and identity negotiation. I came to the work from a personal place spurred by professional experiences rather than any attempt to address research gaps in the education of students learning ESL.

After many years of researching within this area, it has become sadly clear that these gaps do however exist as a result of several factors. International economic restructuring, for example, has increased the mobility of labor markets and cross-cultural contact on a global scale (Burbules & Torres, 2000; Cummins, 2005) resulting in currently 375 million ESL learners worldwide (Beale, 2007). Locally, students in North American elementary schools have become increasingly more culturally and linguistically diverse (Obiakor, 2001). Within the Canadian context for example, a significant number of children in elementary schools located in urban centres speak a first language (L1) other than English or French (Citizenship & Immigration Canada, 2003; Roberts-Fiati, 1997). Specifically, Ontario has experienced a 29 percent increase of students learning ESL within elementary schools since 2000 (People for Education, 2007). Further, the population of Ontario is expected to grow from roughly 12 million in 2001 to 16 million in 2028, with 75 percent of this growth coming from immigration (Glaze, 2007). Despite these demographics, Ontario schools like the ones who participated in this study, have felt the impact of decreased ESL programming and staffing since 1997/98 (People for Education, 2003). Although field work for this study occurred during the 2002-2003 school year, this issue has yet to be addressed in any significant way (People for Education, 2008). What has also remained the same are the standardized, coverage-oriented curriculum and assessment regimes born of neo-liberal, neo-conservative educational reforms that have furthered universal and deficit constructions of young children, both those learning ESL and native speakers.

Educational researchers have also noted a dearth of research about culturally and linguistically diverse students in early childhood education and disparity in providing for these students (Bernhard, Lefebvre, Chud, & Lang, 1995; Falconer & Byrnes, 2003; Suárez-Orozco, 2001; Toohey, 2000). The limited scholarship about young children who are ESL learners has traditionally been methods focused with very little arising from socio-cultural and critical perspectives (Toohey, 2000). In contrast, this study contributes to the more recent and growing body of work in early years literacy research grounded in socio-cultural theory (Bourne, 2001; Boyd & Brock, 2004; Gee, 2001). In addition, it draws on critical multiculturalism as an analytic lens (Kincheloe & Steinburg, 1997; Ladson-Billings, 2004; May, 1999; McLaren, 1994).

Theoretical Framing

As described in previous studies (Iannacci, 2005; Heydon & Iannacci, 2008), two basic tenets of socio-cultural theory highlight its relevance and applicability to this research. The first tenet is that "the mind is social in nature" (Wertsch as cited in Boyd & Brock, 2004, p. 4); the second is that "language in use plays a central role in mediating our actions as humans. Consequently, the uses of language in the context of interactions, and the various analytical ways of looking at that language, become central when considering human learning" (p. 4). Literacy is conceptualized as a social practice that is socially mediated. As such, coming to literacy is not exclusively about the acquisition of a code, but also, and more importantly, a culture. Classroom literacy practices can therefore be understood as a particular set of cultural events. It is consequently important to critically examine what students appropriate as they encounter school literacy as well as the impact this appropriation has on their identities. To this end, critical multiculturalism further informs an analysis of the literacy practices and events encountered by CLD students in their elementary school classrooms. In addition, it allows for an examination of what they appropriated as well as the effect this appropriation has on their identities.

Critical multiculturalism is based in critical theory and as such, "especially concerned with how domination takes place, the way human relations are shaped in the workplace, the schools and everyday life" (Kincheloe & Steinburg, 1997, p. 23). Translated into education, critical theory can help educators explore how "pedagogy functions as a cultural practice that produces rather than merely transmits knowledge within uneven relations of power, which informs teacher student relations" (Sleeter & Bernal, 2004). The influence of critical pedagogy has helped link multicultural education with wider socio-economic and political inequality. This link has traditionally been absent from discussions about and conceptualizations of multiculturalism and multicultural education (May, 1999).

Methods/Methodology:

This study uses Critical Narrative Research (CNR) as an expression of ethnography to address key questions. CNR is an emerging genre of inquiry that frequently border crosses a variety of theoretical orientations (c.g., social constructivist, critical, decolonial) and borrows from ethnographic traditions while maintaining an awareness of its colonial underpinnings (Clair, 2003). CNR is concerned with culture, language, and participation as issues of power in need of critique with the intent of change in the direction of social justice (Moss, 2004). Taken-for-granted relations of power experienced by those constructed as the Other are interrogated through an analysis of observed phenomenon (Iannacci, 2007b). Within this study, ethnographic and autobiographical data are used to construct narratives that were then deconstructed through reflection about and a distancing from prejudices and power relations that informed what was observed during fieldwork. Reconceptualized understandings about the data are developed as a result of this threefold mimesis (Ricoeur, 1992). The process involves constructing the world in narrative form, deconstructing what had been narrated, and finally reconceptualizing by providing insights to a refigured future in an effort to put forward an "opening up of possible new worlds" (Herda, 1999, p. 77). Reconceptualization (as outlined in the introduction of this volume) is thus fostered through a process of construction, deconstruction, and reconstruction.

As previously mentioned, CNR explores connections between the researcher and his/her research and, as such, demands that researchers remain "autobiographically conscious" throughout the research process (Viruru & Cannella, 2001, p. 168). Critical narrative researchers are therefore deeply interested in exploring the relationship between "their life experience and the theoretical underpinnings of their scholarship" (Grant as cited in Burdell & Swadener, 1999, p. 24). As critical researchers, they "describe ways in which their life histories, political involvement, moments of insight, and desire to work in alliances for social change made an impact on their research agenda and professional growth" (p. 24). In short, they "conduct research in a way that demystifies the systems of reasoning behind why they do what they do" (Grant, 1999, p. 1). The "resultant knowing that is discovered is multidimensional, partial, and critical" (Moss, 2004, p. 364). These approaches to knowledge formation resist colonial traditions of inquiry that have constructed identities, the Other, and phenomena in general as unified and, in contrast, are concerned with uncovering the subtleties, complexities, and biases that come with representing culture (Clair, 2003).

Data collection involved long-term, sustained engagement in the field (Hatch, 1998) that consisted of two phases of observation in four early years classrooms in two schools. During both phases of the research, I engaged in "overt participant observation" (Wallen & Fraenkel, 2001, p. 436), identified myself as a researcher, and ensured that research subjects I observed knew that they were being observed. During my fieldwork, I collected field notes, school documents, photographs, and children's work. Interviews with teachers, parents, school board personnel, and students were also conducted throughout the year. This data helped formulate narratives about various dimensions of schooling (e.g. assessment and pedagogy, cultural and linguistic incorporation and community participation) (Cummins, 2001). Literacy events, practices, themes, and salient issues that emerged from the narratives were discussed after they had been juxtaposed, contextualized, and interrogated for inconsistencies and contradictions. In CNR this placing does not seek to validate predetermined theoretical understandings or the proclivities and biases of the researcher but, rather, furthers a multivocal stance that calls into question what has been observed as it further explains and expounds upon interpretations and observations made by various "voices" within the study that include participants, research, theory, and the researcher. These connections are born out of a need to help clarify, contradict, and finally formulate further questioning into the researched phenomenon. This can foster the interrogation of preconceptions and taken-for-granted assumptions that shape and affect the researched experience. Destabilizing the dominant "story" or "grand narrative" creates the potential for personal, professional, and societal change and reconceptualization. As critical narrative researchers deconstruct and challenge dominant narratives, new storylines hopefully begin to emerge.

The aforementioned personal and professional experiences and theoretical and methodological framing informed the year-long ethnography (Iannacci, 2005) discussed in this chapter. The study generally explored gaps in the provision of responsive education for CLD children in two kindergarten and two grade one classrooms.

One of the specific issues that emerged was the forms of colonization CLD students and their teachers encountered in their early years classrooms. Cannella and Viruru (2004) point out that "Postcolonial perspectives result in an awareness of the oblique and indirect ways in which power is used to control and colonize groups of human beings, power that may be exhibited by physical, material practice, but also through discourse and representation" (p. 109). This colonizing power also reveals itself through exerting power over the body of colonized people. Leavitt and Power (1997) argue that "how children's bodies are treated and how their bodied lives are lived are indicative of contemporary social, political, and cultural constructions of the child" (p. 40). The specific purpose of this chapter is, therefore, to critically analyze the ways in which CLD students and their teachers encountered colonization as a result of relations of power and subsequent configurations of literacy practices influenced by material and human resources that were regulated and enforced through imposed curricular mandates. First, narratives constructed from field data are offered to shed light on the conditions of children's bodied lives and their teacher's reactions to these conditions within the early childhood education classrooms observed. Social, political, and cultural implications of these narratives and decolonizing practices and curricula that address issues that emerged in the data are then discussed. Parts of these narratives have appeared in (Heydon & Iannacci, 2008) and have been edited and excerpted to serve the focus of this chapter.

Elmwood Public School

Elmwood Public School[2] is located in Ontario in the centre of one of Canada's largest cities. The building itself is old and in need of repairs and renovations. It is not uncommon to find a maintenance van in the parking lot of the school on a call to "patch-up" yet another problem. The socio-economic status of most of the families in the community is working-class or working-poor and generally considered disadvantaged. Elmwood's overall achievement on provincial tests of literacy designated it a "compensatory school." While these poor scores did qualify Elmwood for resources that it would not otherwise have received, these resources only served to focus even further on the children's weaknesses. The purchase of speech and language pathologists' time for instance was spent administering a phonemic awareness screening to every child in senior kindergarten which resulted in more poor scores.

Given these deficit-driven forms of data, many teachers felt great pressure to improve their students' performance. Grade one teachers, for example, called several meetings with the Kindergarten teachers and administration to push for instructional remedies. Elmwood's labeled status already gave it resources such as speech and language pathology time for phonemic awareness therapy, Educational Assistant time to administer phonemic awareness programs to students, resource teacher time to administer a scripted synthetic phonics program, and an early literacy teacher who worked with support personnel to monitor and help deliver the school district's literacy mandates. Regardless of these resources, the meetings headed by the grade one teachers resulted in additional phonemic awareness and phonics-intensive instruction for all children in Junior and Senior Kindergarten in the form of literacy group sessions headed by the early literacy teacher. The belief was that the sessions would address the students' deficits so that by the time they left kindergarten, they would be better prepared to meet the grade one curricular expectations.

Cindy, the kindergarten teacher, was especially cognizant of and increasingly vocal about the ways these new steps constrained her program, affected the quality of her interactions with her students, and ultimately the learning that occurred within her classroom. As she discussed the literacy centres in her classroom, it became apparent that the decision to implement them was not her own.

> We were called to a meeting with the Principal and literacy teacher, and the Kindergarten teachers were ... the grade one teachers – because they had results from the phonemic awareness test [administered in September] – said that they were not very pleased with the results and wanted to improve the results of the children.

> We looked at the scores and when we looked at, you know, comparisons of other schools or where they

should be, I mean, they might be one percentage off. So, whose fault is that? I just, I don't know. I take it very personally because that's the way that I feel that it's coming.

... I heard a lot of, "They can't do this. They can't even do this," you know, "I don't think they know anything, and they come into grade one and they don't know how to do this, they don't know how to do that." It was almost like the teachers were expecting them to be able to do everything it said in that grade one curriculum when they got to grade one.

So, the literacy teacher suggested that we have these literacy groups twice a day with the children and divide them into three groups. So, this was implemented in October, the beginning of October. So, this happens twice a day for half an hour everyday . . . The literacy teacher comes in, an EA comes in, and I am in and have a group of children. Six children in each group, and we are to help them improve in word awareness, phonemic awareness, and reading skills. It's very, very long for the children, I think. And just for an example today, we had it once today. The EA was away, so I had two groups with me at the carpet and [the literacy teacher] had one group, and they had more of the play activity time. And, at the end of the day, May [an ESL student in this study] commented that today was a "quick day," which I found interesting, and I wonder if they thought it was a quick day because they had more time at the activity centres and it didn't seem so long and drawn out . . . We are never all sitting at tables at the same time with pencils doing work, except now at these literacy times. And, I think that's maybe what they find, you know, long because May wasn't the only one who commented on that. [Another student, not ESL] also at the table, asked if she could go the water table at three o'clock and I said no because it's near your time to go home, and she couldn't believe it: "Really?" So, which I found really interesting . . .

I don't think they should be – sorry, manhandled too much . . . I think direct instruction is good when they're ready for it and depending on what activity it is that you want them to do. . . . I just think that sometimes the adults take too much responsibility for what they think, where they think the child should be.

I observed a number of the phonics and phonemic awareness focused literacy group sessions that caused Cindy such concern. The following story crafted from field notes is not atypical of what occurred during these sessions. However, since it was the last literacy group session I observed during my fieldwork, it is perhaps most significant in demonstrating the frustrations the students as well as Cindy and I had with this configuration of practice.

The ABC's of Literacy

I entered Cindy's Kindergarten classroom a bit early at the tail end of the lunch period. The EA (educational assistant) relieved Cindy so she could eat as well. As the children had finished eating, the EA had them seated on the carpet playing bingo. After the bingo match, she read them a book as they squirmed quietly in front of her. Cindy arrived and began to organize for literacy groups. She called out the names of children who would be working with the EA, the literacy teacher, or herself. I asked the literacy teacher if I could observe her session, she agreed. I noticed that Junior Kindergarten students, some of whom were three years old at the beginning of the year comprised most of the children in the group.

The literacy teacher began by writing "R" on a big sheet, which she shows students. She then shared a small book containing pictures, some of which are things that start with /r/. The students are asked to identify items that begin with /r/ and echo what sound /r/ makes. A couple of students do so successfully, then she called on Amet who sat silently and grinned but did not respond.

Amet, the youngest child in an Albanian speaking family, lives with his parents and older sister Janna, also a participant in this study. Born in Canada, Amet began Junior Kindergarten shortly after turning four. Although his English utterances were often restricted to echoing things his classmates and I said, his oral pro ficiency in English improved a great deal as the year progressed. Highly communicative, demonstrative, rambunctious, and excitable during play, "No" was one of the first words he used independently in January. I also observed Amet code switching (switching between languages) into Albanian to himself during individual and partnered play situations. A common strategy Amet used to quickly finish the mandatory *Jolly Phonics* (Lloyd, 1992) work sheet was quickly writing a few of the letters the sheet required then, using one crayon, furiously "coloring" the featured picture with a hand full of broad strokes. He would then quickly put the work on Cindy's desk and rush to his preferred sand, water, or construction activity. The time spent at these activities was highly productive. On many occasions, Amet, his classmates, and I explored and discussed concepts such as volume and capacity, colors, directionality, and materiality as he built and experimented.

I usually sit right beside Amet during literacy groups since he has needed one-on-one assistance to benefit from them. Whenever I have moved to sit next to other students, Amet tunes out and fidgets. The teacher repeatedly refocuses his and others attention to keep them on task. At times she leaves her seat to direct Amet through the task in hand-over-hand fashion.

On this day the literacy teacher asks Amet a second time for an "R" word. When I remove my ring and give it to him, he rolls it around in his hand. I ask him what it is. "Ring" he replies. After a slight pause, he looks up at the literacy teacher and repeats "Ring, /rrr/!" The literacy teacher affirms his answer with praise. She then asks another student to write "R" on chart paper with a picture of an "R' item under it. On individual sheets of paper each student is asked to copy "R" and draw pictures of "R" items. The entire activity lasts for forty minutes. Between Bingo, the story with the EA, and the literacy group session, students have been seated for well over an hour. Toward the end of the session, Amet looked directly at the teacher and said, "Too long." The literacy teacher giggled nervously and replied, "Ok" but proceeded despite having to plea for the children's stillness and attention.

At the end of the lesson the literacy teacher declared, "Phew, this was a struggle. I think the OT (occupational therapist) has to be called – Do you think? Or is it just they don't get enough practice? Yeah, I'm going to have to check if their brothers [a few of the student's older brothers] had OT. They're the same way." I offer, "It's hard to sit that long." She takes note, "Yeah, but I used to do stuff like this all the time with my classes. I mean they couldn't even hold paper. They should know how to do that."

By this time Cindy has joined our conversation. As the literacy teacher leaves, she looks at me intently and says, "There will be many changes next year." I smile back and say, "I figured there would be." Before I join the students for a much needed gym class, I write the following:

a) Sit still

b) Sit up

c) Have both feet on the floor

d) Pull up your chair

e) Listen to me

f) Look here

g) Don't talk

h) Don't interrupt

i) Don't move

j) Don't touch things

k) Pay attention

l) Answer the question

m) Don't look at people

n) Don't touch people

o) Don't giggle

p) Listen carefully

q) Don't rock

r) Print neatly

s) Don't guess

t) Think

u) Wait

v) Stop

w) Copy neatly

x) Hold pencil properly

y) Take your time

z) Hurry up

When gym is over, the students have recess. Again, the EA comes in to relieve Cindy. The time is used for the students to have a scheduled snack. Once again, they are required to be seated in chairs in tables. Recess is fifteen minutes.

"Inattentive" Alita

Like Amet, Alita was in the very early stages of acquiring English, yet her language proficiency and inexperience with school did not exempt her from participating in the literacy groups, nor were her circumstances taken into consideration in terms of English literacy assessment.

Alita had immigrated to Canada six months before starting junior kindergarten and had turned four just before starting school. She lived with her parents and older sister Ines, also a participant in this study. Fluent in Spanish, Alita also tended to code switch into her first language during play. Her spoken English was extremely limited and at times created difficulties for her at school (e.g., asking to use the bathroom).

Like Amet, Alita also tended to rush through phonics work sheets in order to get to an activity as well as squirm and lose focus during literacy groups without intensive one-on-one support. Yet, attention was not the issue. Cindy for example, had read the class "The Gingerbread Man" and had followed up the story with a hunt to find him. Cindy placed gingerbread man "footsteps" around the school and had the students follow them. The footsteps led to the staff room and a baking tray where he and several of his friends lay ready for snack. Alita was absolutely enthralled by the morning's events and after two and a half months of near verbal silence, began animatedly retelling me the events of the story and recounting the follow-up activity as she painted using a combination of English, Spanish, and onomatopoeia for well over forty minutes.

Alita's first painting fulfilled Cindy's requirement that the students paint the gingerbread man's face and his three buttons on gingerbread man shaped paper she had prepared. Cindy was trying to reinforce expectations related to student's ability to properly illustrate facial features and the concept of three. When Alita finished the required painting, she wanted to continue to tell me about the gingerbread man story and activity. Unfortunately there was a line up of children who were ready to do the required gingerbread man painting, and although there were two painting aisles, only one had paint in it. Cindy walked by and said, "There isn't any paint Alita, you need to go to another activity." Alita remained committed to painting and talking about the ginger-bread man. Her classmates were getting impatient. Remembering an activity a kindergarten teacher once showed me called "magic paint" (using water instead of paint), I quickly grabbed a piece of paper and put it on the second aisle. I filled a baby food jar with water and handed Alita a clean paintbrush. She quizzically looked at me for a split second and then proceeded to paint and retell the morning's events. She remained focused and committed through-out the entire episode. Although no one could actually see the breakthrough painting Alita's concentrated efforts produced, she meticulously and tenderly picked it up and placed in on the drying rack when she was done.

As previously mentioned, Alita's limited English proficiency and her inexperience with school did not exempt her from partic-ipation in literacy group sessions, nor were her circumstances taken into consideration in terms of the ways her English literacy was assessed. The following story crafted from my field notes once again demonstrates Cindy's discomfort with the ways in which students like Alita were consistently constructed as deficient through unresponsive assessment that neither accounted for their assets or English language proficiency.

> I am intimately aware of feelings of anxiety and frenzy that come with the distribution of second-term report cards to parents as I talk with Cindy who is concerned with the report comments the literacy teacher has made based on students' performance during the literacy group sessions. From previous interviews, I knew that Cindy believed the report card should be a place to describe what students can do and the progress they have made throughout the term in a positive and encouraging manner while identifying next steps they need to take.
>
> During this conversation, she indicates she does not agree with some of the comments made about ESL students, in particular one of the comments about

Alita: "Due to her lack of attention during literacy groups, Alita's progress has been hindered." Cindy notes that the focus of the comment is Alita's behavior rather than literacy and indicates that Alita has in no way exhibited problems with regards to behavior. Cindy believes the real issue is Alita's understanding of English and as such, the relevancy of the literacy sessions. She also reiterates that the sessions have become far too long since what was originally scheduled as twenty minutes, became thirty and finally even forty-five minutes. Cindy questions how punitive the remarks on the report card can be towards children who a) have a limited understanding of English and b) are expected to sit for extended periods of time. She decides that the comment will not appear on Alita's report card.

Discussion

Cannella & Viruru (2004) argue that the obvious "method through which colonization is accomplished is when one group places restrictions on the human bodies of another group" (p. 206). They believe that "historic reasoning and contemporary practice illustrate the intrinsic tendency for education to be conceptualized as control of the 'other' (whether physically, socially, intellectually, or in the construction of desire), especially regarding those who are younger" (p. 209). The data that has been shared thus far demonstrates the ways in which *both* teachers' practices and children's bodies were often controlled and colonized through material and human resources that were regulated and enforced through mandates made at board and school levels developed in response to management issues and assessment results (e.g., supervision, standardized curriculum, phonemic awareness screening, literacy group sessions, the *Jolly Phonics* program). The subsequent colonization of Cindy's classroom and her literacy practices meant that transmission-based pedagogies were more privileged and prevalent than she was comfortable with as these practices stressed physical colonization of her students' bodies. Some of the *body work* (Leavitt & Power, 1997) students were subjected to was as a result of the impact of a full day kindergarten program. Full day programs are steadily becoming the norm within Ontario schools which has led to new workload and supervision issues as ECE teachers are required to have uninterrupted planning and down time. It is evident that these changes to Ontario Kindergarten programs will have to address the fact that children cannot be expected to remain sedentary as their teachers receive contractual and much needed planning time.

More importantly, the forms of colonization teachers and students encountered in the data occurred as a result of the proliferation of sedentary approaches emphasized by commercial literacy materials that "efficiently" organized ways for adults to foster print-based literacy skills *at* children who were deemed to be deficient and in need of fixing. As students were understood as not meeting literacy norms, they were rendered deficient and/or pathological and were subsequently stilled under the premise that they could be instilled with literacy to meet expectations efficiently and quickly. Teachers were subsequently responsible for controlling bodies in the hopes of ensuring desired results (print-centric literacy). This was problematic on many levels. From a psychological perspective, "children's identities are connected to their failure or success in managing their bodies in accord with their teacher's demands" (Leavitt & Power, 1997, p. 66) and as such, the demands concerning body work being placed on students such as Alita and Amet communicated how they continually failed to meet teachers expectations regarding the management of their bodies. From a biomedical perspective (Heydon & Iannacci, 2006), colonizing bodies was understood as necessary in inoculating students with literacy interventions to remedy their literacy deficiencies. Through this process, CLD students (and their classmates) were constructed as unfinished, incomplete, and in need of transmission-based technologies (e.g., literacy groups) and interventions (e.g., occupational therapy) that would prompt them toward "normal' development in order to "cure" them. Ultimately, both of these perspectives indicate that the body literacy students were acquiring was based on compliance and physical and cognitive surrender (e.g., Amet and the literacy teacher's hand over hand moments) as a result of their inability to manage and use their bodies in ways that were acceptable to adults.

The focus on accelerating students' ability to perform normally was also reflective of a pushed down, quantitatively overwhelming, and coverage-focussed approach to curriculum that required students to demonstrate knowledge and skills within ten-month time frames in order to meet ministry standards. The organizational framework of the Ontario Kindergarten curriculum and the sheer number of expectations within it meant that children had to navigate and demonstrate conventional print literacy and many prescribed learning outcomes and, as such, compromise the autonomy they had over their bodies and learning.

Although the pedagogical imposition of these age-and-stage expectations were clear during the /r/ lesson Amet experienced, they were also evident in the ways Cindy configured a follow up activity to the Gingerbread Man story by restricting responses to ensure that students demonstrated specific expectations (e.g., the concept of three). What Alita really wanted to do during scheduled play time was retell the story as she depicted in her painting what had happened during the gingerbread man hunt. In order to do this, she first had to comply with Cindy's requests (e.g., her first painting), and then negotiate a way to continue painting unadulterated. As such, she completed the sanctioned work and then continued her multimodal retelling, which consisted of animated strokes on a blank canvas and verbal play using sounds and words from the language she knew (Spanish) and the one she was learning (English). The shift from silent mandatory work to a full-body response meant that Alita could regain control of her play, her body, and ultimately her learning.

Data also demonstrate the importance of destabilizing uncritical stances toward certain forms of play that forward the notion that play is in and of itself a decolonizing practice. Like all configurations of practice and educational philosophies, it is essential that it be seen through a critical lens and understood "as the artifact of a particular culture whose beliefs about human beings are not necessarily applicable to all" (Cannella, 1997, p. 124). Thus, the ways in which play has been colonized by Western science and understood as normal or natural learning behavior for students must be made explicit. For example, the use of verbal and sensorimotor play devoid of objects are cross-cultural examples that challenge dominant constructions of play (Cannella, 1997). The adult/child distinction perpetuated in Western ideas about play is also challenged by the ways in which Europeans of all ages once engaged in play (Aries as cited in Cannella, 1997). It is also important to note that the adult construct of play as a child's work fosters "environments for children that reflect their constructions of what is appropriate through play, their own culturally created agendas for controlling children" (p. 127). It is essential to recognize that play is in fact neither free nor unhindered since adults construct, regulate, and evaluate sanctioned forms of play and, therefore, retain control over the ways in which children are allowed or not allowed to explore and make sense of their world and use their bodies to do so (Cannella, 1997).

I recognize that it may appear as if I am privileging social constructivist notions of learning and disparaging direct instruction, and that the personal experiences I shared at the beginning of this chapter of being an ESL learner have confined me to this disposition. I am, however, aware of how physical colonization of students' bodies has also been observed during events that have employed "progressive" early literacy pedagogy (Luke, 1996). Thus, the issues I have raised are not solely about how pedagogically limiting or unresponsive coverage-focused pedagogy and commercial resources are for CLD students; rather, these issues alert us to the taken-for-granted notions that ensured the pedagogical determinism and colonial relations of power that CLD children experienced as a result of being deemed in need of commercial programs or pedagogy informed by these programs. Further, responsive instruction necessitates valuing and employing explicit instruction within a classroom environment that provides students opportunities to become empowered in their learning through interactions that capitalize on their experiences and identities. Socio-cultural approaches to literacy do in fact recognize the invaluable role guidance plays in addressing children's zone of proximal development (Vygotsky, 1978) and the transfer of scaffolded skills. The use of direct instruction within a classroom that facilitates and supports meaningful, purposeful, context-embedded literacy events can therefore be extremely beneficial to young children.

In contrast, much of what I observed revealed the ways in which direct instruction was frequently used to teach isolated and artificially sequenced phonics with commercially prepared materials that were unresponsive to students' needs and interests, while other pedagogical approaches were assigned a marginal, insignificant role (e.g., context-embedded phonics instruction/activity). Again, the argument I am making should not be understood as a testament to play and the vilification of direct instruction, nor as a reinscription of the debates about developmentally appropriate practice (DAP) outlined in the introduction of this volume. My concerns are about the impoverished nature of the literacy practices and events assigned to students in response to their perceived deficiencies and the disempowering effects of these practices and events. The context-reduced communication (Cummins, 2001) used throughout the isolated phonics and phonemic awareness instruction, for example, meant that interactions that allowed CLD students to learn from and negotiate learning with more experienced communicative partners (e.g., Amet at the sand table, Alita at the painting easel) were diminished. The types of language and literacy experiences engineered as a result of limited and limiting curriculum models, assessment practices, and subsequent transmission-based pedagogy limited students' ability to decide how to use their bodies to engage with a variety of literacies and hence challenge their ascribed school identities from that of deficient and passive knowledge recipients to autonomous, able learners in possession of valuable resources which included their language, culture, and body – all of which remained subjugated throughout many of the events described in the data. My concerns about these dominant forms of curriculum and assessment practices stem from the colonial relations of power they foster and the ways they privilege certain ways of knowing and being while marginalizing others.

Although I am concerned about how constructions of the children in my study effected the body work and body literacy they experienced, I am also aware and want to emphasize that data also demonstrate how "children are not always passive recipients of classroom body rules; sometimes they actively mediate them" (Leavitt & Power, 1997, p. 57). For example, Amet and Alita did manage to subvert unresponsive practices and subsequently establish moments when they were able to negotiate their school identities (e.g., rushing through the mandatory phonics sheet in order to get to activities that made use of their assets and furthered their language acquisition). The comments made by several children about time also demonstrated this active negotiation. Amet's comment that the literacy group session was "too long" showed his unwillingness to be stilled for purposes that were unresponsive to his resources and needs. Two other student's in Cindy's room also commented on how "quick" the day was when the literacy centres were minimized and play was extended. Although Amet's comments specifically demonstrate a refusal to be passive when confronted with excessive body work, his classmates' comments also illustrate how curriculum is lived and negotiated through children's bodies. Kirova (2001) has specifically examined this phenomena in relation to CLD children's experiences of loneliness within school and argues that "feelings of loneliness and isolation that immigrant children experience because of their inability to communicate appropriately with their peers affects how they experience time while they are at school" (p. 263). Given the discursive conditions Amet faced, it is not surprising that he objected to how long he had to endure these conditions and that his classmates were cognizant of the days quick passing when conditions changed. Unfortunately, the narrow and constrictive literacy curriculum did not often provide Amet, Alita, or their classmates many opportunities to alter discursive conditions within their classrooms as they were asked to demonstrate and learn compliance rather than become active participants in their literacy learning.

Like Amet and Alita, Cindy also did not always passively accept the "rules" placed on her. Rather, she was aware and critical of the ways in which adults constructed children and made decisions about their learning based on these problematic constructions. Her comments about how she felt that adults took "too much responsibility" for what and where they think children should be and not wanting children to be too "manhandled" clearly demonstrate this critical stance. Further, her refusal to include the comment about Alita on her report card and her disallowing the literacy groups to continue during the following school year also demonstrated how her critique of the practices led her to negotiating how influential they would be after they proved unsuccessful in her classroom.

The ways in which ECE teachers like Cindy have negotiated mandates that have narrowed curriculum have been documented by Leung (2003) who reported a shift away from multimodal expression in an American kindergarten classroom as a response to standardized statewide goals and district mandates. A study by Wien (2002) also explored how an experienced kindergarten teacher in Ontario was coping with the standardized curriculum. The study found that the document was not central to how she constructed curriculum. Remarks the teacher made indicated that she was not using the official curriculum to guide her planning, but rather students' interests and needs. When asked how she was able to maintain this practice, the teacher credited her fellow teachers and administration at the school for supporting her approach. This is especially significant when we consider the anxiety, pressure and instructional remedies teachers at Elmwood had to reconcile in order to ensure that they were covering expectations while monitoring and reporting students' ability to perform them.

It is important to note that I am aware that body work and the learning of body rules have always been present in early childhood education (Leavitt & Power, 1997). As a former ECE teacher, I have of course had to enforce body rules. What I am objecting to is an unreasonable amount of *overcivilizing* (Leavitt & Power, 1997) that occurs when the potentially dynamic relationships between CLD students and teachers remains underdeveloped as other foci informed by colonial relations of power determine sanctioned interactions and identities. What was particularly disconcerting were the ways in which unexamined perspectives about the children fostered curriculum that kept them from developing a sense of how they were fully able to use their bodies successfully to make choices that furthered their own learning. These perspectives ultimately upheld the construction of children as "a group of people who must be observed and who are in opposition, at least in intellectual ability, agency, and behaviour to adults . . . [a group of] people who must be controlled and administered over until they progress developmentally, mature, and become self-disciplined" (Viruru & Cannella, 2001, p. 162).

What is also objectionable are the ways in which these perspectives were grounded in the Ontario Kindergarten curriculum document (1998, 2006). An overarching analysis of the document reveals how children's bodies are positioned as things to be controlled by their teachers. Expectations about children's bodies mostly appear in areas such as Physical Education and Health and are linked to what physiological and biological understandings children need to have about what their bodies should or should not do (e.g., exhibit gross motor control, partake in healthy living, avoid harmful substances). There is however, a diametrically opposing view and positioning of children's bodies within other examples of ECE curriculum. The Te Whariki (1996) developed and currently in place in New Zealand, for example, demonstrates a philosophically opposing construction of children's bodies. They are depicted as something that children need to have control over and need to learn to control rather than things to be controlled by adults. The goals of the document are to help ECE educators encourage children to utilize their bodies in ways that make use of and develop their resources and their literacies. The body is therefore something to learn through and with and understood as helpful in furthering a child's ability to communicate, to understand, to listen, to share, and to reciprocate in communication and, as such, something to gain confidence in and power over.

The adult's role in supporting and fostering the child's use of their body for communication is based on their ability to organize semiotic rich environments for children, recognize the various ways children are communicating using their bodies, use their own bodies to foster positive relationships with children, and to use a variety of texts to communicate with them. These understandings are extremely helpful as they provide educators with possibilities that address the current limited and limiting ways children's bodies are understood and constructed in dominant ECE curricula. A few of these possibilities include literacy instruction (including phonics and phomemic awareness instruction) that makes use of environmental print, songs, rhymes, poems, visual texts, books, and so forth. Multilingual environmental print can be used to name common items (e.g. blackboard, window, etc.) and concepts (e.g. colors, numbers) found in classrooms, and open up spaces for CLD students to use their first languages as well as teach it to their peers, thus making their assets apparent and valuable. Cummins (2001) also suggests inviting students to bring in a word in their first language that is particularly meaningful to them so that they can teach the word to their classmates. Further, various "identity texts" (texts in which CLD students have invested their identities and reflect who they are) (Cummins, 2005) can also be brought in and accessed (e.g., photos, movement pictures, personal artifacts, etc.). Multilingual posters, alphabets of the languages spoken by children, the children's names, common phrases in various languages, and work done by students in their first language can also be posted and brought into the classroom to create a multilingual environment and facilitate responsive literacy instruction (Schwarzer, Haywood, & Lorenzen, 2003). Children's experiences and resources ultimately become the impetus for deciding what literacy opportunities are presented and organized for and with them. Literacy instruction emerges as a result of these assets as opposed to being set by a predetermined instructional scope and sequence, which exists outside of the context of the classroom and is distanced from children's bodies, literacies, and lives.

Conclusion

At Elmwood P.S, colonizing bodies and teachers practices was understood as necessary in inoculating students with literacy interventions that would remedy their literacy deficiencies. Through this pathologizing process, CLD students experienced an unreasonable and harmful amount of overcivilizing (Leavitt & Power, 1997). Although Alita, Amet, and their teacher managed to subvert colonizing practices and subsequently create moments that allowed for negotiated school identities, the narrow literacy curriculum often prevented them from doing so. As such, the children (and their teacher) were often asked to demonstrate and learn compliance rather than become active participants in their learning and teaching. Ultimately, the impact of this form of ECE curriculum subjugated their funds of knowledge and compromised the autonomy they had over their bodies, literacy practices, and learning. This compliance has ramifications not only in terms of identity, but also to critical and democratic participation. I began this chapter by sharing personal experiences, and so I will end by being personal. Compliance has often curtailed my ability to think. It has caused me to feel the need to please others at my own expense and to perform the "good" son, student, friend, partner, teacher, professor, researcher. This compliance has compromised me and ultimately, caused me to suffer. It is this suffering that I wish to eradicate and therefore advocate for ameliorating children's lives in ways that foster autonomy over their minds, bodies, and spirits.

Notes

[1] I use the term culturally and linguistically diverse (CLD) (Herrera & Murry, 2005) to refer to children who elsewhere are designated as English as a Second Language (ESL), English Language Learners (ELL), or English as an Additional Language learners (EAL). At the time of the research for this study, ESL was the official designation in Ontario of children for whom English was not their first language. It has subsequently changed to ELL. However, ESL, EAL, and ELL are problematic since they focus on the language the child is acquiring rather than their existing "funds of knowledge" (Moll, 1992). Consequently, these labels are deficit oriented. While CLD is not without its problems as it uses the dominant language and culture as the referent, it is a preferred option as it makes explicit children's resources (Heydon & Iannacci, 2008).

[2] All names are pseudonyms.

References

Beale, K. (2007). *How many people learn English globally?* Retrieved December 13, 2005, from http://esl.about.com/od/englishlearningresources/f/f_eslmarket.htm

Bernhard, J. K., Lefebvre, M. L., Chud, G., & Lange, R. (1995). *Paths to equity: Cultural, linguistic and racial diversity in Canadian early childhood education.* Toronto: York Lanes Press. Reprinted in CLAS Early Childhood Research Institute

Bourne, J. (2001). Discourses and identities in a multi-lingual primary classroom. *Oxford Review of Education, 27*(1), 103-114.

Boyd, F. B., & Brock, C. H. (2004). Constructing pedagogies of empowerment in multicultural and multilingual classrooms: Implications for theory and practice. In F. B. Boyd, C. H. Brock, & M. S. Rozendal (Eds.), *Multicultural and multilingual literacy and language* (pp. 1-11). New York: The Guilford Press.

Burbules, N. C., & Torres, C. A. (2000). Globalization and education: An introduction. In N. C. Burbules & C. A. Torres (Eds.), *Globalization and education: Critical perspectives* (pp. 1-26). New York: Routledge, 2000.

Burdell, P., & Swadener, B. B. (1999). Critical personal narrative and autoethnography in education: Reflections on a genre. *Educational Researcher, 28,* 21-26.

Cannella, G. S. (1997). *Deconstructing early childhood education: Social justice & revolution.* New York: Peter Lang.

Cannella, G. S., & Viruru, R. (2004). *Childhood and postcolonization: Power, education, and contemporary practice.* New York: RoutledgeFalmer.

Citizenship & Immigration Canada. (2003). *Facts and Figures: Immigration Overview.* Retrieved July 21, 2005, from http://www.cic.gc.ca/english/pub/facts2003/permanent/6.html

Clair, R. P. (2003). The changing story of ethnography. In R. P. Clair (Ed.), *Expressions of ethnography: Novel approaches to qualitative methods* (pp. 3-28). Albany, NY: State University of New York Press.

Clandinin, J., & Connelly, M., (2000) *Narrative inquiry: Experience and story in qualitative research.* San Francisco, CA: Jossey-Bass.

Cummins, J. (2001). *Negotiating identities: Education for empowerment in a diverse society* (2nd ed.). Los Angeles: California Association for Bilingual Education.

Cummins, J. (2005, April). *Diverse futures: Rethinking the image of the child in Canadian schools.* Paper presented at the Joan Pederson Distinguished Lecture Series. University of Western Ontario.

Deluca, S. (2000). *Finding meaning places for healing: Toward a vigilant subjectivity in the practice of a nurse educator.* Unpublished doctoral dissertation, University of Toronto, Toronto.

Falconer, R. C., & Byrnes. D. A. (2003). When good intentions are not enough: A response to increasing diversity in an early childhood setting. *Journal of Research in Childhood Education, 17*(2), 188-200.

Gee, J. P. (2001). A sociocultural perspective on early literacy development. In S. B. Newman, D. K. Dickinson (Eds.), *Handbook of early literacy research* (pp. 30-42). New York: Guilford Press.

Glaze, A. (2007, December). English language learners: Will we deliver? Paper presented at the "From the roots up: Supporting English Language Learners in Every Classroom" Provincial Symposium, Ontario Ministry of Education, Toronto.

Herda, E. A. (1999). *Research conversations and narrative: A critical hermeneutic orientation in participatory inquiry.* Wesport, CT: Praeger.

Herrera, S. G., & Murry, K. G. (2005). *Mastering ESL and bilingual methods: Differentiated instruction for culturally and linguistically diverse (CLD) students.* Boston, MA: Allyn and Bacon.

Heydon, R., & Iannacci, L. (2006). Biomedical approaches to literacy: Two curriculum teachers challenge the treatment of dis/ability in contemporary early literacy education. *Language & Literacy, Special Print Edition,* 32-39.

Heydon, R., & Iannacci, L. (2008). *Early childhood curricula and the depathologizing of childhood.* Toronto: University of Toronto Press.

Iannacci, L. (2005). *Othered among others: A critical narrative of culturally and linguistically diverse (CLD) children's literacy and identity in early childhood education (ECE).* Unpublished doctoral dissertation, University of Western Ontario, London, Ontario.

Iannacci, L. (2007a). Critical narrative research (CNR): Conceptualizing and furthering the validity of an emerging methodology. *Vitae Scholasticae, 24,* 55-76.

Iannacci, L. (2007b). *Stories that must be told: Reclaiming teacher Otherness through critical autobiographical research.* In W. Smale & K. Young (Eds.) Approaches to educational leadership and practice (pp. 141-155). Calgary, AB: Detselig Enterprises Ltd.

Kincheloe, J., & Steinburg, S. (1997). *Changing multiculturalism.* Philadelphia, PA: Open University Press.

Kirova, A. (2001). Loneliness in immigrant children: Implications for classroom practice. *Childhood Education, 77*(5) 260-267.

Ladson-Billings, G. (2004). New directions in multicultural education. In J. Banks & C. Banks (Eds.), *Handbook of research on multicultural education* (2nd ed., pp. 50-65). San Francisco, CA: Jossey-Bass.

Leavitt, R. L., & Power, M. B. (1997). Civilizing bodies: Children in day care. In J. L. Tobin (Ed.), *Making a place for pleasure in early childhood education* (pp. 39-75). New Haven, CT: Yale University Press.

Leung, C. B. (2003, April). *The narrowing of literacy curriculum from multimodal to verbocentric during a year in kindergarten.* Paper presented at the Annual Meeting of AERA, Chicago, IL.

Lloyd, S. (1992). *The jolly phonics handbook.* Essex, UK: Jolly Learning.

Luke, A. (1996). The body literate: Discourse and inscription in early literacy training. In P. Cobley (Ed.), *The communication reader* (pp. 384-395). London: Routledge.

May, S. (1999). Introduction: Towards critical multiculturalism. In S. May (Ed.), *Critical multiculturalism* (pp. 1-41). London: Falmer Press.

McLaren, P. (1994). White terror and oppositional agency: Towards a critical multiculturalism. In D. T. Goldberg (Ed.), *Multiculturalism: A critical reader* (pp. 45-74). Cambridge, MA: Blackwell.

Moll, L. (1992). Funds of knowledge for teaching: Using a qualitative approach to connect homes and classrooms. *Theory into Practice, 31*(2), 132-41.

Moss, G. (2004). Provisions of trustworthiness in critical narrative research: Bridging intersubjectivity and fidelity. *The Qualitative Report, 9*(2), 359-374.

New Zealand Ministry of Education (1996). *Te Whariki: Early childhood curriculum.* Wellington, NZ: Learning Media Ltd.

Obiakor, F. E. (2001). Research on culturally and linguistically diverse populations. *Multicultural Perspectives, 3*(4), 5-10.

Ontario Ministry of Education and Training. (1998). The kindergarten program. Toronto: Queen's Printer for Ontario.

Ontario Ministry of Education and Training. (2006). The kindergarten program (revised). Toronto: Queen's Printer for Ontario.

People For Education. (2003). *The 2003 elementary school tracking report: Six years of the funding formula.* Retrieved May 2, 2005, from http://www.people foreducation.com/tracking/summrpts/elem/2003/Elem_03_TrackingRe port.PDF

People for Education. (2007). *The annual report on Ontario's public schools.* Retrieved December 14, 2005, from http://www.peopleforeduation.com/ adx/aspx/adxGetMedia.aspx?DocID=634

People for Education, (2008). *The annual report on Ontario's public schools.* Retrieved February 25, 2009, from http://www.peopleforeducation.com/ school_survey

Reay, D. (1998). *Class work: Mother's involvement in their children's primary schooling.* London: Routledge.

Ricoeur, P. (1992). *Oneself as another.* Chicago, IL: University of Chicago Press.

Roberts-Fiati, G. (1997). Observing and assessing young children. In K. M. Kilbride (Ed.), *Include me too! Human diversity in early childhood* (pp. 122-140). Toronto: Harcourt Brace & Company.

Schwarzer, D., Haywood, A., & Lorenzen, C. (2003). Fostering multiliteracy in linguistically diverse classroom. *Language Arts, 80*(6), 453-460.

Sleeter, C. E., & Bernal, D. D. (2004). Critical pedagogy, critical race theory, and antiracist education. In J. Banks & C. Banks (Eds.), *Handbook of research on multicultural education* (2nd ed., pp. 240-258). San Francisco, CA: Jossey-Bass.

Suárez-Orozco, C. (2001). Afterword: Understanding and serving the children of immigrants. *Harvard Educational Review, 71*(3), 579-589.

Toohey, K. (2000). *Learning English at school: Identity, social relations and classroom practice.* Clevedon, UK: Multilingual Matters Ltd.

Vygotsky, L. (1978) *Mind and society: The development of higher psychological Processes.* Cambridge, MA: Harvard University Press.

Viruru, R., & Cannella, G. S., (2001). Postcolonial ethnography, young children, and voice. In S. Grieshaber & G. Cannella (Eds.), *Embracing identities in early childhood education; Diversity and possibilities* (pp. 158-172). New York: Teachers College Press.

Wallen, N. E., & Fraenkel, J. R. (2001). *Educational research: A guide to the process.* San Francisco, CA: Lea Publications.

Wien, C. A. (2002). Coping with standardized curriculum in kindergarten: Portrait of an exemplary early childhood educator. *Early Childhood Education, 35*(1), 14-21.

Authors

Emily Ashton is a Masters student in the Critical Studies of Education program at the University of New Brunswick. Her research interests include feminist poststructuralism, postdevelopment studies, and critical media literacies. As a member of the UNB Early Childhood Centre curriculum team, Emily works as researcher, editor, and writer, along with teaching the Cultural Constructions of Childhood course in the undergraduate education program. Emily can be reached at emily.ashton@unb.ca

Kimberly Bezaire is an Early Childhood Education specialist and Doctoral Candidate at the Ontario Institute for Studies in Education, University of Toronto. Her research/writing interests include children's classroom play, multiliteracies, and the children's toy market. Having taught in early years settings, as well as teacher education, Kimberly's work includes consulting on projects relating to kindergarten and the arts in early childhood. Kimberly can be reached at kbezaire@oise.utoronto.ca

Linda Cameron is an Associate Professor at the Ontario Institute for Studies in Education, University of Toronto. Her work in Early Childhood has spanned four decades, ten countries, and every level from birth to higher education. During this time, her interests have spanned play, early literacy, parenting, and conditions of learning. Linda can be contacted at lcameron@oise.utoronto.ca

Christine Chan is a teacher at a preschool in Vancouver, British Columbia. She works with children between the ages of three to five years. Since 2006, Christine has been involved with a research initiative entitled Investigating Quality Early Childhood Environments. Christine can be reached at christineskchan@hotmail.com

Rachel Heydon is an Associate Professor in the Faculty of Education at The University of Western Ontario. She teaches courses in language and literacy education and curriculum. A former special education teacher, Rachel's research now focuses on multimodal literacy, early childhood curriculum, and intergenerational learning. She is about to undertake a large-scale study of intergenerational singing. Rachel can be reached at rheydon@uwo.ca

Luigi Iannacci is an Assistant Professor in the School of Education and Professional Learning at Trent University in Peterborough, Ontario. He teaches courses that focus on language and literacy as well as special needs learners. He has taught mainstream and special education in a range of elementary grades in Ontario. His research interests include first and second language and literacy acquisition, critical multiculturalism, early childhood education, and critical narrative research. Luigi can be reached at luigiiannacci@trentu.ca

Maureen Kendrick is an Associate Professor in the Language and Literacy Education Department at the University of British Columbia. She teaches courses that focus on literacy and multimodality in cross-cultural contexts, and literacy and inquiry-based learning. Her research interests include literacy and multimodality in diverse contexts; digital literacies, youth, and pedagogy; and family literacy. Maureen can be reached at maureen.kendrick@ubc.ca

Laurie Kocher teaches in the Faculty of Child, Family, and Community Studies at Douglas College near Vancouver, British Columbia. Most of the courses she teaches are in the early childhood teacher education programme. She has worked in a number of contexts with children and families, and at a variety of college and university settings. Laurie's doctoral work was based on the pedagogy and philosophy of the Reggio Emilia approach, and specifically on the practice of pedagogical documentation. She has been involved at several levels with the development of B.C. Early Learning Framework and the University of Victoria's Investigating Quality Project. Laurie can be reached at lkocher@telus.net

Veronica Pacini-Ketchabaw is Associate Professor and Coordinator of the Early Years Specialization in the School of Child and Youth Care at the University of Victoria, and the co-director of the Investigating Quality Project and the B.C. Early Learning Implementation Framework Project. She has worked professionally in the field of early childhood education for over fifteen years and taught at different levels in a variety of educational settings in Argentina and Canada. She teaches and conducts research on issues related to poststructural, feminist, and postcolonial theory-practice in early childhood education. Veronica can be reached at vpacinik@uvic.ca

Sherry Rose is a PhD student in the Early Childhood Centre at the University of New Brunswick working as a member of the Early Childhood Research and Development Team. She has taught undergraduate and graduate courses in Curriculum and Critical Studies, administered the UNB Children's Centre, and conducted research for the Early Learning and Care Curriculum Framework (English) for New Brunswick. Sherry's teaching experience includes Kindergarten to grade nine. Her research interests include critical literacies and narrative documentation. Sherry can be reached at srose@unb.ca

Alejandra Sanchez is an Instructor & Practicum Coordinator in the Early Childhood Education Department at Douglas College, New Westminster, BC. Her teaching and research focus on examining children's learning and teachers' pedagogical practices using post-structural theories. She uses the Collaborative Critical Reflective Protocol as a methodological strategy to deconstruct pedagogical documentation with student teachers. She is also involved in the University of Victoria's Investigating Quality Project. Alejandra can be reached at sancheza@douglas.bc.ca

Tara-Lynn Scheffel is an Assistant Professor in the Faculty of Education at Nippising University in North Bay. She teaches courses that focus on language and literacy, and she formally taught elementary school in Ontario. Her research interests include literacy engagement, researcher/participant identity negotiation, and research with young children. She was part of a team working on a provincial early childhood curriculum framework for New Brunswick. Tara-Lynn can be reached at taralyns@nipissingu.ca

Roz Stooke is an Assistant Professor in the Faculty of Education at the University of Western Ontario in London, Ontario where she teaches courses in children's literature, language arts, and curriculum studies. Roz has also worked as an elementary teacher, family literacy facilitator, and children's librarian. Her research interests focus on early childhood literacies, the social organization of early childhood education and care (ECEC) work, and in particular, the institutional technologies that currently organize ECEC in Canada. Roz can be reached at rstooke@uwo.ca

Pam Whitty is a Professor in the Faculty of Education, Fredericton, New Brunswick. She is Director of the UNB Early Childhood Centre. Her areas of expertise include early literacies, cultural constructions of childhood and curriculum. She has been funded for numerous projects in early literacies and most recently was co-director of the New Brunswick Curriculum Project for Early Learning and Child Care. She can be reached at whitty@unb.ca

Kelly Young is an Associate Professor in the School of Education and Professional Learning at Trent University in Peterborough, Ontario. She teaches courses that focus on language and literacy as well as classroom management. She taught in a range of elementary and secondary grades in Ontario. Her research interests include language and literacy, curriculum theorizing, and eco-justice and environmental educational leadership. Kelly can be reached at kellyyoung@trentu.ca